Imperfect Believers

Imperfect Believers

Ambiguous Characters in the Gospel of John

Susan E. Hylen

WESTMINSTER
JOHN KNOX PRESS
LOUISVILLE • KENTUCKY

First edition
Published by Westminster John Knox Press
Louisville, Kentucky

09 10 11 12 13 14 15 16 17 18—10 9 8 7 6 5 4 3 2 1

Book design by Drew Stevens
Cover design by Night & Day Design
Cover Art: Henry Tresham (painter); Robert Shipster (engraver), The Macklin Bible—
Nicodemus Came to Jesus by Night, 1800, Plate from The Macklin Bible,
Special Collections, Vanderbilt University

Library of Congress Cataloging-in-Publication Data

Hylen, Susan.
  Imperfect believers : ambiguous characters in the Gospel of John / Susan E. Hylen.
      p.   cm.
  Includes bibliographical references and indexes.
  ISBN 978-0-664-23372-3 (alk. paper)
  1. Bible. N. T. John—Criticism, interpretation, etc.   2. Bible. N. T. John—Biography.   I. Title.
  BS2615.52.H95   2009
  226.5'066—dc22

                                                                          2009011996

For Bennett and Tobias

Contents

Acknowledgments

In the completion of this book, I am indebted to both individuals and institutions. I would like to thank Allen Vantrease for his assistance in researching the book, and the Vanderbilt University Summer Research Program, which made his work possible. I am grateful to my colleagues in Vanderbilt's Department of Religious Studies and Divinity School for their support and friendship. In particular, Robin Jensen and Anne Richardson Womack provided me with a wonderful array of artwork possibilities for the cover; I only wish I could use them all. I appreciate their readiness to share their expertise. Fernando Segovia read and commented on chapter 4. His gracious response helped me to clarify my own understanding of my argument, particularly regarding the role of Judas and the future of the disciples. As I was researching chapter 4, a conversation with Ted Smith helped me to better articulate my understanding of the disciples. Ted's written comments on chapter 7 also helped me to tighten and clarify my argument. A.-J. Levine responded to chapter 7 both in writing and conversation. She helped me to differentiate my argument from that of others and to be explicit about the problem of exculpating the text. I am grateful to each of my colleagues for their encouraging and helpful feedback.

Outside of Vanderbilt, Bill Wright generously read and commented on four of my chapters. His comments helped me to restructure the introduction and provided additional examples and references in a number of cases. A conversation with Gail O'Day helped me to arrive at the current two-part structure to the book and pointed me to a couple of articles I had missed that proved very useful. Stephanie Egnotovich's editing improved the logic and readability of the book, and I am thankful for her collaboration and encouragement. Finally, I am grateful to my partner, Ted Smith, and our sons, Bennett and Tobias. Their acceptance and even love of my own imperfections are a means of grace for which I give thanks.

1

Introduction

Many of the characters in John appear rather briefly, engage Jesus on one topic, and then disappear. As a result, many interpreters argue that these characters are "flat" or one-sided, display a single attribute, and rarely show development throughout the course of the narrative. Thus Alan Culpepper writes, "Thomas doubts, Pilate wrestles with the claims of truth and political expediency, Peter is impulsive, the Beloved Disciple is perceptive."[1] John's characters, the argument goes, are an object lesson, placed in the narrative to embody a single trait. And according to Culpepper, the character's response to Jesus—particularly, the response of belief or disbelief—determines their character: "The characters represent a continuum of responses to Jesus. . . . Given the pervasive dualism of the Fourth Gospel, the choice is either/or. All situations are reduced to two clear-cut alternatives, and all the characters eventually make their choice."[2] The disciples believe, the Jews disbelieve. Nicodemus begins with some openness to Jesus on account of his signs, but ultimately he cannot comprehend Jesus. The blind man begins uncomprehending but rapidly comes to "see" Jesus. What shapes the reader's overall impression of each character is that character's bottom-line response of faith or disbelief.

According to this view, characters are each a "type" of believer. The character's response to Jesus does not belong only to that character and their role in the narrative; it also represents a larger class of believers. Nicodemus's response represents those who believe on the basis of

Jesus' signs but later turn away. Likewise, the Samaritan woman is a spokesperson for her village yet represents a more positive response to Jesus. The disciples represent true believers or the Johannine community; the Jews represent unbelievers or Jewish authorities hostile to the Christian community.[3]

Scholarly opinion is not unanimous on this, however, and some interpreters have questioned the simple either/or categorization of characters. Colleen Conway identifies one difficulty: "If these characters are so transparent, embodying only a single trait, one would expect that such traits could be readily discerned. At least, one should be able to determine whether a particular character represents a faithful response to Jesus."[4] But this determination often proves difficult. For example, Nicodemus approaches Jesus with the statement, "Rabbi, we know that you are a teacher sent from God" (John 3:2; all translations are mine unless indicated otherwise). This may not represent a full confession of faith in Jesus, but Nicodemus does seem to be on the right track. The Gospel elsewhere uses similar terms to describe Jesus (e.g., 1:38; 5:30). However, the conversation between Nicodemus ends with Jesus saying, "Are you a teacher of Israel, and yet you do not understand these things?" (3:10). Some elements of Nicodemus's story imply belief, others disbelief. Identifying which character trait should define Nicodemus's character can prove to be difficult.

The history of interpretation bears evidence of the difficulty of evaluating John's characters. To some the Samaritan woman is an exemplary believer; to others she never fully understands Jesus. Even interpreters who identify a character clearly as one type of believer often note variations in that character. Alan Culpepper, while seeing the disciples as "marked especially by their recognition of Jesus and belief in his claims,"[5] also recognizes that they often misunderstand Jesus and at crucial moments turn away from following his teaching. Wayne Meeks's interpretation of Nicodemus and the disciples shows a similar tension. Meeks concludes that Nicodemus is uncomprehending and unbelieving,[6] yet he sees both positive and negative attributes in the character of Nicodemus. Nicodemus comes "by night" (3:2), placing him within the realm of darkness. Yet he "comes to the light," with positive implications. And according to Meeks, he shows some understanding of Jesus: "Nicodemus's opening statement to Jesus is, in effect, a declaration of faith."[7] The analysis of these two scholars reveals greater complexity than their bottom-line assessment of each character allows.

While such indications of complexity in John's characters suggest that a reevaluation of character may be fruitful, the interpretation of John's characters as flat has been compelling for many readers of the Gospel. In reading the characters as flat, interpreters have presented a coherent understanding of the Gospel that accounts for much of the language of John. Their reading does four things that all good interpretations should do: (1) it situates the language of the Gospel in its first-century literary and social context, (2) it accounts for the dualistic and symbolic nature of John's language, (3) it relates characterization and plot, and (4) it draws on literary theory to explain how readers construct characters. In reading John's characters differently, I have made different decisions regarding each of these four categories. Here I address each one to explain why I reject the decisions other interpreters have made and to outline the implications for reading John's characters in a different way.

CHARACTERS IN CONTEXT

First-century readers of John did not approach the Gospel's characters in a vacuum; they had expectations of character formed by their literary and cultural context. Scholarly interpretations of John try to make sense of the Gospel as a product of the first-century Greco-Roman world. In particular, interpreters compare John's characters to other ancient literary figures and try to imagine a social and historical context in which John's language makes sense.

Literary Context

Reading John's characters as flat situates the Gospel's language within the context of other ancient literature. The flat reading of character is consistent with one prominent way that ancient characterization has been understood. As Robert Scholes and Robert Kellogg have observed, "Characters in primitive stories are invariably 'flat,' 'static,' and quite 'opaque.'"[8] Many scholars attribute this understanding of character to Aristotle. He suggested that characters in tragedy are subordinate to plot, and that the author should try to convey general truths through the portrayal of individual characters.[9] Many of the characters of Greek drama have been read in this manner. For example, Scholes and Kellogg argue, "Homer's Achilles . . . is presented to us almost exclusively in terms of one facet of life—the emotion of anger."[10] When interpreters read John's characters as flat, they are making sense of John's characters in relationship to other ancient literature.

Recently a more nuanced understanding of ancient characterization has developed.[11] Ancient narratives do not convey concern with the interior psychological state of a character: as Scholes and Kellogg note, this is a phenomenon of the modern novel. However, there are other ways that the characters of ancient narratives appear complex rather than flat. Many narratives portray changes in a character over the course of time. Ancient characters are also easily differentiated from one another. This is true even when their identifiable character traits overlap, as Christopher Pelling argues: "Certainly their heroic isolation and intransigence show some similarities—Ajax, Antigone, Oedipus, Philoctetes, Electra—but it would surely be inadequate to regard these as straightforward repetitions of a single 'type.'"[12] The circumstances of each character lead to differentiation between them. Simply reading ancient characters as "flat, static, and opaque" may ignore important elements of ancient characterization.

Biblical scholars have also long recognized complexity in the characters of the Hebrew Bible. Most agree that Old Testament characters do not fit the flat/round typology.[13] The question then arises that if neither Greek nor Hebrew characters are simply flat, static, and opaque, why must John's characters be read in this way? While there are one-sided characters in antiquity, this no longer appears to be the only available option, and the reader of John should be prepared to encounter other possibilities.

Social Context

Understanding John's characters as representative figures allows the reader to situate the Gospel in a likely first-century context: characters are mirrors of the social context in which the Gospel was produced. For example, C. K. Barrett writes that in the interchange between Nicodemus and Jesus, "we are made to hear not a conversation between two persons but the dialogue of Church and Synagogue."[14] Nicodemus, in this view, stands in for a "typical" Jewish perspective at the time of the Gospel's writing, and Jesus stands for that of the church. Nicodemus need not have been an actual person who spoke to Jesus, but he represents actual people in John's community.[15]

One problem with this approach is that it renders literary characters as real people. Literary theorists describe the view of characters as real-life figures as "mimesis."[16] However, most scholars now agree that characters are not easily equated with their flesh-and-blood counterparts. Characters are, rather, constructed through the act of writing and reading and do not have lives outside of a literary work, except perhaps in the minds of their readers.[17] The reader's experience of reading may bring a character to life; yet this is not the same as saying that these characters are real people. Even characters who are constructed as historical figures are creations of the literary work and do not correspond completely with actual people. Historical judgments are a necessary part of scholarship: they help the reader to understand the background against which a first-century reader might understand John's metaphorical language and Old Testament allusions. But the characters of the Gospel do not give readers direct access to the author or the author's location.

At the same time, one important aspect of reading characters as representative should not be lost: it captures the way John's language invites readers to make judgments about characters. If the conversation between Jesus and Nicodemus is a conversation between church and synagogue, the first readers of the Gospel could have applied the fruits of that conversation directly to their own lives, an impulse that seems to correspond to much of the Gospel's language. From the beginning, John sets up categories against which one may judge various responses to Jesus: "He came to what was his own, and his own people did not accept him. But to all who received him, who believed in his name, he gave power to become children of God" (1:11–12). In general terms, the prologue sets the reader's expectations for how to read the story that follows. Reception and rejection of Jesus are concepts that John gives to readers, which they may use to explore the Gospel's characters. The Gospel sets up categories against which one may judge various responses to Jesus, and characters appear stylized to enact such responses.

In this book, instead of speaking of characters as representative, I explore the ways characters function in the Gospel. Part of the characters' function is to draw the reader into a process of discernment about what counts as true discipleship. Readers might apply this discernment in their own lives, using the categories that John sets forth to evaluate their own or other people's words and actions. Yet one can say this without equating John's characters with historical groups or individuals. Characters do not represent actual people but function to train the reader in making judgments about how words and actions represent belief in Jesus or rejection of him.

THE NATURE OF JOHN'S LANGUAGE

Interpreting John's characters also involves a number of decisions about the nature of John's language. The reader recognizes certain features of John's language—contrasts like "above" and "below," "light" and "dark," or metaphors like "I am the light of the world"—and also decides how this language relates to the overall meaning of the Gospel.

Dualism

John is often described as exhibiting a dualistic worldview: the author sees everything in polarized categories. Language exhibiting such contrasts is found throughout the Gospel:

> What is born of the flesh is flesh, and what is born of the spirit is spirit. (3:6)

> You are from below, I am from above; you are of this world, I am not of this world. (8:23)

> Those who walk during the day do not stumble, because they see the light of this world. But those who walk at night stumble, because the light is not in them. (11:9–10)

This language sets up sharp contrasts—flesh/spirit, above/below, day/ night—and in each of these cases, the contrasts apply to people in some way. It is not simply that "above" and "below" exist, but that Jesus speaks of people as being "from above" or "from below." In assessing John's characters as flat, scholars have used these contrasts as standards against which characters are judged. Against this background, belief in Jesus is understood to be an all-or-nothing affair.[18] In this view, John's dualistic language plays a defining role in understanding character. The notion that characters correspond to polar opposites like above and below predetermines the interpretive result: no matter how varied the evidence, in the end characters must either believe or not. Thus Jouette Bassler argues that Nicodemus is an ambiguous character, but he does not remain ambiguous to her, for "to be anything less than fully committed to the Johannine Jesus . . . is to retain the damning and dangerous connections with darkness, the 'Jews,' and the world."[19] To Bassler, dualism turns ambiguity into simple disbelief.

Interpreters of John confront stark contrasts alongside characters who show much greater ambiguity than the contrasts will allow. The flat reading of John's characters privileges the contrasts. They provide a rigid framework into which characters ultimately fit. In this book I have tried to allow this paradox to exist without trying to "solve" it: on the one hand, John describes people in either/or terms; on the other hand, he portrays characters who do not fit neatly into these categories. In the conclusion I return to a discussion of whether John's outlook is sharply dualistic. Delaying this decision allows me to bring the ambiguities in John's characters to the forefront.

Symbol and Metaphor

Viewing John's characters as representative figures has been persuasive because interpreters have similarly understood John's language as symbolic. In Craig Koester's words, "A symbol, in the most general sense, is something that stands for something else."[20] In John 6, when Jesus identifies himself as "bread of life" (6:35) and says, "Whoever eats of this bread will live forever" (6:51), "bread" stands for "spiritual nourishment" and "eating" symbolizes believing. Thus, as Koester explains, "to partake of Jesus as the bread of life is to believe that the crucified Messiah is the source of eternal life with God."[21] The reader substitutes "belief in Jesus" for "eating bread."[22] Similarly, in terms of characters, understanding characters as "types" is a symbolic reading of character: the characters stand in for different types of believers.

In contrast to symbol, metaphor emphasizes the conceptual nature of figurative language. A metaphor understands one thing in terms of another.[23] When Jesus is described as "bread," the metaphor draws on a specific understanding of bread as a way to shed light on the identity of Jesus. This is not mere substitution of the idea of "bread" for Jesus; it requires that the reader draw on common cultural understandings of bread to understand what is being said about Jesus. The conventions associated with bread in John's culture give depth to the metaphor. In John 6, the metaphor "I am the bread of life" is related explicitly to the story of manna (6:30–31). Readers familiar with the exodus story (as John's first readers likely were) would draw on conventional aspects of that story to understand "bread" in a relationship to Jesus. The manna was "bread from heaven" that God sent to the Israelites so that they would not die of hunger (Exod. 16:3–4). Early on, manna was also associated with God's word or Wisdom. The Israelites had to follow God's instructions to collect it (Exod. 16:4–5, 16–20), and the manna itself became a metaphor for the word of God (see Deut. 8:3; Wis. 16:26). John draws on these aspects of the manna story to elaborate the metaphor "Jesus is manna." Like the manna, Jesus "comes down from heaven and gives life to the world" (6:33). The manna was a gift of God to sustain the Israelites, and so is Jesus. As such, he is associated with teaching and learning (6:45). The life that Jesus brings as bread differs from the manna, however, in that those who eat it never die (6:50–51). Because metaphors are conceptual, the reader draws on the language of the Gospel and on conventional knowledge of the exodus story to understand what it means for Jesus to be "bread of life."[24]

Awareness of the metaphorical or symbolic nature of John's language is important to the reader's understanding of characters. First, aspects of characterization are metaphorical. This is clearly the case with Jesus' "I am" statements. John's Jesus describes himself alternately as "bread" (6:35); "light" (8:12); "gate" (10:7); "shepherd" (10:11); "the resurrection and the life" (11:25); "the way, the truth, and the life" (14:6); and "vine" (15:1).[25] Other characters also assume metaphorical attributes. A character's actions can be understood metaphorically—for example, Jesus speaks of Mary's anointing of his feet as a preparation for his burial (12:7). Her act may also be understood as prefiguring the washing of feet, to which Jesus calls his disciples (13:14). Either way, the action contributes to the reader's understanding of Mary and what she understands about her relationship to Jesus and his identity.

Second, characterization and metaphor interact on a complex level when characters' actions or words are read in relationship to the metaphors used to understand Jesus. For example, Jesus is presented as "light" many times in the Gospel, beginning with the prologue: "The true light, which enlightens all people, was coming into the world" (1:9). The reader is prepared to understand Jesus as light (cf. 1:5; 8:12; 9:5). When Nicodemus is introduced, part of the description is that he comes to Jesus "by night" (3:2). Along with Meeks (above), many interpreters read the timing of this story metaphorically. The detail "by night" suggests a relationship between the action of Nicodemus and the metaphor "Jesus is light." Something similar happens in John 4:10–15, where Jesus speaks to the Samaritan woman of his gift of living water.

When the woman departs, she leaves her water jug at the well (4:28). Many interpreters read this detail in relation to the water metaphor that the earlier discussion with Jesus sets up. Abandoning her water jar shows that the woman has received Jesus' gift of water. As Jesus has indicated, "Those who drink of the water that I will give them will never be thirsty" (4:14). In assessing characters, readers make judgments about the characters on the basis of other metaphors in the Gospel.[26]

Reading John's language as metaphor rather than symbol helps to explain how the act of evaluating character draws the reader into John's worldview.[27] In terms of Nicodemus the metaphor "Jesus is light" is frequently used to judge Nicodemus's character. The word "night," used in reference to Nicodemus, may characterize him as someone who does not understand Jesus. The question then is whether Nicodemus's act of "coming to Jesus" is enough to bring him out of the darkness and into light. Making judgments about characters in this way is not simply a matter of categorizing characters according to type, but rather involves reasoning according to the terms of the metaphor. This act of judgment draws the reader into the Gospel's worldview. A modern example, explored by Lakoff and Johnson, may be useful: In the 1970s, the Carter administration described the energy crisis as "war." "Suppose Carter announces that his administration has won a major energy battle. Is this claim true or false? Even to address oneself to the question requires accepting at least the central parts of the metaphor."[28] Something similar happens through John's characterization. To ask if Nicodemus has come to the light, a reader first accepts the metaphor "Jesus is light" and begins to reason in its terms. Understanding John's language as metaphor helps to shed light on the way the Gospel involves readers in the evaluation of character. In assessing characters, readers engage John's metaphors and come to understand them more deeply.

THE RELATIONSHIP OF CHARACTER AND PLOT

Character and plot are closely related: characters are known in part by their actions.[29] The flat reading of John's characters incorporates a commonly held understanding of the plot of the Gospel. Since Rudolf Bultmann, the plot of John has widely been read as Jesus' revelation of God. Bultmann drew on a mythic pattern found in later gnostic texts in which a redeemer figure comes down from heaven and reveals saving knowledge. Bultmann saw parallels in the way John tells the story of Jesus: Jesus comes down from heaven and reveals knowledge about himself. His acts and speech are all aimed toward this goal. The development of the plot of the Gospel "is a matter of how Jesus' identity comes to be recognized and how it fails to be recognized."[30] Characters are given a choice to respond to Jesus with either belief or unbelief. Their response determines their character.

This reading of John's plot highlights some important themes and literary features of the Gospel. Belief and unbelief are important categories of John's Gospel, and the reader's own belief is the book's stated goal (20:31). Many aspects of John's literary style contribute to the goal of belief. From the beginning, the reader is assumed to know the events of the story. Already in chapter 2, Jesus responds to his mother's suggestion that he can help with the wine supply: "My hour has not yet come" (2:4). Even if a reader does not yet know that "hour" is John's way of referring to the events of Jesus' crucifixion and glorification, the narrative sets the expectation for an important pending event. Soon afterward, the narrator specifically indicates that Jesus will rise from the dead (2:22). The offhand nature of the comment suggests that this is not new information for the implied reader. The reader of the Gospel is not reading to discover the events of the Gospel so much as to learn what they mean. The discovery of meaning is also suggested by coupling Jesus' signs with explanatory discourse. Jesus not only performs a miraculous feeding of five thousand people; he also goes on to describe himself in relation to manna. This combination of signs and discourse leaves the impression that John emphasizes the deeper meaning of the signs rather than the miracles themselves. In this literary context, it makes sense to see a character's understanding of Jesus as an important attribute.

Yet limiting the plot of John to revelation and belief has two main drawbacks. First, it may overstate the importance of belief and unbelief. The plot of John is not only one of Jesus' revelation and people's responses. It is also a story of the life, death, and resurrection of Jesus. Even if the reader knows the events of Jesus' death from the outset of the Gospel, they are nonetheless important to the narrative. Many characters have a relationship to this plot as well. Judas, for example, cannot be fully understood without reference to Jesus' arrest, trial, and crucifixion. His betrayal of Jesus is not simply an act of disbelief; it also sets in motion the final events of the Gospel. Judas moves the plot of the story forward by bringing the police and soldiers to arrest Jesus (18:2–3). In addition, the emphasis on belief and unbelief as the plot of John excludes other character traits from consideration. Is

Judas's betrayal of Jesus really a simple failure of belief? The Gospel never describes it explicitly in these terms. Judas's betrayal might also be described as a failure to "love," or to "abide in" Jesus. This language is also prominent within the Gospel and can serve as an alternative means of evaluating characters.

Keeping a broader view of the plot in mind can change the reader's understanding of character. For example, one of the important turns in the plot of the Gospel is the specific plan to put Jesus to death that develops following the raising of Lazarus. Prior to John 11, there are attempts to kill Jesus, but he easily circumvents them. The belief of the Jews that results from the raising of Lazarus leads directly to this more coordinated plot to kill Jesus (11:45, 48). Most interpreters characterize the Jews as unbelieving: they grumble against Jesus' teaching about the bread of life (6:41, 52), and they try to stone him in 8:59. Yet in chapter 11 it is the widespread belief among the Jews that turns the direction of the narrative decidedly toward the crucifixion. Belief plays both positive and negative roles in the overall story of the Gospel. A new understanding of the character of the Jews might result from a different way of relating them to the Gospel's plot.

The second drawback to emphasizing only revelation and belief as plot is that it focuses on the act of belief at the expense of the content of belief. When a character's choice is described as either belief or unbelief, the content of their belief is often assumed or ignored. In Bultmann's interpretation of John, Jesus acts as the redeemer figure who reveals saving knowledge to humans: for Jesus, it is knowledge of himself. Humans who accept such knowledge (who in John's terms "believe") find salvation ("eternal life"). Scholars have discredited aspects of Bultmann's thesis, but his comprehensive theological understanding of the Gospel, and especially his description of the plot as revelation and response, has had tremendous staying power. Yet his understanding of Jesus as the Redeemer strangely eliminates the content of belief in Jesus: as Bultmann himself indicates, Jesus *reveals nothing but that he is the Revealer.*[31] Characters are called to an affirmation of Jesus without additional substance.

John's Gospel has a great deal to offer regarding the substance of belief, and John provides a variety of metaphors to help the reader understand who Jesus is: he is water, shepherd, vine, and manna, just to name a few. The emphasis on belief, however, flattens out the diversity and usefulness of these metaphors. For example, Culpepper's statement of plot makes the individual scenes of the Gospel redundant:

"Each episode has essentially the same plot as the story as a whole. Will Nicodemus, the Samaritan woman, or the lame man recognize Jesus and thereby receive eternal life? The story is repeated over and over."[32] The particularity of each of these stories fades into the background. Yet Nicodemus's interaction with Jesus introduces an important metaphor for thinking about belief in Jesus: being born from above. The Samaritan woman's interaction has a different metaphor: water of life. Interpreters like Culpepper would not deny this. Yet the emphasis on revelation and response mutes the content of each story: the important thing is the response of faith. In this approach, drinking the water of life expresses the same thing as being born from above. While it seems right to say that these metaphors are both used to understand one complex concept, something is lost when the two become synonyms for "belief in Jesus." The metaphor of new birth suggests that following Jesus initiates a whole new life, one that is tied to the nature of its parent, the Spirit. The water metaphor ties the gift of Jesus to the experience of thirst, and to the Old Testament stories of God's miraculous provision of water for the Israelites. Attention to plot should not detract from the particularity and substance of John's metaphors.

LITERARY ANALYSIS OF CHARACTER

Scholars who study John's characters try to read John's Gospel as literature and understand its characters as being constructed and read much the way other literary characters are. Interpreting John's characters as flat makes sense in terms of certain literary theories of characterization. E. M. Forster's distinction between "flat" and "round" characters and W. J. Harvey's definition of a *ficelle* have influenced the interpretation of John's characters.[33] Forster identified flat characters as those who exhibit only one idea or quality; round characters are more lifelike. Harvey distinguished between protagonists, background characters, and intermediate characters, one of which is the ficelle, a character whose purpose is to serve a particular function in the plot, and who may have special symbolic or representative value. Against the background of these options, John's characters may appear most like flat characters or ficelles.

There has, not surprisingly, been expansion and criticism of Forster's flat/round typology for character. Baruch Hochman analyzes characters with regard to eight different features, each of which operates on a spectrum. Characters can be highly stylized or naturalistic, coherent or incoherent, whole or fragmentary, literal or metaphorical, complex or simple, transparent or opaque, dynamic or static, closed or open.[34] Although I do not explicitly employ Hochman's categories in this book, I find his work helpful because it changes the expectation that characters should be simply flat or round. A character might display only one primary trait yet also develop over time. Another character might be metaphorical but also open-ended. For example, in John 6 the Jews "grumble" (or complain, ἐγόγγυζον, *egongyzon*, 6:42) against Jesus. The Greek word is an allusion to the exodus story, where the Israelites grumble (e.g., Exod. 16:2 LXX, διεγόγγυζε, *diegongyze*) against Moses and God. The allusion indicates a figurative aspect of their character: they are metaphorically like the Israelites who grumble. At the same time, their character appears somewhat incoherent: like the Israelites, they both believe and grumble.[35] Hochman's work points to a variety in characterization that opens up new ways of conceiving John's characters. If characters need not be simply flat or round, John's characters may appear in a new light.

Other theorists address questions of how a reader constructs or analyzes character. My own analysis of John's characters has benefited greatly from the work of David Gowler and others. Gowler argues that characterization occurs through both direct and indirect modes of presentation.[36] Direct modes include the attribution of adjectives or other description with reference to specific characters. An example is found in Luke's portrayal of Simeon: "This man was righteous and devout, waiting for the consolation of Israel, and the Holy Spirit was upon him" (Luke 2:25). "Righteous" and "devout" are direct statements of Simeon's character. Such explicit characterization is rarely found in the Gospel of John. John uses indirect modes of characterization, which include speech by or to a character, the actions of characters, their environment, and comparison with other characters. For example, the Jews "grumble" about Jesus' teachings in John 6–7; Nicodemus approaches Jesus "by night"; Peter's second denial of Jesus, "I am not" (18:25), contrasts with Jesus' bold "I am" (18:5–6). None of these details provides unfiltered information about a character; rather, the reader is left to decide what each piece contributes to characterization.

In this analysis I follow a two-part method. First, I have initially categorized what John says about each according to these indirect modes of characterization: What language does John use to portray the characters' actions? What is said about them? What words do they say? Is the character portrayed in relationship to others? Laying out the evidence in this way is often what persuaded me to reject some of the traditional interpretations of John's characters, which did not fit what I saw. In the example from John 6 noted above, it is not only the Jews who grumble against Jesus; the disciples do so as well (6:61). The action of grumbling is itself significant, as I noted above. It characterizes the disciples and the Jews as the Israelites from the exodus story. It is also significant that these characters—often the primary exemplars of belief and unbelief—are in this instance described in the same terms. The disciples and the Jews seem less like polar opposites when their behavior is the same. Analysis of modes of characterization helps to identify a full range of possibilities before drawing conclusions about a particular character.

The second step in my analysis of character is to identify the decisions that other interpreters are making as they evaluate John's characters.[37] Modern readers make both historical and literary judgments. On a historical level, the interpreter tries to understand how a reader in John's community might have understood the language of the Gospel. The characterization of the disciples and Jews as "grumbling" takes on new meaning in a first-century context where readers would be likely to recognize the allusion to Exodus.[38]

In terms of literary judgments, readers judge the words and actions of characters against standards that John's language suggests. The contrasting language of above and below makes it easy for readers to say what the standards are: one must be born of the Spirit; one must be "from above." But other than Jesus, the characters are not identified explicitly in these terms. The reader is left to decide which words or actions meet the standards. Another literary judgment is the question of tone. A character's words give the reader some information about that character, but those words will be assessed differently based on the understanding of their tone. Is the Samaritan woman's request for water (4:15) serious or mocking? Such determinations make a tremendous difference in the conclusions a reader draws. Because so much of John's characterization is indirect, noticing what literary decisions other readers have made helps me to identify the choices that John's indirect characterization makes available to readers.

In large part, I find evidence of such choices in the interpretations of other scholars. (In the endnotes, I have cited a few examples of each interpretive option that I discuss. These examples are not exhaustive, but I have tried over the course of each chapter to cite a variety of interpreters.) As I do so, I disagree with very good interpreters of John, as I have above: scholars like Wayne Meeks, Alan Culpepper, and Craig

Koester. I notice ways in which their readings of character flatten out the ambiguities of John's language. That this intrigues me may say more about myself as a reader than any inherent deficiencies in their readings. Interpretations change over time, as do readers. By offering a new interpretation, I do not expect to exclude all other past and future readings of John; instead, I seek to enter into a larger conversation about the meaning of John. In the end, however, I hope to persuade the reader that my interpretation is a good one, by which I mean that it accounts for the language of John in its literary and historical milieu, and it speaks to the interpreter's context in a meaningful and ethical way. Comparison with other readers is important because the disagreements point to decisions that readers make in assessing character.

In the chapters that follow, I argue that John's characters are ambiguous and complex. John's indirect modes of characterization leave a great deal of room for ambiguity. Many characters have conflicting attributes: they both believe and do not believe; they understand some things and misunderstand others. They act in good ways—testifying or following Jesus—yet without perfect understanding of what they do or who Jesus is. Because indirect characterization takes a number of forms, readers assess what a character does alongside what they say, what is said about them, and the environment in which these words or actions occur. Many qualities can shape a given character. Ambiguity in characterization draws the reader into the theological worldview of the Gospel.[39] In making judgments about a character, the reader begins to reason according to the terms the Gospel sets forth. Readers may ultimately reject John's call to believe in Jesus or to testify to Jesus. But in evaluating characters, they nevertheless accept belief and testimony as standards against which characters are judged. The process of reading John's characters is one of formation: through it John positions readers to see Jesus—and the world—the way John sees them.

ORGANIZATION OF THE BOOK

Many scholars who study characters subdivide them in some way, such as major and minor characters, or individual and corporate characters. I have ignored such distinctions in this book largely because I find that they make little contribution to the reader's understanding of the modes of characterization that John employs or the conclusions that interpreters draw regarding the character's significance. The division in this book is not due to considerations of literary technique but to the peculiar difficulties that contemporary readers encounter with certain characters. The characters of part 1 are figures who are often read as flat, yet for whom I find textual evidence that suggests greater complexity. I am not arguing that none of John's characters are flat. However, I hope that the same method might be fruitful when applied to characters that I have not included. I have also selected these characters because I find them to be ambiguous in different ways. The variety allows me to explore the ways John's ambiguous characters may function for the reader.

The characters of the Jews and Jesus raise a number of questions particular to those characters. First, John's portrayal of each of these characters encompasses virtually the entire Gospel. Many scholars have interpreted each of these passages and the larger question of John's overall message about their character. A complete consideration would require a much longer treatment of the subject. Second, external considerations of history and theology intervene with these characters to a much greater extent than with other characters. The history of Christian anti-Semitism and its consequences push back against any attempts to dismiss John's harsh language about the Jews. With the character of Jesus, the weight of Christian theology and doctrine intervenes to shape the range of possibilities under consideration. In each case, interpreters must not only assess the character but also situate their interpretation within the ideological consequences it inevitably evokes.

For these reasons, the chapters in part 2 differ from the other chapters of the book. They are less exegetical and more conceptual. Regarding the Jews, I hope to show how thinking about the Jews as a character might raise new questions as well as new resources for answering old ones. I suggest that ambiguity in this character may open up new potential for the reader's relationship to the Jews. With Jesus, I hope simply to explore one important aspect of John's characterization of Jesus: his use of metaphor. I address the question of how to view John's metaphorical language rather than offering an overarching view of Jesus' character.

BIBLIOGRAPHY

Alter, Robert. *The Art of Biblical Narrative*. New York: Basic Books, 1981.

Auerbach, Erich. *Mimesis: The Representation of Reality in Western Literature*. Translated by Willard R. Trask. 1953. Reprint, Princeton, N.J.: Princeton University Press, 2003.

Bar-Efrat, Shimon. *Narrative Art in the Bible.* Journal for the Study of the Old Testament: Supplement Series 70. Sheffield: Almond Press, 1989.

Barrett, C. K. *The Gospel according to St. John.* Philadelphia: Westminster Press, 1978.

Bassler, Jouette M. "Mixed Signals: Nicodemus in the Fourth Gospel." *Journal of Biblical Literature* 108 (1989): 635–46.

Berlin, Adele. *Poetics and Interpretation of Biblical Narrative.* Bible and Literature Series 9. Sheffield: Almond Press, 1983.

Black, Max. "Metaphor." *Proceedings of the Aristotelian Society* 55 (1954–55): 273–94.

Bradley, A. C. *Shakespearean Tragedy: Lectures on Hamlet, Othello, King Lear, Macbeth.* 1904. Reprint, London: MacMillan Education, 1986.

Brown, Jeannine K. *The Disciples in Narrative Perspective: The Portrayal and Function of the Matthean Disciples.* Academia Biblica 9. Leiden: E. J. Brill, 2002.

Bultmann, Rudolf. *The Gospel of John.* Philadelphia: Westminster Press, 1971.

———. *Theology of the New Testament.* 2 vols. New York: Scribner, 1951–55.

Burnett, Fred. W. "Characterization and Reader Construction of Characters in the Gospels." *Semeia* 63 (1993): 1–28.

Chatman, Seymour. *Story and Discourse: Narrative Structure in Fiction and Film.* Ithaca, N.Y.: Cornell University Press, 1978.

Collins, Raymond F. "The Representative Figures of the Fourth Gospel—I." *Downside Review* 94 (1976): 26–46.

Conway, Colleen M. *Men and Women in the Fourth Gospel: Gender and Johannine Characterization.* SBL Dissertation Series 167. Atlanta: Society of Biblical Literature, 1999.

———. "Speaking through Ambiguity: Minor Characters in the Fourth Gospel." *Biblical Interpretation* 10 (2002): 324–41.

Culpepper, R. Alan. *Anatomy of the Fourth Gospel: A Study in Literary Design.* Philadelphia: Fortress Press, 1983.

Darr, John A. "Narrator as Character: Mapping a Reader-Oriented Approach to Narration in Luke-Acts." *Semeia* 63 (1993): 43–60.

———. *On Character Building: The Reader and the Rhetoric of Characterization in Luke-Acts.* Louisville, KY: Westminster/John Knox Press, 1992.

Fehribach, Adeline. *The Women in the Life of the Bridegroom: A Feminist Historical-Literary Analysis of the Female Characters in the Fourth Gospel.* Collegeville, MN: Liturgical Press, 1998.

Forster, E. M. *Aspects of the Novel.* New York: Harcourt, Brace & World, 1927.

Gibbs, Raymond W. *The Poetics of Mind: Figurative Thought, Language, and Understanding.* Cambridge: Cambridge University Press, 1994.

Gill, Christopher. "Character-Development in Plutarch and Tacitus." *Classical Quarterly* 77 (1983): 469–87.

Ginsberg, Warren. *The Cast of Character: The Representation of Personality in Ancient and Medieval Literature.* Toronto: University of Toronto Press, 1983.

Gowler, David B. *Host, Guest, Enemy, and Friend: Portraits of the Pharisees in Luke and Acts.* Emory Studies in Early Christianity 2. New York: Peter Lang, 1991.

Greimas, Algirdas Julien. *Sémantique structurale: Recherche de méthode.* Paris: Librairie Larousse, 1966.

Hakola, Raimo. "A Character Resurrected: Lazarus in the Fourth Gospel and Afterwards." Pages 223–63 in *Characterization in the Gospels: Reconceiving Narrative Criticism.* Edited by David Rhoads and Kari Syreeni. Sheffield: Sheffield Academic Press, 1999.

Harvey, W. J. *Character and the Novel.* London: Chatto & Windus, 1965.

Hays, Richard B. *Echoes of Scripture in the Letters of Paul.* New Haven, CT: Yale University Press, 1989.

Heath, Malcolm. *The Poetics of Greek Tragedy.* Stanford, CA: Stanford University Press, 1987.

Hochman, Baruch. *Character in Literature.* Ithaca, NY: Cornell University Press, 1985.

Hylen, Susan. *Allusion and Meaning in John 6.* Beiheifte zur Zeitschrift für die neutestamentliche Wissenschaft 137. Berlin: Walter de Gruyter, 2005.

Johnson, David H. "The Characterization of Jesus in Mark." *Didaskalia* 10 (1999): 79–92.

Johnson, Mark. *The Body in the Mind: The Bodily Basis of Meaning, Imagination, and Reason.* Chicago: University of Chicago Press, 1987.

Jones, John. *On Aristotle and Greek Tragedy.* New York: Oxford University Press, 1962.

Kermode, Frank. *The Genesis of Secrecy: On the Interpretation of Narrative.* Cambridge: Harvard University Press, 1979.

Koester, Craig R. *Symbolism in the Fourth Gospel: Meaning, Mystery, Community.* 2nd ed. Minneapolis: Fortress Press, 2003.

Lakoff, George, and Mark Johnson. *Metaphors We Live By.* Chicago: University of Chicago Press, 1980.

Lakoff, George, and Mark Turner. *More Than Cool Reason: A Field Guide to Poetic Metaphor.* Chicago: University of Chicago Press, 1989.

Lockwood, Peter F. "The Woman at the Well: Does the Traditional Reading Still Hold Water?" *Lutheran Theological Journal* 36 (2002): 12–24.

Malbon, Elizabeth Struthers. *In the Company of Jesus: Characters in Mark's Gospel.* Louisville, KY: Westminster John Knox Press, 2000.

Meeks, Wayne A. "The Man from Heaven in Johannine Sectarianism." *Journal of Biblical Literature* 91 (1972): 44–72.

Merenlahti, Petri. "Characters in the Making: Individuality and Ideology in the Gospels." Pages 49–72 in *Characterization in the Gospels: Reconceiving Narrative Criticism.* Edited by David Rhoads and Kari Syreeni. Sheffield: Sheffield Academic Press, 1999.

Moloney, Francis J. *Belief in the Word: Reading the Fourth Gospel: John 1–4.* Minneapolis: Fortress Press, 1993.

Morgann, Maurice. "Essay on the Dramatic Character of Sir John Falstaff." Pages 143–215 in *Shakespearian Criticism*. 1777. Edited by Daniel A. Fineman. Oxford: Clarendon Press, 1972.

O'Day, Gail R. *Revelation in the Fourth Gospel: Narrative Mode and Theological Claim*. Philadelphia: Fortress Press, 1986.

Pelling, Christopher. "Conclusion." Pages 245–62 in *Characterization and Individuality in Greek Literature*. Edited by Christopher Pelling. Oxford: Clarendon Press, 1990.

Powell, Mark Alan. *What Is Narrative Criticism?* Minneapolis: Fortress Press, 1990.

Propp, Vladimir. *Morphology of the Folktale*. Translated by Laurence Scott. 2nd ed. Austin: University of Texas Press, 1968.

Resseguie, James L. *The Strange Gospel: Narrative Design and Point of View in John*. Biblical Interpretation 56. Leiden: E. J. Brill, 2001.

Rhoads, David, Joanna Dewey, and Donald Michie. *Mark as Story: An Introduction to the Narrative of a Gospel*. 2nd ed. Minneapolis: Fortress Press, 1999.

Rimmon-Kenan, Shlomith. *Narrative Fiction: Contemporary Poetics*. 2nd ed. New York: Routledge, 2002.

Schaberg, Jane. *The Resurrection of Mary Magdalene: Legends, Apocrypha, and the Christian Testament*. New York: Continuum, 2004.

Schneiders, Sandra M. "Feminist Hermeneutics." Pages 349–69 in *Hearing the New Testament: Strategies for Interpretation*. Edited by Joel B. Green. Grand Rapids: Wm. B. Eerdmans Publishing Co., 1995.

Scholes, Robert, and Robert Kellogg. *The Nature of Narrative*. New York: Oxford University Press, 1966.

Shepherd, William H. *The Narrative Function of the Holy Spirit as a Character in Luke-Acts*. SBL Dissertation Series 147. Atlanta: Scholars Press, 1994.

Staley, Jeffrey L. "Stumbling in the Dark, Reaching for the Light: Reading Character in John 5 and 9." *Semeia* 52 (1991): 55–80.

Sternberg, Meir. *Expositional Modes and Temporal Ordering in Fiction*. Baltimore: Johns Hopkins University Press, 1978.

———. *The Poetics of Biblical Narrative: Ideological Literature and the Drama of Reading*. Bloomington, IN: Indiana University Press, 1985.

Thompson, Marianne Meye. "When the Ending Is Not the End." Pages 65–76 in *The Ending of Mark and the Ends of God*. Edited by Beverly Roberts Gaventa and Patrick D. Miller. Louisville, KY: Westminster John Knox Press, 2005.

Thompson, Richard P. "Reading beyond the Text, Part II: Literary Creativity and Characterization in Narrative Religious Texts of the Greco-Roman World." *ARC: The Journal of the Faculty of Religious Studies* [McGill University] 29 (2001): 81–122.

Tolmie, D. François. "The (Not So) Good Shepherd: The Use of Shepherd Imagery in the Characterisation of Peter in the Fourth Gospel." Pages

353–67 in *Imagery in the Gospel of John: Terms, Forms, Themes, and Theology of Johannine Figurative Language.* Edited by Jörg Frey, Jan G. van der Watt, and Ruben Zimmerman. Wissenschaftliche Untersuchungen zum Neuen Testament 200. Tübingen: Mohr Siebeck, 2006.

Turner, Mark. *The Literary Mind.* New York: Oxford University Press, 1996.

Williams, Joel F. *Other Followers of Jesus: Minor Characters as Major Figures in Mark's Gospel.* Journal for the Study of the New Testament: Supplement Series 102. Sheffield: JSOT Press, 1994.

PART I

2

Nicodemus

Nicodemus is a difficult character to evaluate, but a good one with which to begin this study, for he is surely one of the Gospel's most ambiguous characters. Almost every phrase that characterizes him raises more questions than it answers. Nicodemus "comes to" Jesus (cf. 3:2), which may indicate belief in him. But he also comes "at night," which associates him with the darkness that John has already said does not understand the light (1:5). At the end of their dialogue, Jesus indicates that Nicodemus does not understand "these things" (3:10). Though the dialogue ends, Nicodemus's story does not. His later speech and actions in chapters 7 and 19 suggest—but do not clearly confirm—that he develops further understanding about Jesus.

Not surprisingly, then, interpreters arrive at a variety of conclusions about Nicodemus. He is rarely seen as a positive character throughout the Gospel.[1] Overwhelmingly, commentators agree that he is portrayed negatively in John 3.[2] Some, however, see development in his character, so that he comes to be a more positive figure by the end of the Gospel.[3] Yet others maintain his lack of understanding through the end of the story.[4] A few interpreters understand Nicodemus as an ambiguous character. Details like the description of Nicodemus coming to Jesus by night make it difficult to reach a conclusion about his character. Jouette Bassler argues that "Nicodemus makes a series of appearances that seem to be fraught with significance, but the nature of that significance remains elusive. He appears in the narrative often enough

23

to evoke curiosity, but not, it seems, often enough to satisfy it."[5] In
the end it is not possible to say for sure what Nicodemus understands
or believes, and this ambiguity is usually evaluated negatively. If characters are meant to encounter Jesus and believe in him, Nicodemus's
wavering is negative. He starts out a Pharisee and perhaps flirts with
discipleship. But in the end he is still a Pharisee: "Nicodemus moves
through the narrative with one foot in each world, and in this Gospel
that is just not good enough."[6] In this reading, ambiguity in the character of Nicodemus points to his refusal to commit fully to Christian
discipleship. Readers assess Nicodemus's character in different ways,
but there is general agreement that he can ultimately be categorized as
a believer or an unbeliever.

In my view, Nicodemus is simply an ambiguous character. I see this
ambiguity even in his initial encounter with Jesus in chapter 3. Nicodemus first appears ambiguous because he is clearly equipped to understand Jesus and shows a strong initial understanding; but at the same
time he seems resistant to parts of Jesus' teaching. But the ambiguity in
Nicodemus's character is not simply a matter of his wavering decision.
The language of the Gospel makes it difficult to tell what Nicodemus
understands or believes. His reappearances in the Gospel narrative bring
the reader back to this character with uncertain results. His words and
actions may show some understanding of Jesus, but it is difficult to say
how much he understands or whether he has any self-awareness of the
way his actions display belief. Readers need not resolve the ambiguities
in Nicodemus's character.[7] Instead of deciding that ambiguity makes
him an unbeliever, I argue that he is simply an ambiguous character,
and I view this ambiguity as productive for the Gospel. The portrayal
of Nicodemus helps the reader explore ideas like Jesus as light and king,
and discipleship as birth. Through the character of Nicodemus, the
reader learns to reason according to John's worldview.

A BELIEVER IN SIGNS

The verses that precede the introduction of Nicodemus link him with
those who believe in Jesus' signs. The Greek indicates a connection
between 2:23–25 and the story of Nicodemus, one that the chapter
break and most English translations obscure. The language of verse
25—literally, "[Jesus] had no need for someone to witness concerning
a man; for he knew what was in a man"—leads directly into the story

of chapter 3: "There was a man of the Pharisees, named Nicodemus."
The repetition of the word "man" (or "person," ἄνθρωπος, *anthrōpos*)
invites the reader to understand Nicodemus as one such person, about
whom the previous verses speak. He can therefore be understood as one
of those who "believed in his name because they saw the signs that he
was doing" (2:23), but to whom Jesus does not entrust himself, because
he knows all people (2:24–25).[8]

The juxtaposition of Jesus' mistrust and the people's belief in his
signs raises questions about Nicodemus's character. Although John
gives no indication of what causes Jesus not to entrust himself, one
way to understand the language is that Jesus mistrusts the people's
belief because it is based on signs. Belief in signs indicates incomplete
understanding. The conversation with Nicodemus may be evidence of
this: he shows some initial understanding but is unwilling or unable
to understand all that Jesus says. Yet belief in signs is not necessarily a
negative thing in John's perspective. Elsewhere in John, belief in signs
is mentioned without judgment: not only the crowd (6:2, 14) but also
Jesus' disciples (2:11) believe in him on the basis of signs. The belief
attributed to Nicodemus, then, is not necessarily negative.[9] Taken by
itself, 2:23 gives no evaluation of the people's belief. It is the "but" that
follows in verse 24 that qualifies the reader's view of their understanding: they believe, yet Jesus knows something more. The verses function
in part to draw attention to Jesus' knowledge of people, a point to
which the stories of Nicodemus and the Samaritan woman also draw
attention. Jesus' knowledge does not necessarily mean that the people's
belief is wrong or ill founded. It may simply mean that belief by itself
does not lead Jesus to trust people. Nicodemus then serves as an example of this. Jesus engages him initially, and when Nicodemus does not
progress, Jesus cuts off the conversation.

Nicodemus's initial belief on the basis of signs may even be a positive aspect of his character. Elsewhere John indicates that belief on
the basis of signs is an important component of understanding who
Jesus is. The statement of the Gospel's purpose in 20:30–31 indicates
directly that "these [signs] are written so that you may believe that Jesus
is the Messiah, the Son of God." Signs may lead to belief in Jesus. The
performance of signs seems to have been part of the expectations people
had of the Messiah (7:31). By recognizing the importance of Jesus'
signs, the reader may come to understand his identity. With a parallel
term, "works" (ἔργα, *erga*), John indicates that Jesus' acts testify to his
relationship to God (see 5:36; 10:37–38). Jesus is sent by God, and

part of his mission is the performance of works. Belief in the works indicates understanding of Jesus' origins.

The most important question may not be whether Nicodemus believes on the basis of signs, but what the signs lead him to believe.[10] Nicodemus's first words to Jesus elaborate what belief on the basis of signs means in his case. The signs suggest Jesus' relationship to God: "We know that you are a teacher who has come from God; for no one can do these signs that you do, unless God is with that person" (3:2). A number of commentators see this as an incomplete understanding of Jesus.[11] Yet Nicodemus's words are not far from expressing belief that the Gospel upholds.[12] The identification of Jesus as a teacher (or rabbi) is also found on the lips of the disciples in 1:38.[13] One of these disciples says shortly thereafter, "We have found the Messiah" (1:41). The juxtaposition of terms suggests that for the disciples, they are complementary rather than contradictory titles. "Teacher" may not be a complete understanding of Jesus' role, but neither is it incorrect. Teaching is an important aspect of Jesus' role (e.g., 7:15–17; 18:19–20). Calling Jesus "teacher" may indicate understanding on Nicodemus's part.

Nicodemus shows understanding by identifying Jesus as a teacher "who has come from God" (3:2). This phrase directly parallels what the Gospel claims Jesus knows about himself: "that he had come from God" (13:3). The question of Jesus' origin also comes up repeatedly in this Gospel. In John 6, the Jews say that they know Jesus' mother and father: "How can he now say, 'I have come down from heaven'?" (6:42). In chapter 7, the question of the Messiah's origins resurfaces (see 7:26–27, 41–42, 52). While the crowd debates if Jesus can be the Messiah based on his hometown, the reader knows that the most important thing in answering this question is that Jesus is from God and is sent by God (7:28–29). In the light of these later debates, Nicodemus's statement that Jesus is a teacher who has come from God represents an early and accurate understanding of Jesus' origins.[14]

Likewise, Nicodemus's statement that Jesus' signs indicate that "God is with him" (3:2) also shows understanding. Jesus' signs testify that he is sent from God (5:36; 10:25). Although the exact Greek phrasing, "God is with him" (ὁ θεὸς μετ' αὐτοῦ, *ho theos met autou*) does not occur elsewhere in John, parallel phrases are found in 1:1 (with God, πρὸς τὸν θεόν, *pros ton theon*) and 6:46 (from God, παρὰ τοῦ θεοῦ, *para tou theou*, cf. 9:16, 33).[15] Nicodemus's words convey his understanding that God is the source of Jesus' acts. In this, he expresses something important about Jesus.

Nicodemus's entry into the Gospel aligns him with those who believe based on signs. But this in itself does not give a decisively negative quality to his character. It may even prepare the reader to see Nicodemus in a positive light, as one who understands the signs and believes from the very beginning. If this is the case, what is at issue in the following verses is the extent of Nicodemus's belief and his willingness to deepen his understanding of Jesus on the basis of his teaching. In light of this, what is striking is that Nicodemus does not continue to understand Jesus. This difficulty should not necessarily lead to a rejection of Nicodemus's initial faith.[16] It may be that the dialogue with Nicodemus leads the reader to consider this situation: Nicodemus has all the resources he needs to understand Jesus and yet does not.

ONE OF THE PHARISEES

Nicodemus might well be expected to progress in his understanding: he is "one of the Pharisees," and "a leader of the Jews" (3:1). These descriptions complicate his portrayal, because readers must decide what the association with other groups means for Nicodemus's character. On the basis of verse 1, many interpreters understand Nicodemus as representative of the Pharisees and their response to Jesus.[17] The reader of the Gospel must decide how the identification of Nicodemus as a Pharisee contributes to his characterization. Some argue that John has already depicted the Pharisees negatively at this point in the narrative.[18] In 1:24, the Pharisees have sent people to question John the Baptist. Many view their approach as hostile from the start: Raymond Brown describes this interchange as an "interrogation."[19] He argues that, unlike the Synoptic Gospels, John has no trial before the Sanhedrin prior to Jesus' crucifixion (see Matt. 26:57–68; Mark 14:53–65; Luke 22:66–71), but intersperses trial language throughout John. This suggests that even the questioning of John the Baptist in John 1 should be read as a trial similar to the one that ends in Jesus' condemnation. The reader should presume that the Pharisees are already antagonistic to Jesus. Yet their question to John the Baptist reads simply, "Who are you?" (1:19). It is not necessarily hostile. It can be read as an open question. The follow-up questions posed by the priests and Levites even seem to indicate a positive impression of John the Baptist. When he says he is not the Messiah, they respond by asking, "Are you Elijah? . . . Are you the prophet?" (1:20–21). These questions suggest that they are considering John's behavior in the light of other important figures. When the Pharisees are seen in this way, Nicodemus's initial belief in Jesus is less surprising.

Since Nicodemus is also a "leader of the Jews," the same question can be asked of him in relationship to the Jews. In John 2:18–20, the Jews question Jesus about his overturning tables and driving people out of the temple. Their questions are skeptical, although much milder than one might expect, given the scope of Jesus' actions. They first ask him for a sign, for a way of understanding what he has done or his authority to do it. After Jesus' rather cryptic reply about the temple, they ask, "Will you raise it up in three days?" (verse 20). In Greek grammar a question may be phrased to imply that it is tentative or expects a negative answer. John employs this construction a number of times in the Gospel (with μή, *mē*, 4:29; 7:51), but not in this case. The open construction suggests that their question may be genuine. In addition, the narrator's comment—"Therefore, when he was raised from the dead, his disciples remembered that he had said this, and they believed the scripture and the word that Jesus had spoken" (2:22)—implies that even the disciples do not understand Jesus' words at this point. The disciples remember his words and believe only after the resurrection. Questioning Jesus' statement about the temple is natural, given the strangeness of what he says. Thus the Jews in the Gospel may not be strongly opposed to Jesus at this point; their questions may even be taken as genuine.

The presentation of the Pharisees and the Jews in latter parts of the Gospel also influences interpreters' decisions about the ways they understand Nicodemus's character. Most interpreters assess John's overall presentation of these characters as negative. Bassler's view is typical: "Though the Fourth Gospel refers to the 'Jews' in a variety of contexts and ways, a characteristically Johannine usage emerges in which the term loses its nationalistic meaning and comes to designate unreceptivity— even hostility—toward Jesus."[20] A full discussion of the Jews deserves its own chapter (see chap. 7). As a corporate character, the Jews are characterized as much by their divided response to Jesus as by hostility. They are repeatedly said to believe in him (8:31; 11:45; 12:11). At other times, some of them seek to kill him (5:18; 7:1; 8:59; 10:31). It thus is difficult to tell from the outset how Nicodemus's membership in this group should color the reader's understanding of his character.

Ambiguity in Nicodemus's character arises in part from his association with these groups. The reader must decide what it means for Nicodemus to be a Pharisee and a leader of the Jews. Readers who view the Pharisees negatively will likely be suspicious of Nicodemus from the outset. Yet if the Pharisees are more ambiguous, Nicodemus's openness to Jesus might contribute to the divided nature of the group's portrait. The terms John uses to characterize Nicodemus do not simply decide the matter of his character; yet these terms open questions for the reader.

UNDERSTANDING AND MISUNDERSTANDING

What does Nicodemus understand about Jesus? This question is at the heart of assessing his character, for belief in Jesus would certainly qualify him for a positive evaluation. It is difficult to say what Nicodemus believes or does not believe, or how much he understands of what Jesus says. Nicodemus's speech is one of the most reliable sources for his understanding or lack thereof, yet his language also gives rise to multiple interpretations.

Nicodemus's second speaking part (verse 4) may show less understanding than his first, in which he declared Jesus to be sent by God. Jesus tells him that to enter the kingdom of God, one must be born *anōthen*. The Greek word *anōthen* means either "from above" or "again," depending on the context. Nicodemus responds, "How is it possible for a man to be born once he has grown old? He cannot enter into his mother's womb a second time and be born, can he?" (3:4). The interpretation of Nicodemus's response depends on what it suggests about his understanding of birth *anōthen*. For some interpreters, Nicodemus's mistake is to understand Jesus' words only on a physical or material level.[21] He thinks Jesus speaks of a physical second birth (born again), while Jesus speaks of spiritual birth (born from above). The way in which Nicodemus misunderstands is then illuminated by Jesus' words: "What is born of the flesh is flesh, and what is born of the spirit is spirit" (verse 6). Nicodemus is of the flesh. It is not simply that he does not understand Jesus: he cannot understand.

Yet verse 4 may show that Nicodemus has a certain basic level of understanding. For a majority of scholars, the misunderstanding in verses 3–4 is not that Jesus means one thing (born from above) and Nicodemus understands another (born again), but that Jesus means *both* born from above and born again.[22] If Jesus means both, then Nicodemus has understood a piece of the equation. He is not entirely off track in asking about a second birth, even if he has not fully grasped the metaphor of birth "from above." When Jesus is understood to support both aspects of birth *anōthen*, the dualism of this passage is minimized to some extent. While many scholars identify Nicodemus as being one of those born of "the flesh," his response in this verse should not place him on one side of a dualistic divide. There is still more that Nicodemus should understand, but his question shows that he understands to some extent and seeks greater understanding.

It is even possible that Nicodemus understands Jesus' metaphorical speech. His response can be read as addressing Jesus on a metaphorical level. Jesus draws on a conventional metaphor of spiritual parentage, which is something that Nicodemus could and probably should understand. Numerous Old Testament texts speak of Israel as God's child.[23] Just as modern-day readers have little problem identifying Jesus' words as metaphorical, it is quite likely that Nicodemus grasps the birth metaphor. In response, he picks up the vocabulary that Jesus has used and questions him further. The reader must imagine a tone of openness in Nicodemus's question: "You say that one must be born *anōthen*. How does such birth happen? It's not possible to reenter the womb. . . ." Nicodemus questions the teacher about how this process takes place.[24] Nicodemus is portrayed as naive: he does not understand how one is born *anōthen*, something a Pharisee might be expected to know. But he is not so naive that he does not understand this to be metaphorical language.

Verses 5–10 support the possibility of openness and sincerity in Nicodemus's approach to Jesus. Many read Jesus' response in verse 5 as intentionally evasive. Jesus does not address Nicodemus's question directly. Instead, he replies: "Truly, truly, I say to you, unless one is born of water and the Spirit, one cannot enter the kingdom of God" (verse 5). Nicodemus has misunderstood so completely that Jesus does not bother to engage him directly.[25] Hoskyns writes, "Jesus discourses openly and without reserve. He does not, however, discourse *with* Nicodemus, but *to* him; and *through* him to the readers of the gospel."[26] If Jesus does not take Nicodemus's question seriously, neither should the reader.

Yet another way to read verse 5 is that Jesus is explaining what it means to be born *anōthen*. He begins with one metaphorical understanding of the life of the believer—being born *anōthen*—and elaborates that idea with an additional metaphor, birth by water and Spirit.[27] If this is the case, then Jesus' words may be understood as a response to Nicodemus's question. How can one be born *anōthen*? There are two answers combined in Jesus' response. First, one is born "by water and the

Spirit." Second, this birth is a parallel concept to entry into the kingdom of God. In each case, Jesus elaborates the metaphor of birth *anōthen* by using additional metaphors available to Nicodemus from Jewish tradition. Renewal by the pouring out of God's Spirit, or by cleansing with water, are also familiar Old Testament concepts.[28] If Jesus engages Nicodemus seriously, then it makes sense to read Nicodemus's question in verse 4 as a real question about the process of rebirth.

In verse 6 Jesus continues to engage Nicodemus regarding the nature of rebirth. Many interpreters read this verse as a pronouncement that bears directly—and negatively—on Nicodemus's character: When Jesus says, "What is born of the flesh is flesh, and what is born of the Spirit is spirit" (verse 6), he speaks directly of Nicodemus. Nicodemus is "born of the flesh" and therefore cannot understand things of the Spirit.[29] But the Greek syntax of this sentence makes this reading unlikely. John uses the neuter participle, "what is born of the flesh" (τὸ γεγεννημένον, *to gegennēmenon*) rather than the masculine, "the one who is born of the flesh" (ὁ γεγεννημένος, *ho gegennēmenos*). The use of the neuter may mean that John does not have the whole person in mind. Jesus is not categorizing humans into two separate and opposite groups: some fleshly, some spiritual. Rather, the language continues to elaborate the metaphor of birth *anōthen*. Being born *anōthen* does not mean an additional physical birth, as Nicodemus's question has implied. Humans are already born of the flesh. To connect to the Spirit of God, a part of the person is born "of the Spirit." Jesus continues to teach Nicodemus about birth *anōthen* by drawing a distinction between the former birth and this new birth.

Nicodemus's third question casts doubt on the level of his understanding. Jesus speaks of being born of the Spirit, and Nicodemus replies, "How can these things be?" (3:9). On the one hand, Nicodemus again appears incredulous. His question may represent a complete lack of understanding or resistance to understanding.[30] He has not really been able to follow Jesus' remarks and now questions how any of it can even be possible. Yet another way to translate verse 9 is "How can these things happen?"[31] If this is the case, Nicodemus is following the conversation to some extent but is still asking the question "How does one achieve spiritual rebirth?" Interpreted either way, Nicodemus still seems to end up understanding less than someone in his position should.

Jesus' answer in verse 10 can be read as supporting either of the above options. He says, "You are a teacher of Israel, and you do not understand these things?" (3:10). The reminder of Nicodemus's status as a Pharisee and leader of the Jews underscores the idea that there is something here that Nicodemus should be able to understand yet has not. On the one hand, it may be that Nicodemus has not understood any of the conversation and does not even grasp the possibility of rebirth. On the other, Nicodemus may understand that there is birth *anōthen* but not have any idea how to achieve it. Jesus' words imply that Nicodemus's background gives him the means to answer these questions. Nicodemus understands that Jesus is speaking metaphorically and should be able to converse with Jesus on a deeper level. Instead, he remains stuck in a series of procedural questions.

Yet Jesus' words in verse 11 imply that Nicodemus has ultimately not grasped the heart of the conversation: "Truly, truly, I say to you, we speak about what we know, and witness to what we have seen, and you do not receive our teaching." If Nicodemus has been seeking understanding, he now is characterized as rejecting Jesus' teaching. Jesus' response does not supply the content of what Nicodemus has missed. Perhaps he has understood nothing and is not capable of understanding. But perhaps Nicodemus, while not a firm believer, understands certain things and resists others.

AN OPEN-ENDED STORY

Nicodemus's dialogue with Jesus in John 3 dissipates rather than ends. This makes it difficult to reach a bottom-line assessment of Nicodemus at this point. The reader last hears Nicodemus speak in verse 9, but Jesus goes on for eleven more verses. The Gospel gives no indication what, if anything, Nicodemus learns from what Jesus says. But the reader comes across this character two more times as the Gospel progresses. In each case, ambiguities remain regarding what Nicodemus understands or believes about Jesus.

Nicodemus's appearance at the end of chapter 7 does not clarify what he understands about Jesus. He appears amid his fellow Pharisees, who with the chief priests have sent out the temple police to arrest Jesus. The police return empty-handed, and they seem impressed by Jesus: "Never has anyone spoken like this!" (7:46). The Pharisees chide the police, likening them to the masses, who do not know the law. Nicodemus interjects: "Our law does not judge people without first giving them a hearing, . . . does it?" If this is a defense of Jesus, it is tentative. Nicodemus makes a single attempt to reason with his fellow

Pharisees and frames his objection as a question. The Gospel records no rebuttal to the Pharisees' reply, "You are not also from Galilee, are you? Search and see that a prophet does not arise out of Galilee" (7:52). So here Nicodemus reappears in the Gospel story only to reiterate a lukewarm approach to Jesus.

Yet other elements of his characterization suggest that Nicodemus now believes in Jesus. The Pharisees pose their argument to the police as a rhetorical question, whose answer should be apparent: "Has any one of the authorities or of the Pharisees believed in him?" (7:48). In this context, Nicodemus's reply may indicate that he is precisely that: one of the authorities or of the Pharisees who believes in Jesus.[32] The reader is reminded about Nicodemus with two phrases that characterize him as "one who had come to Jesus before" and "who was one of them" (7:50). The first phrase echoes the language of 3:2, in which Nicodemus "came to Jesus by night." For readers who have understood this description negatively, the language reinforces Nicodemus's prior lack of understanding. However, as noted earlier, "coming to Jesus" is also a metaphor for having faith. The second phrase may also be negative or positive: Nicodemus is "one of them." If "they" are seen as entirely negative, this means that Nicodemus cannot be a believer.[33] Another possibility is that the identification of Nicodemus as "one of them" underscores the irony of the Pharisees' statement to the police.[34] They assume that none of the Pharisees believes in Jesus. And their question suggests that if Pharisees did believe, then the police would have grounds to do so. Immediately "one of them" speaks on Jesus' behalf. The Pharisees are shown to be wrong on two levels: some of the Pharisees or authorities do believe, and this gives credence to what the police have witnessed.

Not only does one of the Pharisees defend Jesus at this point, but he also does so on the basis of the law: "Our law does not judge people without first giving them a hearing, . . . does it?" (7:51). Because the Pharisees have just cursed the crowd for not knowing the law, Nicodemus's response is doubly ironic. One who knows the law believes in Jesus. Yet scholars have differed over whether Nicodemus's words are an accurate statement of the law. Deuteronomy 1:16 and 17:4 provide that both sides should be given a fair hearing, and 17:6 and 19:15 instruct that two or more witnesses be heard. Yet nowhere in the law does it say that the defendant must be given a hearing.[35] In John 5:31–47, Jesus seems to reinforce this idea by saying that he does not testify to himself, but John the Baptist, Jesus' works, his Father, and the Scriptures all testify on his behalf. Yet in 8:14, Jesus will argue that his own testimony is valid "because I know where I have come from and where I am going." Nicodemus's words anticipate this latter statement.[36] His defense of Jesus shows significant understanding.

The Pharisees' hostile response to Nicodemus also points in favor of his understanding. They immediately seek to discredit him, suggesting that they see his statement as a defense of Jesus. Their characterization of Nicodemus as being from Galilee is likely intended as an insult, but it also aligns Nicodemus with Jesus. They understand Nicodemus's words to imply the validity of Jesus' speech and suggest that Nicodemus must be like Jesus in his origins. This is a bad thing from the Pharisees' perspective, but not from the perspective of the Gospel. The believer knows where Jesus is "from" (e.g., 7:33), and the birth metaphor suggests that believers share that identity in being born *anōthen* (cf. 14:3). Perhaps the Pharisees are correct in a way they do not understand: Nicodemus has come to share in Jesus' origins.

A SECRET BELIEVER

Like his defense of Jesus in chapter 7, Nicodemus's final appearance is difficult to interpret. He appears alongside Joseph of Arimathea, who has requested the body of Jesus for burial (19:38). Nicodemus comes bringing a great quantity of spices (19:39), and together they lay Jesus' body in a new tomb (19:42).

On the one hand, the presentation of Nicodemus as a secret disciple is negative. Nicodemus is characterized by his association with Joseph of Arimathea, whom the Gospel says is "a disciple of Jesus, but secretly, because of the fear of the Jews" (19:38). Nicodemus's close association with Joseph suggests that he may be a secret disciple as well.[37] Interpreters usually assess this secrecy negatively. Although Jesus himself acts in secret (ἐν κρυπτῷ, *en kryptō*, 7:10) or hides himself (from the related Greek verb *kryptō*; see 8:59; 12:36), these appear as momentary episodes between which Jesus acts and teaches openly (7:26; 18:20). Jesus is certainly never said to act out of fear; it is secrecy due to fear toward which John is critical. Many are said to believe in Jesus but do not confess because of their fear. These, the Gospel indicates, "loved the glory of humans more than the glory of God" (12:43). Through his association with Joseph, Nicodemus may be one such character. He acts in secret and perhaps out of fear. "He remains, therefore, 'one of them,' not one of the children of God."[38] If discipleship is an either/or proposition, Nicodemus has failed.

Other aspects of his characterization, however, contribute to a more positive assessment. Like Joseph, Nicodemus's belief may be secret to the Pharisees as a group. But the request for Jesus' body and his burial are public acts.[39] Even if Nicodemus does not confess belief, his actions may be understood to be a witness. Jesus' own actions witness to himself (5:36), and the earlier conversation with Nicodemus indicates that "those who do what is true come to the light, so that it may be shown that their deeds have been done in God" (3:21). The reader must assess whether Nicodemus's final actions qualify as something "true."

Scholars disagree regarding what Nicodemus's actions imply about his understanding. For some, the expensive burial places too much emphasis on Jesus' death. Nicodemus does not understand that Jesus will rise again, or that his "lifting up" is both crucifixion and glorification.[40] Other readers see comprehension here. John's trial scene has centered on the question "Are you the king of the Jews?" (18:33; cf. 18:37, 39; 19:14, 19–22). Nicodemus enacts a burial fit for a king: he brings an overly large quantity of spices. His actions may suggest that he knows the answer to Pilate's question. Yet how does the reader assess such implicit actions? Even the more positive aspects of Nicodemus's character may be accidental. Other characters unwittingly testify to Jesus' identity (see e.g., Pilate's inscription on the cross; 19:19–22), and that may be the case here as well. Because the Gospel gives no motivations for his actions, the reader is left to make a determination based on what is implicit.

CONCLUSION

Nicodemus's character can be assessed in multiple ways. He is often seen initially as a character who either willfully misunderstands or is not capable of understanding Jesus. He is "of the flesh" rather than of the Spirit. When this is the case, Nicodemus's character is valuable as an example of those who reject Jesus. His initial understanding of Jesus is not enough, and he resists further instruction. Even if he defends Jesus to some extent, whatever belief he has is secret and therefore inadequate. He represents both the enemies of Jesus during his lifetime and those who rejected John's community. Yet other interpreters see a positive development in Nicodemus's character. He may not understand Jesus initially, but by the end he enacts a significant level of understanding. As I have argued, Nicodemus can also be read ambiguously, with both positive and negative attributes. He understands that Jesus speaks metaphorically of spiritual birth, but he resists delving deeper into Jesus' teaching. And in his final appearances, it is not possible to say for sure what Nicodemus understands or believes.

The ambiguity of Nicodemus's character leads readers to reflect on the identity of Jesus. Nicodemus comes to Jesus "by night." Whatever that means for Nicodemus's character, interpreters agree that Jesus is light. They go on to understand Nicodemus in different ways. In one version he is a representative of the forces of unbelief, and he emerges from this darkness only briefly before returning again. In another, his approach to the light portrays him as one sincerely open to understanding Jesus. Having to decide what the detail of night brings to the character of Nicodemus leads readers to rely on John's understanding of Jesus elsewhere: he is "the light." Something similar happens at Jesus' burial. John supplies only Nicodemus's actions, not his intentions. This puts the reader in the position of reflecting on the meaning of these actions. Nicodemus gives Jesus a royal burial. He may do so because he misunderstands and is focused on Jesus' death, yet even so his actions testify to Jesus' identity as king. Even when seen as an unwitting and not an intentional witness to Jesus, Nicodemus has served an instructive purpose.

In evaluating Nicodemus's understanding, readers also make judgments about Jesus' relationship to Judaism. If Nicodemus has the resources to understand what Jesus says, what is the reader to make of his lack of understanding? One option is that Nicodemus is a representative of Jewish leadership, and the knowledge he has is not an adequate basis on which to understand Jesus' identity. The point is that "Jesus cannot be understood by old standards, even those of the traditional Judaism represented by Nicodemus."[41] He must be comprehended on his own terms.

My interpretation suggests instead that Nicodemus's failure to understand is an example of Johannine irony. If Nicodemus understands a good deal of what Jesus says, then his failure is not a failure of the concepts of Jewish tradition but of his own ability to understand how Jesus' teaching carries forward that tradition. The importance of reading Nicodemus as understanding is not that it makes him an ideal believer but that it puts him into a different relationship to Jesus' metaphorical speech. The birth metaphor of chapter 3 is continuous with Jewish tradition. Jesus is not creating a new religion ex nihilo. Nicodemus's knowledge prepares him to understand a good deal about Jesus' teaching, yet he does not fully accept Jesus' testimony. The irony is that such a great teacher of Israel does not grasp Jesus' teaching about rebirth. The critical portrayal of Nicodemus in his first appearance underscores how Jesus' teaching builds on rather than rejects Jewish conceptions of spiritual birth.

Ambiguity may also lead the reader to reflection on the nature of discipleship in John. Many scholars claim that reading the story of Nicodemus functions to form the reading community as a group of "insiders."[42] The reader understands what characters like Nicodemus do not. Only the believer with special knowledge of Jesus truly understands. Readers who believe in Jesus come to understand themselves in opposition to unbelieving characters like Nicodemus.

If Nicodemus remains ambiguous, the reader learns something different about being a disciple of Jesus. First, there is more to discipleship than belief in Jesus. If belief is the only category that matters, Nicodemus fails miserably as a disciple. Yet even without clear evidence of belief, Nicodemus's actions show evidence of discipleship. Jesus indicates that his followers should expect persecution by the world (15:18–25), and Nicodemus suffers ridicule because of his defense of Jesus. The disciple's role is to testify or witness, an activity that aligns the believer with one of the Spirit's roles (15:26–27). Nicodemus's final actions witness to Jesus' kingship. One who is "born of the Spirit" (3:8) might be identified by just such actions.

Second, through the metaphor of birth *anōthen*, the reader may reflect on the process of becoming a disciple. Metaphorical speech is appropriate to the subject of the life of faith and difficult to avoid. Parallel metaphors John employs are "seeing" or "entering into" the kingdom of God (3:3, 5). These metaphors illumine the life of discipleship in different ways. Birth *anōthen* emphasizes the believer's entry into light and life. It suggests a transformation like that of human birth, but one that initiates life in the Spirit. Because of the parallel to human birth, birth *anōthen* may be interpreted as a onetime event. Modern Christians often speak of being "born again" as an all-or-nothing affair. Yet the juxtaposition with Nicodemus raises questions about whether this is the case. Nicodemus begins by understanding quite a bit about Jesus' identity, but then he resists Jesus' teaching. Later he seems to understand more than his first encounter suggested.

If Nicodemus is a disciple at all, he comes to it in bits and pieces. The characterization of Nicodemus presents the reader with an idea of discipleship as an event (like birth) and as a slow and uncertain process. Both metaphors illumine aspects of human religious experience. Many Christians experience a particular moment of enlightenment through which they come into deeper understanding of the divine. Others experience spurts of understanding. Still others would say that both are true: moments of illumination are only the beginning (or the middle) of a lifetime of growing closer to God. The characterization of Nicodemus suggests a creative tension between singular and progressive understanding. He fails to grasp some things and succeeds at others. Interacting with Nicodemus's character brings the reader to a place of reflection on the complexities of following Jesus.

BIBLIOGRAPHY

Auwers, Jean-Marie. "La nuit de Nicodème (Jean 3, 2; 19, 39) ou l'ombre du langage." *Revue biblique* 97 (1990): 481–503.

Barrett, C. K. *The Gospel according to St. John*. Philadelphia: Westminster Press, 1978.

Bassler, Jouette M. "Mixed Signals: Nicodemus in the Fourth Gospel." *Journal of Biblical Literature* 108 (1989): 635–46.

Bligh, John. "Four Studies in St. John, II: Nicodemus." *Heythrop Journal* 8 (1967): 40–51.

Blomberg, Craig L. "The Globalization of Biblical Interpretation: A Test Case— John 3–4." *Bulletin for Biblical Research* 5 (1995): 1–15.

Borgen, Peder. *Bread from Heaven: An Exegetical Study of the Concept of Manna in the Gospel of John and the Writings of Philo*. Novum Testamentum Supplement 10. Leiden: E. J. Brill, 1965.

Born, J. Bryan. "Literary Features in the Gospel of John (An Analysis of John 3:1–12)." *Direction* 17, no. 2 (1988): 3–17.

Brown, Raymond. *The Community of the Beloved Disciple*. New York: Paulist Press, 1979.

———. *The Gospel according to John*. 2 vols. Anchor Bible 29–29A. New York: Doubleday, 1966–70.

Bultmann, Rudolf. *The Gospel of John*. Philadelphia: Westminster Press, 1971.

Carson, D. A. *The Gospel according to John*. Grand Rapids: Wm. B. Eerdmans Publishing Co., 1991.

Collins, Raymond F. "The Representative Figures of the Fourth Gospel—I." *Downside Review* 94 (1976): 26–46.

Conway, Colleen M. *Men and Women in the Fourth Gospel: Gender and Johannine Characterization.* Society of Biblical Literature Dissertation Series 167. Atlanta: Society of Biblical Literature, 1999.

Cotterell, F. P. "The Nicodemus Conversation: A Fresh Appraisal." *Expository Times* 96 (1984–85): 237–42.

Culpepper, R. Alan. *Anatomy of the Fourth Gospel: A Study in Literary Design.* Philadelphia: Fortress Press, 1983.

De Jonge, Marinus. *Jesus: Stranger from Heaven and Son of God: Jesus Christ and the Christians in the Johannine Perspective.* Translated by John E. Steely. Society of Biblical Literature Sources for Biblical Study 11. Missoula, MT: Scholars Press, 1977.

Derrett, J. Duncan M. "Correcting Nicodemus (John 3:2, 21)." *Expository Times* 112 (2001): 126.

Dodd, C. H. *The Interpretation of the Fourth Gospel.* Cambridge: Cambridge University Press, 1953.

Graf, Julius. "Nikodemus." *Theologische Quartalschrift* 132 (1952): 62–86.

Grese, William C. "'Unless One Is Born Again': The Use of a Heavenly Journey in John 3." *Journal of Biblical Literature* 107 (1988): 677–93.

Hoskyns, Edwyn Clement. *The Fourth Gospel.* Edited by F. N. Davey. London: Faber & Faber, 1947.

Koester, Craig R. "Hearing, Seeing, and Believing in the Gospel of John." *Biblica* 70 (1989): 327–48.

———. *Symbolism in the Fourth Gospel: Meaning, Mystery, Community.* 2nd ed. Minneapolis: Fortress Press, 2003.

———. "What Does It Mean to Be Human? Imagery and the Human Condition in John's Gospel." Pages 403–20 in *Imagery in the Gospel of John: Terms, Forms, Themes, and Theology of Johannine Figurative Language.* Edited by Jörg Frey, Jan G. van der Watt, and Ruben Zimmerman. Tübingen: Mohr Siebeck, 2006.

Köstenberger, Andreas J. *John.* Grand Rapids: Baker Academic, 2004.

Kysar, Robert. "The Making of Metaphor: Another Reading of John 3:1–15." Pages 21–41 in *"What Is John?" Readers and Readings of the Fourth Gospel.* Edited by Fernando F. Segovia. SBL Symposium Series 3. Atlanta: Scholars Press, 1996.

Lindars, Barnabas. *The Gospel of John.* New Century Bible. London: Oliphants, 1972.

Martyn, J. Louis. *History and Theology in the Fourth Gospel.* 3rd ed. Louisville, KY: Westminster John Knox Press, 2003.

Meeks, Wayne A. "The Man from Heaven in Johannine Sectarianism." *Journal of Biblical Literature* 91 (1972): 44–72.

Michel, M. "Nicodème ou le non-lieu de la vérité." *Revue des sciences religieuses* 55 (1981): 227–36.

Moloney, Francis J. *Belief in the Word: Reading the Fourth Gospel: John 1–4.* Minneapolis: Fortress Press, 1993.

———. *The Gospel of John*. Sacra pagina 4. Collegeville, MN: Liturgical Press, 1988.

Mosur, Félix. "Missverständnis und Ironie in der johanneischen Argumentation und ihr Gebrauch in der heutigen pfarramtlichen Praxis." Pages 47–73 in *Johannes-Studien: Interdisziplinäre Zugänge zum Johannes-Evangelium*. Edited by Martin Rose. Zurich: Theologischer Verlag, 1991.

Neyrey, Jerome H. "John III—A Debate over Johannine Epistemology and Christology." *Novum Testamentum* 23 (1981): 115–27.

O'Day, Gail R. *The Gospel of John*. New Interpreter's Bible 9. Nashville: Abingdon Press, 1995.

Odeberg, Hugo. *The Fourth Gospel: Interpreted in Its Relation to Contemporaneous Religious Currents in Palestine and the Hellenistic-Oriental World*. Chicago: Argonaut, 1968.

Pamment, Margaret. "Focus in the Fourth Gospel." *Expository Times* 97 (1985): 71–5.

Pancaro, Severino. *The Law in the Fourth Gospel: The Torah and the Gospel, Moses and Jesus, Judaism and Christianity according to John*. Supplements to Novum Testamentum 42. Leiden: E. J. Brill, 1975.

———. "The Metamorphosis of a Legal Principle in the Fourth Gospel: A Closer Look at Jn 7, 51." *Biblica* 53 (1972): 340–61.

Rensberger, David. *Johannine Faith and Liberating Community*. Louisville, KY: Westminster John Knox Press, 1996.

Renz, Gabi. "Nicodemus: An Ambiguous Disciple? A Narrative Sensitive Investigation." Pages 255–83 in *Challenging Perspectives on the Gospel of John*. Edited by John Lierman. Wissenschaftliche Untersuchungen zum Neuen Testament 219. Tübingen: Mohr Siebeck, 2006.

Resseguie, James L. *The Strange Gospel: Narrative Design and Point of View in John*. Biblical Interpretation 56. Leiden: E. J. Brill, 2001.

Sandnes, Karl Olav. "Whence and Whither: A Narrative Perspective on Birth ἄνωθεν (John 3, 3–8)." *Biblica* 86 (2005): 153–73.

Schnackenburg, Rudolf. *The Gospel according to St. John*. 3 vols. New York: Seabury Press, 1982–90.

Smith, D. Moody. *John*. Abingdon New Testament Commentaries. Nashville: Abingdon Press, 1999.

Sylva, Dennis D. "Nicodemus and His Spices." *New Testament Studies* 34 (1988): 148–51.

Tsuchido, Kiyoshi. "The Composition of the Nicodemus-Episode, John ii 23–iii 21." *Annual of the Japanese Biblical Institute* 1 (1975): 91–103.

Wellhausen, Julius. *Das Evangelium Johannes*. Berlin: Georg Reimer, 1908.

Whitters, Mark F. "Discipleship in John: Four Profiles." *Word and World* 18 (1998): 422–27.

Williford, Don. "John 3:1–15—*gennēthēnai anōthen*: A Radical Departure, a New Beginning." *Review and Expositor* 96 (1999): 451–61.

3

The Samaritan Woman

The Samaritan woman is another character who offers a range of interpretive choices. Like Nicodemus, she enters into conversation with Jesus around a metaphor he offers—in this case, the water of life. Their conversation gradually reveals information about the water that Jesus offers, the woman's unusual marital history, and the location of "true worship." The conversation ends abruptly with the arrival of the disciples, but the story does not end. The Samaritan woman goes on to become an effective witness, leading her entire city to faith in Jesus. Her character has been assessed in a number of ways. Interpreters' conclusions range widely: for some, she is "not completely unresponsive" to Jesus' teachings; for others her response is "a model for faith and witness."[1]

Amid a great deal of variety in interpretations, there are two common negative judgments of the Samaritan woman's character: she is a sinner, and she misunderstands Jesus. A familiar reading is that the woman is a sinner to whom Jesus offers repentance: the waters of life. She understands little of what he says until he jolts her into recognition of her sin through the command, "Go, call your husband" (4:16). By calling the woman's attention to her need for salvation from sin, Jesus enables her to understand that he is the Messiah (verse 26). While some recent interpreters challenge the notion of the Samaritan's sinfulness, all concur that she misunderstands Jesus' words in their discussion of the "water" he offers her. At best, she is "a quick study"[2] who starts out uncomprehending but easily catches on. Yet some interpreters argue that the Samaritan woman never understands Jesus; her testimony to her village (verse 29) contains only a tentative suggestion of belief in him, and while the villagers come to believe, the narrator makes no further indication of the woman's belief. The Samaritan woman, this argument goes, cannot be a model disciple because she consistently fails to understand Jesus.

In this chapter, I challenge both of these judgments. Although the notion of the woman's sinfulness is prominent in many people's imaginations of the Samaritan woman, it is not an explicit association made by the text, as I discuss further below. Perhaps more important, the woman understands a great deal of what Jesus says from the very beginning. She does not have prior knowledge of him, nor does she intuit his identity. But the woman does understand that Jesus speaks to her on a metaphorical level. She questions him about the "water" he offers her and rapidly comes to understand what Jesus is trying to communicate about this gift. The Samaritan woman starts off with no knowledge of Jesus and yet shortly becomes a witness to her entire city. Her achievement is remarkable. She engages Jesus in theological dialogue, comes to believe in him, and witnesses to others about her experience. There is a great reversal here in the story of Jesus and the Samaritan woman, but it is not the familiar one of the excluded sinner graciously offered repentance. It is the story of a woman who is spiritually more astute than the great Pharisee Nicodemus. It is the story of a Samaritan woman whose witness to Jesus brings her whole village to the true worship of God.

The ambiguity in the character of the Samaritan woman is not like Nicodemus's ambiguity. Ambiguity in Nicodemus's character leads the reader to ask important and basic questions: "Is he a disciple or not?" "Does he believe or not?" In the end, even these basic questions cannot be clearly answered. The Samaritan woman, on the other hand, does appear to be a follower of Jesus. Even so, she is not without ambiguity. The ambiguity in the Samaritan woman's character is that her testimony to Jesus occurs in the absence of clear belief in him. Her only expression of belief is tentative: "He cannot be the Messiah, can he?" (4:29). Yet her actions are positive: she witnesses to her city, and people believe as a result of her testimony (4:39). The Samaritan woman appears to be a disciple of Jesus, but the ambiguity in her character leads to different questions: What kind of a follower is she? What does it mean to witness?

THE SAMARITAN WOMAN'S UNDERSTANDING

The Samaritan woman is characterized by the attributes that have come to serve in place of her name. She is a Samaritan and a woman, features that raise questions about her character from the outset. As a Samaritan, she is one with whom Jews would not usually share things in common (4:9), perhaps especially eating utensils or water jugs.[3] As a woman, she is an unlikely conversation partner for Jesus, at least in the estimation of his disciples (verse 27). Both of these aspects of the Samaritan woman stand in marked contrast to the characterization of Nicodemus.[4] As not only a Jew but also a prominent male authority, Nicodemus's visit to Jesus might be said to bring Jesus honor or prestige. His interaction with the Samaritan woman presumably can bring him no such repute. She has no name, no authority. Yet it is this latter conversation that bears fruit.

The Samaritan is also characterized by the time frame of this story: "It was about noon" (verse 6). Potentially, at least, such contextual clues play a role in John's characterization of the woman. In the case of Nicodemus, I argued that it is ambiguous to what extent his approaching Jesus "by night" should lead the reader to associate Nicodemus with "those who walk in darkness." The emphasis could be either on the darkness or on the act of "coming to Jesus," a metaphor for belief. The time frame is ambiguous with regard to the Samaritan woman, but for different reasons. In the former case, the time frame modifies Nicodemus's actions: "He came to Jesus by night" (3:2). The noon setting is not as clearly connected to the Samaritan woman. She does not approach Jesus but merely finds him sitting at her village well, and "it was about noon" (4:6). Because of this, it may seem odd to attribute anything positive or negative to her character. Yet even if it is not attached to her actions, the time frame creates a contrast with the Nicodemus story and is a further indication that the reader is to read these two stories in tandem. He comes by night, and she encounters Jesus by day.[5] By itself, neither time setting provides a clear clue to the individual's character. But just as "night" may signal to the reader that Nicodemus will not entirely understand Jesus, so "noon" may indicate that the woman will become one who "walks in the light."[6]

"LIVING WATER" (JOHN 4:8–14)

Although it is Jesus who initially approaches the woman, her immediate response shows both curiosity and understanding. The conversation begins with Jesus' request for a drink (4:7). The woman responds, "How is it that you, a Jew, ask a drink of me, a woman of Samaria?" (verse 9). In evaluating her character, interpreters gauge the tone of the woman's question. Some see it as a rejection of Jesus' request for water.[7] Yet at face value it is just a question prompted by unusual circumstances. Her surprise reflects the division between Jews and Samaritans. This context suggests that her response is normal: the woman recognizes that Jesus is breaching social conventions. Jesus' response takes her question seriously: "If you knew the gift of God, and who it is that is saying to you, 'Give me a drink,' you would have asked him, and he would have given you living water" (verse 10). He indicates that not only is he asking her for a drink, but also that she might rightly request from him "living water."

The woman's curiosity emerges strongly in her next response. Modern interpreters read the woman's next response as a complete misunderstanding: "You have no bucket, and the well is deep. Where do you get the living water?" (verse 11). She thinks Jesus speaks of running water (an equally good interpretation of the Greek, ὕδωρ ζῶν, hydōr zōn), and wonders how he will provide it. She has missed the metaphorical nature of Jesus' speech.[8] A different understanding of the Samaritan's response emerges when Jesus' words "living water" are understood as a conventional metaphor. Metaphors are an everyday part of language, in which one concept is understood in terms of another. Many metaphors are conventional: they are used commonly and effortlessly by both speakers and hearers. A conventional metaphor in modern American culture is ARGUMENT IS WAR.* If I speak of "defending my argument against attack," hearers understand, without conscious reflection, that I am speaking metaphorically. Read in this light, the woman may understand that Jesus speaks metaphorically.

The Samaritan woman would have been likely to understand "living water" as a conventional metaphor. Samaritans were familiar with the stories of God's provision of water to the Israelites in the desert (Exod. 15:22–27; 17:1–7). Like the Israelites, they probably also remembered these stories as part of God's sustenance of the people (e.g., Pss. 78:15–16; 105:41; 1 Cor. 10:4). Elsewhere in the Jewish Scriptures, the metaphor communicates God's gift of abundance, wisdom, and life (see Prov. 13:14; 18:4; Isa. 35:6–7; 41:17–18; 55:1–2; 58:11; Jer.

*The use of small capital letters is a convention of conceptual metaphor theory that helps the reader to distinguish between root metaphors (e.g., ARGUMENT IS WAR) and their verbal expressions ("defending my argument").

2:13; 17:7–8, 13). Water also appears as a metaphor in later Samaritan writings.[9] Although the Samaritans only accepted the Pentateuch as Scripture, the familiar imagery in both traditions suggests that the Samaritan woman could comprehend Jesus' words as a conventional metaphor. Just as modern readers are not likely to be duped into thinking that Jesus speaks about physical water, so also the woman could easily identify Jesus' speech as metaphorical.[10]

The setting of this story at Jacob's well (verses 5–6) supports the reading of living water as a conventional metaphor. The Old Testament reports that Jacob purchased a parcel of land (Gen. 33:18–20) and later gave it to Joseph (48:22). The well and its relationship to Jacob are clearly known and important to her, as she points out: "Our ancestor Jacob . . . gave us the well" (verse 12). Jacob's well is already a source of religious identity for her community. Although Jews disputed the point, the Samaritans understood themselves as true followers of the God of Jacob. When Jesus offers "living water," she could naturally understand him to be making reference not simply to the water of the well before them, but also to its metaphorical associations, which include the spiritual source and nourishment of her community. She already thinks of Jacob's well as a metaphor for the foundation of the Samaritan people and their faith in God.

In her response, the woman takes up Jesus' conventional metaphor and begins to reason in its terms. When speakers draw on conventional metaphors, reasoning proceeds in the terms offered by the metaphor. A listener who heard me speak of "defending my argument" might respond by making a suggestion that will help me "strengthen my position." In doing so, the hearer has accepted the terms of the metaphor ARGUMENT IS WAR and begins to reason in those terms. If an argument is war, then it may be won and lost; we can think about strategies for an effective defense. Yet arguments need not be conceived as war. They might be conceived as mere conversation. In the metaphor ARGUMENT IS WAR, cultural conventions about "war" structure the way "argument" is understood.[11] In suggesting how I might "strengthen my position," the listener grasps that I have been speaking metaphorically and uses what they know about war to elaborate. Likewise, the Samaritan woman discerns immediately that Jesus is speaking on a metaphorical level and responds in kind: "Sir, you have no bucket, and the well is deep; where do you get the living water?" (4:11). Her statement builds on attributes of physical water: "You have no bucket, and the well is deep." Since he has begun the comparison, she finishes it: the water that she would give him requires a bucket. And since he has none, what is the source of the water that he is offering? Read as conventional metaphor, her response "Where do you get this living water?" asks for information about Jesus' origins or authority. She has understood that he is offering spiritual sustenance, and she is curious about its source.

The woman's response to Jesus may thus be understood as a creative elaboration of the metaphorical terms that Jesus has laid out. Her response to Jesus shows creative understanding of the water metaphor. Jesus has offered her "the water of life." The specificity of the woman's response adds content to his metaphor: such water must have a source. Her question also offers a challenge. She already understands her well as spiritual and suggests its depth. She seems willing to believe that Jesus offers her "living water" but wants to know its source. Can Jesus provide water superior to this? Refashioning Jesus' metaphor characterizes the woman as one who is actively challenging Jesus and trying to understand him.

The woman's next question can also be understood as asking Jesus to elaborate on the metaphor of living water. "Are you greater than our ancestor Jacob, who gave us the well, and drank from it, along with his children and his flocks?" (verse 12). Her language compares Jesus to Jacob, "our ancestor," a religious authority. Granted, she does not expect Jesus to say that he is greater than Jacob. Nevertheless, the question conveys understanding of her conversation with Jesus. Notice that she does not question whether Jesus can provide water; she is again seeking to understand what kind of water he gives. Her question assumes that Jesus can provide water in a spiritual sense. The question is this: Is his water better than the water she already has? Again, the woman understands Jacob's well as a source not simply of physical water, but also of religious identity and nourishment for the community. At the same time, she seems open to Jesus' offer.

The notion that the woman has understood Jesus' metaphor is confirmed by Jesus' response to her. He accepts the woman's contrast between Jacob's well and his own living water and explains to her why she should prefer his water over the spiritual water she already has: "Everyone who drinks of this water will be thirsty again, but those who drink of the water that I will give them will never be thirsty. The water that I will give will become in them a spring of water welling up to eternal life" (verses 13–14). His answer to her question continues to elaborate the metaphor of living water. Jesus' words can be understood as further evidence that what the woman has said represents a certain level of understanding, so he builds on that understanding. His water is like that of Jacob's well, but better: the one who drinks will never be thirsty. On a metaphorical level, Jesus' words indicate that, while Jacob's well is also a spiritual source of nourishment, it is inferior to the water Jesus has to offer. His water transforms the one who drinks so that it becomes "a spring of water welling up to eternal life."

The woman again responds on a metaphorical level. She asks for the water that he has offered: "Sir, give me this water, so that I may not be thirsty nor keep coming here to draw water" (verse 15). Commentators point to this statement as evidence that she still does not understand that Jesus speaks metaphorically. But her words may again be read metaphorically, just as Jesus' words were. Jesus has promised that his water will mean that she is never thirsty (verse 14). Her words "nor keep coming here to draw water" elaborate this aspect of the metaphor. Her response indicates she understands that Jesus' gift of water would render the spiritual water of Jacob's well unnecessary. She asks him for his water, affirming her understanding that it will provide all she needs. Remarkably, she is willing to abandon her ancestors' well in favor of "the gift of God."

Reading the conversation this way implies that the woman understands a remarkable amount in a short period of time. It is surprising, perhaps astonishing, to think that a non-Jewish person with no prior knowledge of Jesus would ask for the water of life so quickly. The extraordinary nature of this interpretation does not make it less plausible. The surprise of the woman's comprehension and later actions may be the point of the story. The conversation with Nicodemus sets up further comparison. He also starts out by speaking with Jesus on a metaphorical level, but his questions do not move beyond mere puzzlement. Here is a Samaritan woman who cannot be expected to be theologically astute, yet she tracks Jesus' conversational moves and extends his line of thought.

THE SAMARITAN RECEIVES LIVING WATER

The subject of the woman's husbands (verses 16–19) complicates her characterization. There are two primary decisions for interpreters of these verses. First, readers must decide how to understand these verses in the flow of the woman's conversation with Jesus. His introduction of the topic in verse 16 seems unconnected to the previous verses. The discussion of living water has been going well. Interpreters ask why Jesus introduces this new topic. This segment of the conversation seems to be a setup: Jesus asks the Samaritan to call her husband (verse 16) although he knows she cannot do so. He is aware that she has no husband (verse 18). Second, these verses offer significant information—the woman's marital history, her declaration of Jesus as a prophet—that readers use to draw conclusions about the Samaritan woman's character. Yet there are many possibilities as to what these details mean. Readers explore the cultural and literary background of these aspects of the woman's character in order to evaluate their significance. There are four common solutions to these questions; two take the husbands literally, two figuratively.[12]

In the most common literal reading, the information about the Samaritan woman's husbands (verses 17–18) is seen as evidence of her sinful nature.[13] Up to this point, the woman has understood little or nothing of what Jesus has said about living water. He turns the subject to her sinful sexual practices, knowing that recognizing her need for forgiveness will enable her to understand Jesus' identity and purpose.[14] An advantage to this interpretation is its power to explain why Jesus makes a request he knows the woman cannot fulfill. He does not want to meet her husband but wants to draw her attention to her sin and need for forgiveness. The approach also has a significant disadvantage: a literal reading of husbands does not demand that the woman be seen as sinful. The language does not indicate that either the woman or Jesus understands her marital history or present state as sinful. Neither the tone of Jesus' statement nor the woman's response conveys condemnation or shame. Readers may easily import the notion of multiple marriages as sinful, but the interpreter's task is not to reiterate their culture's stereotypes about women but to assess the language of the text. In the first-century context, it is possible that the woman's multiple marriages were unusual but seen neither as sinful nor as something for which she was responsible. Her husbands may have died. Multiple husbands could indicate the practice of levirate marriage (cf. Luke 20:27–33).[15] She may also have been divorced, yet it is not clear how this would reflect on her character.[16] In each case it may have been the woman's husband who initiated the divorce, as permitted in Scripture (cf. Deut. 24:1–4). The conversation about the woman's husbands may still be understood literally without implying the woman's sin.

A second option is that the literal discussion of husbands appears in the text to provide an opportunity for Jesus to display prophetic insight. Jesus knows something distinctive about this woman without being told. This interpretation explains the introduction of the subject matter without assuming the woman's sinfulness. Her marital history is notable, though not necessarily sinful. Jesus introduces the subject of the woman's husband in order to lead the woman to a deeper under-standing of him. This reading also fits the literary context. Such displays of knowledge appear with some frequency in John (e.g., 1:47–48; 2:25). Jesus' revelation of his knowledge plays a role in the subplot of this passage. On the basis of Jesus' knowledge of her, the Samaritan woman comes to recognize him as a prophet (4:19). Her later testimony reinforces the significance of his knowledge of her.

Many interpreters also understand these verses figuratively, reading the reference to "husbands" as an allusion to Old Testament language. Two allusions are possible. The first sees John 4 as evoking stories where a betrothal begins with an encounter at a well (Gen. 24:10–20; 29:1–14; Exod. 2:15b–21). Ancient readers would have been familiar with the general arc of such well-known stories:

> The betrothal scene unfolds in a predictable though mutable way. Upon leaving his family circle and journeying to a foreign land, a prospective bridegroom encounters a marriageable woman at a well. After water has been drawn from the well and news of his arrival has been hurriedly reported to the woman's home, the stranger is invited to dinner. Soon thereafter, the couple is betrothed.[17]

Understood against this background, John 4 re-creates significant aspects of the betrothal "type story." The story is different in one way: literal marriage does not result. Yet early Christian readers might understand the resulting belief of the Samaritans in light of the notion of Christ as "bridegroom." This concept was clearly known to readers of John: John the Baptist has just made reference to Jesus metaphorically as the bridegroom (3:29). The idea of the well encounter as type story helps explain the introduction of the woman's husbands. For an ancient reader, the topic would not seem disconnected from other parts of the passage, which have already evoked the Old Testament stories. This part of the conversation continues to set the reader's expectation for the "marriage" that follows.

A second figurative interpretation is that the language of "husbands" alludes to Old Testament language of God as "husband" to Israel and Israel's marital "infidelity" (Isa. 54:5; Jer. 3:20; 31:32). In pointing out the woman's five husbands, John suggests that the Samaritans have not retained their true "husband," God. The discussion of worship that follows (John 4:20–24) supports the identification of an allusion.[18] In their infidelity, the Samaritans have strayed from the true worship of God.

All but the first of these options appear to be good readings of the text. Both of the Old Testament allusions are possible. An early reader of John would be likely to recognize these allusions. Both sets of imagery were accessible in the Old Testament texts and were likely to be known to Jewish readers. In each case the recurrence of references makes it more likely that a reader would recognize an allusion.[19] There are multiple aspects of the well story to indicate an allusion to the betrothal narratives, while the husband and worship language suggest an allusion to the Samaritans' infidelity to God. The two allusions may even work together: unfaithful to God as husband, the Samaritans now are betrothed to Christ, and therefore regain "true worship" of God.

Understanding either of these Old Testament allusions as present does not exclude a literal reading. Throughout John, layers of imagery add depth and richness to the story's possible meanings. In favor of the literal reading is the woman's later testimony to the people of her city: "He told me everything that I have done" (4:29, 39). The Samaritan woman is presented as understanding Jesus' words in reference to her own life. On the basis of her testimony, many believe. Their response endorses her words as a good understanding of her interaction with Jesus.

The four readings I have summarized here all assume that the Samaritan woman has not understood Jesus up to this point in the dialogue. Jesus' insertion of the strange topic of her husbands is meant to jog the woman from misunderstanding to understanding. Yet I have argued above that the woman does understand Jesus to a large extent, and that her request for water in verse 15 is a genuine request for the water of life. Based on Jesus' words in verse 10, the reader may expect that he will grant her request. My reading raises a new question about verses 16–18: not, "Why does Jesus introduce this strange subject?" but "Why does he withhold the water?"

One possibility is that verses 16–19 enact Jesus' gift of water to the Samaritan woman. This idea is supported by evidence in later verses that she has received living water. By verse 28, the woman leaves her water jug, metaphorically acting out what she and Jesus have said results from Jesus' water: she will "not be thirsty" (verses 14–15).[20] Her later testimony (verses 29–30, 39–42) also underscores the notion that the woman has received Jesus' gift. In the Fourth Gospel, "testimony" is an important goal of discipleship. Testimony is one of the purposes of Jesus' coming (18:37; cf. 3:11, 32). It is the primary function of

John the Baptist (1:7–8, 15, 19, 32, 34; 3:26), and it is identified as the disciples' future role (15:27). Testimony leads people to believe in Jesus (1:7; 19:35), which is the purpose of the writing of the Gospel itself (20:30). The Samaritan woman's testimony likewise leads many Samaritans to believe in Jesus. Their belief is expressed explicitly (verse 39) and also metaphorically. On the basis of her testimony, people "come to" Jesus (verses 30, 40), common metaphorical language in John for believing in him. They also ask Jesus to "stay" with them (verse 39). To stay or "abide" is another way John expresses the relationship between Jesus and believers (e.g., 14:25; 15:4–7). The belief of the Samaritan people, linked specifically to the woman's testimony, confirms that she has received living water. It has "become in [her] a spring of water welling up to eternal life" (4:14).

If the woman has received water, what aspect of verses 16–26 conveys Jesus' gift of water? Most interpreters would say that it is the opportunity to learn of Jesus' identity. "The woman will not be able to interpret ὕδωρ ζῶν [hydōr zōn, living water] correctly until she can recognize the identity of the person with whom she speaks."[21] Jesus' command to call her husband results in the woman's understanding that he is a prophet (verse 19). Her further inquiries of the prophet lead Jesus to reveal that he is the Messiah (verse 26).[22] The question of Jesus' identity is certainly an issue in these verses. Yet equating the gift of living water with knowledge of Jesus creates a problem: the woman does not seem to display accurate knowledge of Jesus.[23] She does declare him to be a prophet, which is a good if partial understanding of Jesus. Yet her later testimony includes only a tentative identification of Jesus as the Messiah: "Can he be the Messiah?" (verse 29).[24] The testimony that evokes such a positive response is not based primarily on the woman's identification of Jesus as the Messiah. She testifies to her experience of Jesus.

Therefore, another option is to understand the woman's experience of Jesus in verses 16–19 as an important part of the gift of water. This corresponds more closely to the content of her testimony: "He told me everything that I have done" (verses 29, 39). Some interpreters deride the woman's statement: she does not confess faith but only reports that Jesus has extraordinary knowledge of her.[25] Yet this does not account for the importance of prophecy in the first century, and the likelihood that, for the woman, Jesus' knowledge of her would indeed be a significant event.[26] The way John tells the story does not denigrate the woman's testimony. Her encounter with Jesus has been transformative. Knowledge of him is an important result of the encounter, but the experience itself is also important. Together they are the "water of life" she receives.

The rest of the conversation reinforces the notion that the woman is on the right track as she seeks further understanding. She understands Jesus to be a prophet (verse 19). This seems a good preliminary understanding of who he is since John elsewhere aligns Jesus with Moses. In verse 20, the Samaritan woman turns the conversation to the issue of the proper location for worshiping God. This was an important religious issue, one to which a prophet might be expected to speak. Her words again characterize her as one who understands a great deal about Jesus and her conversation with him so far. She understands that Jesus has the religious authority to speak to this topic, one of the primary points of disagreement between Jews and Samaritans. Jesus engages her on the subject, speaking to her at some length (verses 21–24). If the woman's question about worship is merely a tactic to divert Jesus from the discovery of her sin, Jesus seems nevertheless eager to follow her lead. It is more likely that his response is evidence that the woman has offered a good extension of the conversation. The contrast with Nicodemus is again instructive: with Nicodemus, Jesus quickly pointed out that Nicodemus lacked understanding and cut off the conversation with him. The extended dialogue with the Samaritan woman suggests progression in her understanding. Jesus speaks eschatologically ("An hour is coming," verses 21, 23) of a time when true worship will not belong to a single location, Samaria or Jerusalem, but will be "in spirit and in truth" (verses 23–24). The woman understands the eschatological tenor of Jesus' speech. She relates what he has said to the coming of the Messiah. Again, this is an appropriate connection. Jesus' claims about worship are best understood within a framework of his identity as the Messiah. Thus far the woman has identified Jesus as a prophet and has not yet determined that he is the Messiah. She nevertheless makes a good attempt at relating what Jesus has said to what she knows. Jesus seems to understand this as a positive thing because he responds by identifying himself as the Messiah.

THE SAMARITAN'S UNDERSTANDING
IN COMPARISON TO THE DISCIPLES

Verses 31–38 interrupt the story of the woman's testimony and implicitly contrast her actions with those of Jesus' disciples. The contrast with the disciples characterizes the Samaritan woman as forthright and open to learning.[27] Initially, the disciples' timid interaction with Jesus contrasts with the woman's bold engagement. They are astonished that Jesus speaks with a woman, yet they do not ask Jesus any questions (verse 27). The Samaritan woman was also surprised that Jesus spoke with her and immediately asked him about it (verse 9). The disciples' unwillingness to engage Jesus directly is reinforced by verse 33, where they question one another—rather than Jesus himself—about his need to eat. The Samaritan questioned Jesus directly when confronted with a metaphor she did not completely understand. She is characterized as open to his teaching, while the disciples do not seem to learn much about Jesus. Interpreting the story in this way is supported by the outcome of each interaction with Jesus. Like Nicodemus, the disciples drop out of the story fairly quickly. Jesus continues speaking to them (verses 34–38), but there is no further indication that they comprehend. Nor are they seen to testify, even to their limited understanding of Jesus. The comparison highlights the ways in which the woman is an exemplary follower of Jesus.

The woman's interaction with Jesus also conveys greater understanding of Jesus' words. The disciples' question to each other shows little comprehension of his statement "I have food to eat that you do not know about" (verse 32). Like "living water," the notion of God or God's word as food is common in the Old Testament (e.g., Ps. 63:5; Prov. 9:1–6; Isa. 25:6; cf. 1 Cor. 3:2; 10:3). Jesus' "food" is also a conventional metaphor that the disciples might be expected to understand without difficulty. Yet their response is vague: "Surely no one has brought him something to eat?" (John 4:33). The disciples' question might be understood to convey a rudimentary understanding that Jesus has spoken metaphorically—they are ruling out the possibility of physical food being offered to Jesus. But they have not grasped the metaphorical meaning of "food," nor are they pushing for deeper understanding based on what they do know. Alongside the woman's immediate response, "Where do you get the living water?" (verse 11), the disciples seem timid and a bit dim-witted.

Jesus' metaphors of food and harvest (verses 34–38) continue to characterize the woman's actions and to contrast them with the disciples' responses. In the disciples' absence, Jesus has partaken of "food" (verse 32): he has done God's will (verse 34). The conversation with the Samaritan woman is an example of Jesus' engaging in God's work. The harvest imagery (verses 35–38) is another conventional metaphor for the gathering of God's people in the last days. Such imagery is found in the Old Testament (as in Isa. 27:12; Joel 3:13), and is often refashioned in the New Testament (as in Matt. 13:24–30; Mark 4:26–29; Rev. 14:14–20). Jesus' words point to the imminence of the harvest: "The fields . . . are ripe for harvest; the reaper is already receiving wages" (John 4:35–36). The Samaritans are about to be "gathered up" as God's people, indicating the arrival of eschatological time.[28] Just as the disciples purchase food that they did not labor to produce (verse 38a), so also they will reap the crop of Samaritan people without laboring (verse 38b). "Others" (verse 38) have labored: in this context, the plural points to both Jesus and the Samaritan woman as "laborers."

The comparison with the disciples characterizes the Samaritan woman in a positive light. She has not clearly grasped Jesus' identity, but even so her actions lead her in the right direction: she questions Jesus and learns from him; she becomes a laborer for the harvest. The disciples also "enter into" the labor of the harvest (verse 38) even though they seem to understand less than the Samaritan woman at this point. Her incomplete understanding does not preclude her discipleship, nor her participation in the activity of witnessing and harvest. The disciples, who have already believed in Jesus (2:11), appear uncomprehending. In the ambiguity of discipleship, the woman's imperfect witness to Jesus brings in a full harvest, and the disciples reap the harvest that they did not sow.

CONCLUSION

The story of the Samaritan woman asks the reader to think in terms of a metaphor: Jesus gives living water. The metaphor draws from the wells of Jewish and Samaritan imagery to suggest nourishment that comes directly from God. The one who drinks this water will never be thirsty, for the water becomes a spring within that person, an ever-present source of life in a land that is often dry. The gift of God that Jesus offers continues God's provision of abundance, wisdom, and life. Through the woman's questioning of Jesus, the reader learns of this gift and what it means. Details of the story, like the abandoned water jar, are left open for the reader's interpretation. Whatever the reader decides about the jar's effect on the woman's character, the question invites the reader to think along with the Gospel's presentation of living water. Asking questions about how much the woman understands, the reader necessarily engages in understanding the water metaphor and thinking through its implications.

The Samaritan woman starts out as an ambiguous character because of her identity: she is a Samaritan and a woman. She ends up as an ambiguous character as well, but for different reasons. The Samaritan woman is an example of faithful discipleship: one who engages Jesus and pushes toward greater understanding. At the same time, she does not fully understand him. Her testimony about Jesus' identity as the Messiah is exploratory rather than confessing. Yet the way John tells her story confirms her exploration as a model for discipleship. "She is a success in spite of herself, in spite of her own tentative faith."[29] Her testimony to her experience of Jesus brings others to faith.

The reader of the Gospel is left to evaluate this ambiguity in the Samaritan woman's character. If characters can only believe or disbelieve in Jesus, her character must be negative. In the end, she is little different from Nicodemus: she does not confess belief in him as the Messiah. But if the Samaritan can be ambiguous, then her character can teach the reader something further about what it means to be a disciple. She witnesses, not to perfect faith in Jesus, but to her experience of him. This witness subsequently attracts others to their own experience and belief: "We have heard for ourselves, and we know that this is truly the Savior of the world" (4:42). The result of her testimony suggests the importance of her encounter with Jesus. The gift of living water transforms the Samaritan woman. Even without full belief, she becomes a well that brings living water to others.

BIBLIOGRAPHY

Aitken, Ellen B. "At the Well of Living Water: Jacob Traditions in John 4." Pages 342–52 in *The Interpretation of Scripture in Early Judaism and Christianity*. Edited by Craig A. Evans. Journal for the Study of the Pseudepigrapha: Supplement Series 33. Sheffield: Sheffield Academic Press, 2000.

Alter, Robert. "Biblical Type-Scenes and the Uses of Convention." Pages 47–62 in *The Art of Biblical Narrative*. New York: Basic Books, 1981.

Aune, David E. *Prophecy in Early Christianity and the Ancient Mediterranean World*. Grand Rapids: Wm. B. Eerdmans Publishing Co., 1983.

Barrett, C. K. *The Gospel according to St. John*. Philadelphia: Westminster Press, 1978.

Beasley-Murray, George R. *John*. Word Bible Commentary 36. Waco, TX: Word, 1987.

Beirne, Margaret M. *Women and Men in the Fourth Gospel: A Genuine Discipleship of Equals*. Sheffield: Sheffield Academic Press, 2003.

Black, Clifton C. "Rhetorical Criticism." Pages 256–77 in *Hearing the New Testament: Strategies for Interpretation*. Edited by Joel B. Green. Grand Rapids: Wm. B. Eerdmans Publishing Co., 1995.

Blass, Friedrich, and Albert Debrunner. *Grammatik des neutestamentlichen Griechisch*. Göttingen: Vandenhoeck & Ruprecht, 14th ed. 1975.

Brown, Raymond. *The Gospel according to John*. 2 vols. Anchor Bible 29–29A. New York: Doubleday, 1966–70.

Bultmann, Rudolf. *The Gospel of John*. Philadelphia: Westminster Press, 1971.

Calvin, Jean. *The Gospel according to St. John 1–10*. Edited by David W. Torrance and Thomas F. Torrance. Calvin's Commentaries. Grand Rapids: Wm. B. Eerdmans Publishing Co., 1961.

Carmichael, Calum M. "Marriage and the Samaritan Woman." *New Testament Studies* 26 (1980): 332–46.

Cook, Joan E. "Wells, Women, and Faith." Pages 11–19 in *Proceedings of the Eastern Great Lakes and Midwest Biblical Societies*. Edited by Benjamin Fiore. Buffalo, NY: Eastern Great Lakes and Midwest Biblical Societies, 1997.

Cuvillier, Élian. "La figure des disciples en Jean 4." *New Testament Studies* 42 (1996): 245–59.

Daube, David. "Jesus and the Samaritan Woman: The Meaning of συγχράομαι." *Journal of Biblical Literature* 69 (1950): 137–47.

Davidson, Jo Ann. "John 4: Another Look at the Samaritan Woman." *Andrews University Seminary Studies* 43 (2005): 159–68.

Dodd, C. H. *The Interpretation of the Fourth Gospel*. Cambridge: Cambridge University Press, 1953.

Farmer, Craig S. "Changing Images of the Samaritan Woman in Early Reformed Commentaries on John." *Church History* 65 (1996): 365–75.

Gench, Frances Taylor. "The Samaritan Woman: John 4:1–42." Pages 109–35 in *Back to the Well: Women's Encounters with Jesus in the Gospels*. Louisville, KY: Westminster John Knox Press, 2004.

Giblin, Charles Homer. "What Was Everything He Told Her She Did? (John 4.17–18, 29, 39)." *New Testament Studies* 45 (1999): 148–52.

Hays, Richard B. *Echoes of Scripture in the Letters of Paul*. New Haven, CT: Yale University Press, 1989.

Hendriksen, William. *Exposition of the Gospel according to John*. Vols. 4–5 of *New Testament Commentary*. Grand Rapids: Baker Book House, 1953–54.

Hoskyns, Edwyn Clement. *The Fourth Gospel*. Edited by F. N. Davey. London: Faber & Faber, 1947.

Hylen, Susan. *Allusion and Meaning in John 6*. Beiheifte zur Zeitschrift für die neutestamentliche Wissenschaft 137. Berlin: Walter de Gruyter, 2005.

Koester, Craig. "The Savior of the World (John 4:42)." *Journal of Biblical Literature* 109 (1990): 665–80.

Lakoff, George, and Mark Johnson. *Metaphors We Live By*. Chicago: University of Chicago Press, 1980.

Lockwood, Peter F. "The Woman at the Well: Does the Traditional Reading Still Hold Water?" *Lutheran Theological Journal* 36 (2002): 12–24.

Maccini, Robert Gordon. *Her Testimony Is True: Women as Witnesses according to John*. Journal for the Study of the New Testament: Supplement Series 125. Sheffield: Sheffield Academic Press, 1996.

MacDonald, John. *Memar Marqah: The Teaching of Marqah*. Beihefte zur Zeitschrift für die alttestamentliche Wissenschaft 84. Berlin: A. Töpelmann, 1963.

MacGregor, George Hogarth Carnaby. *The Gospel of John*. Moffatt New Testament Commentary. 1928. Reprint, New York: Harper & Brothers Publishers, 1937.

Moloney, Francis J. *The Gospel of John*. Sacra pagina 4. Collegeville, MN: Liturgical Press, 1988.

Moore, Stephen D. "Are There Impurities in the Living Water That the Johannine Jesus Dispenses? Deconstruction, Feminism, and the Samaritan Woman." *Biblical Interpretation* 1 (1993): 207–27.

Moulton, James Hope. *A Grammar of New Testament Greek*. Edinburgh: T&T Clark, 1963.

Munro, Winsome. "The Pharisee and the Samaritan in John: Polar or Parallel?" *Catholic Biblical Quarterly* 57 (1995): 710–28.

O'Day, Gail R. *The Gospel of John*. New Interpreter's Bible 9. Nashville: Abingdon Press, 1995.

———. "Narrative Mode and Theological Claim: A Study in the Fourth Gospel." *Journal of Biblical Literature* 105 (1986): 657–68.

———. *Revelation in the Fourth Gospel: Narrative Mode and Theological Claim*. Philadelphia: Fortress Press, 1986.

Okure, Teresa. *The Johannine Approach to Mission: A Contextual Study of John 4:1–42*. Wissenschaftliche Untersuchungen zum Neuen Testament 31. Tübingen: Mohr Siebeck, 1988.

Pazdan, Mary Margaret. "Nicodemus and the Samaritan Woman: Contrasting Models of Discipleship." *Biblical Theology Bulletin* 17 (1987): 145–48.

Scaer, Peter J. "Jesus and the Woman at the Well: Where Mission Meets Worship." *Concordia Theological Quarterly* 67 (2003): 3–18.

Schnackenburg, Rudolf. *The Gospel according to St. John*. 3 vols. New York: Seabury Press, 1982–90.

Schneiders, Sandra M. "Feminist Hermeneutics." Pages 349–69 in *Hearing the New Testament: Strategies for Interpretation*. Edited by Joel B. Green. Grand Rapids: Wm. B. Eerdmans Publishing Co., 1995.

———. *Written That You May Believe: Encountering Jesus in the Fourth Gospel*. New York: Herder & Herder, 1999.

Sheeley, Steven M. "Lift Up Your Eyes: John 4:4–42." *Review and Expositor* 92 (1995): 81–87.

Snyder, Graydon F. "The Social Context of the Ironic Dialogues in the Gospel of John." Pages 3–23 in *Putting Body and Soul Together*. Edited by Virginia Wiles, Alexandra Brown, and Graydon F. Snyder. Valley Forge, PA: Trinity Press International, 1997.

Strack, Hermann L., and Paul Billerbeck. *Kommentar zum Neuen Testament*. Vol. 2. Munich: C. H. Becksche Verlangsbuchhandlung, 1924.

Whitters, Mark F. "Discipleship in John: Four Profiles." *Word and World* 18 (1998): 422–27.

4

The Disciples

The disciples are most often seen as representatives of belief in John.[1] Many scholars observe how, from the beginning, the Gospel presents individual disciples as already possessing significant understanding of Jesus. In the calling narratives of 1:35–51, they use a number of important titles for Jesus that reflect appropriate understandings of who he is: Rabbi (1:38), Messiah (1:41), one about whom Moses in the law and also the prophets wrote (1:45), Son of God (1:49), King of Israel (1:49). The disciples are then said to believe in Jesus following his first sign, changing water into wine at a wedding in Cana (2:11). The disciples' early belief is especially striking for readers of the Synoptic Gospels, where their lack of understanding is notorious (especially in the Gospel of Mark).

At the same time, interpreters recognize that the disciples are a mixed bag. They do not fully believe in Jesus or understand who he is. If the disciples include those who know about Jesus' identity from the beginning, why is their belief only indicated following his sign? John attributes belief to the disciples with one hand and takes it away with the other. This pattern of partial belief—or belief coupled with disbelief—continues throughout the Gospel. Jesus repeatedly indicates that something has happened or will happen "so that you may believe" (ἵνα πιστεύσητε, *hina pisteusēte*: 11:15; 13:19; 14:29).[2] Jesus' words imply that the disciples do not yet believe. Alan Culpepper writes that the disciples "are marked especially by their recognition of Jesus and belief in his claims. Yet, they are not exemplars of perfect faith, but of positive responses and typical misunderstandings."[3] Wayne Meeks likewise recognizes that the disciples are not *pneumatikoi*—spiritual beings who, like Jesus, have "come down from heaven"—but "a small group of believers isolated over against 'the world.'"[4] How is it that the disciples end up being both of these things? They are exemplars of belief who are "not of this world"; at the same time, they do not understand Jesus and often disbelieve.

In this chapter I argue that the disciples are an ambiguous character. I investigate "the disciples" as a corporate character in John. Individual disciples are also important, and separate chapters could be written on each. But "the disciples" also act, speak, and are spoken to as a group and thus warrant their own designation as a character in the Gospel. Rather than being marked especially by belief in Jesus, they are marked by both belief and disbelief. Even as they indicate their belief, their words and actions show misunderstanding and disbelief. They abide with Jesus yet scatter in his time of greatest need.

A common explanation is that the disciples grow into full belief as the Gospel progresses.[5] This would be a good explanation if in fact the reader saw the disciples' belief develop. I argue below that this is not the case. The entire narrative presents the disciples as both believing and disbelieving. My reading offers a narrative of hope instead of a narrative of progress: the disciples remain imperfect believers who are transformed by Jesus' inauguration of the end time.

BELIEF AND DISBELIEF

The disciples' interactions with Jesus display misunderstanding and disbelief. In their first conversation with Jesus (4:27–38), they misunderstand both Jesus' metaphorical speech and the nature of his actions.[6] Jesus says, "I have food to eat that you do not know about," and the disciples respond by saying to one another, "Surely no one has brought him something to eat?" (4:32–33). As in prior conversations with Nicodemus and the Samaritan woman, Jesus' speech draws on a conventional metaphor—here, God's word as food. The disciples assume that Jesus has been speaking of literal food, like that which they had gone to Sychar to purchase (4:8). Jesus' response underscores the disciples' lack of comprehension. He supplies a more direct statement of the metaphor so that they may understand: "My food is to do the will of the one who sent me and to complete his work" (4:34). In saying this, Jesus defines his interaction with the Samaritan woman as doing God's will.[7] The food that the disciples do not know about (4:32) is Jesus' teaching of this woman, an activity that astonishes the disciples (4:27).

The disciples' lack of understanding is underscored by comparing them with other characters. In the chapters on Nicodemus and the Samaritan woman, I argued that their questions in response to Jesus' words (in 3:4 and 4:11, 15 respectively) can be understood as metaphorical themselves: they build on and elaborate the metaphorical terms Jesus initiates. The disciples' response to Jesus in 4:33 is not, however, metaphorical. The most generous reading of it is simply that they are reaching toward a metaphorical understanding by ruling out the literal option. They comprehend little of Jesus' meaning.[8] The disciples are also characterized in comparison to what other characters "know." Jesus' words in 4:32 characterize the disciples as "not knowing" about Jesus' food. Others are more knowledgeable: the Samaritan woman knows "that the Messiah is coming" (4:25), and the people of her village come to know "that this is truly the Savior of the world" (4:42).[9] In John 4 Jesus' disciples show less understanding than the Samaritans or Nicodemus.

Yet in most cases, positive attributes of the disciples' character qualify such negative aspects.[10] In their discussion in chapter 4, Jesus characterizes the disciples as part of his work. He employs imagery of the eschatological harvest (4:35–38), which he applies to the situation with the Samaritans: "Lift up your eyes and see the fields, because they are ripe for harvest" (4:35). Although the disciples have been absent for and then astonished by Jesus' teaching, Jesus calls their attention to what is about to happen. He also includes them as participants in the harvest: "Others have labored, and you enter into their labor." The disciples, though not immediately comprehending this situation, are characterized as workers in the harvest.[11] They will reap a harvest of Samaritan believers for which they did not labor.

The disciples' next appearance (John 6) characterizes them as both believing and unbelieving. After the feeding miracle and Jesus' withdrawal (6:1–15), his disciples cross the sea of Galilee in a boat (6:16–21). John's narration of Jesus' appearance by walking on the sea suggests a theophany: the disciples see Jesus as God.[12] In typical Johannine fashion, this is not stated explicitly but is suggested through a series of allusions to the exodus story. Having just served a meal at the time of the Passover (6:4), Jesus' walking on the sea may suggest

God's powers over the waters of the Red Sea. The disciples recognize Jesus, unlike similar stories in Matthew and Mark, where they think he is a ghost (cf. Matt. 14:26; Mark 6:49). Their response is one of fear, a typical and appropriate response to a vision of God (see, e.g., Exod. 3:6; 15:14; 20:18–20). Jesus' words confirm the theophany. In saying "I am" (6:20), Jesus refers to himself with the divine name (cf. Exod. 3:14).[13] His subsequent reassurance, "Do not be afraid" (6:20), is characteristic speech during an appearance of God (e.g., Gen. 26:24; Isa. 43:1–44:8). The setting and the characters' speech suggest that the story of Jesus' walking on water is crafted by John to communicate more than just a miraculous appearance by Jesus. Rather, in this event the disciples see and experience Jesus as divine.

The disciples seem to understand enough to recognize Jesus and to be afraid. Their characterization in this scene is implicit, however. The reader must interpret the situation and their response to it. The disciples do not clarify their understanding through speech. Their one action, wanting to take Jesus into the boat (6:21), is not fulfilled. This desire is fairly open-ended and may be interpreted in a number of ways. It seems parallel to the prior desire of the crowd, who want to make Jesus king (6:15). Jesus' evasion of their plan makes the desire seem misguided. Yet the understanding that Jesus is king is not incorrect from John's viewpoint. The crowd may understand rightly that Jesus is king but misunderstand what kind of king Jesus is. This is a topic that John takes up again in the trial narrative (see John 18:33–19:22). Like the crowd, the disciples' desire to take Jesus into the boat may represent some understanding of what they have witnessed. It may even represent a desire for Jesus to "abide" with them. The characterization of the disciples is ambiguous, but it leans in the direction of their having some understanding.

When the disciples appear again at the close of Jesus' teaching, they are characterized differently: they disbelieve. This comes through in their own words and the words of Jesus. The disciples are reluctant to accept his teaching: "Many of his disciples who were listening said, 'This teaching is hard. Who can accept it?'" (6:60). Jesus' words contribute to their characterization: "Some of you do not believe" (6:64). The narrator indicates that "many of his disciples turned from following him and no longer went about with him" (6:66). Though they initially believed in Jesus, the end of John 6 presents a somewhat contradictory view of them as unbelieving.

Interpreters have explained this apparent contradiction in the disciples' behavior in a variety of ways. Rudolf Bultmann reorders the

narrative so that 6:60–71 comes at the very end of John 12. As he
reconstructs the text, the disciples initially follow and believe, and then
there is a shift: first "the Jews who had believed in Jesus" (8:30–40)
and then "the disciples" (6:60–71) respond to the offense of Jesus'
self-revelation by turning from him.[14] The rejection by the disciples
in John 6 becomes the decisive turning-away reaction just before the
Last Supper. There is no manuscript evidence to support Bultmann's
reordering of the text, and a majority of scholars have since rejected
his proposal. Other scholars suggest less radical and more satisfying
conclusions. One solution is that the disciples' behavior suggests a rift
within the corporate character "the disciples." It is simply that some
disciples believe and some do not.[15] This is supported by Jesus' words
in 6:64: "Some of you do not believe." But even if this is the case,
"the disciples" as a whole have previously been said to believe (2:11).
The problem of believing disciples who suddenly disbelieve still exists.
Some scholars draw on the understanding of representative characters
to indicate that the text here creates two groups of disciples, believing
and unbelieving, and each group represents factions in John's community. For example, Ludger Schenke sees the disciples who turn away
as representative of early Christians who left the community to return
to Judaism.[16] For other scholars, it is simply a matter of "true" and
"false" belief among Jesus' disciples. According to Rudolf Schnackenburg, "[Jesus'] intention is not to discourage those who are prepared
to believe, but to prove his knowledge of the division beginning in the
group of the disciples."[17] Some disciples remain true to Jesus; others
show themselves to be unbelieving.

An additional possibility is that the disciples are both believing
and unbelieving. This interpretation does not try to solve the apparent contradiction by saying that some individuals in the group believe
while others disbelieve. Instead, the disciples are characterized by this
contradiction: they are both believing and unbelieving. The characterization of the disciples as "grumbling" (γογγύζουσιν, *gongyzousin*,
6:61) about Jesus' teaching provides additional support for this reading. The word "grumbling" characterizes the disciples as resistant to
Jesus' teaching, but it does so in a particular way that makes sense of the
disciples' contradictory behavior here. In a chapter filled with echoes
of the exodus story, "grumbling" is an additional allusion to Exodus.
It is the response of the Israelites in the wilderness. They also believed
what God had done (Exod. 14:31), yet soon afterward they grumbled
(Exod. 16:7; 17:3; Num. 14:2, 27, 36; the LXX uses the same word

group, διαγογγύζω [*diagongyzō*] and ὁ γογγυσμός [*ho gongyzmos*]).
The disciples' resistance to Jesus' teaching stands in a line of believing
people's previous resistance to God's care for them. The disciples are
not characterized simply as grumblers. Along with the Israelites, they
both believe and disbelieve.

Comparison to "the Twelve"[18] reinforces the characterization of the
disciples as both believing and unbelieving. Following the retreat of
many of the disciples, Jesus questions the Twelve: "Do you also wish to
go away?" (6:67). Peter replies on behalf of the group: "Lord, you have
the words of eternal life, and we have come to believe and know that
you are the Holy One of God" (6:68–69). Peter's statement is one of
the few direct confessions by a disciple that the Gospel offers. Yet, as
the next verses point out, the Twelve also includes Judas. John explicitly characterizes him as "one of the Twelve" (6:71). Judas is one of
those who believe and know and have been chosen by Jesus (6:69–70).
He is "a devil" and will betray Jesus (6:70–71). These verses are constructed to communicate Jesus' foreknowledge of Judas's betrayal. He
is already aware that one of his intimate associates will hand him over
to the authorities. Though many interpreters read the response of the
Twelve (represented by Peter) as positive,[19] the description of Judas is
a reminder that even the Twelve do not constitute perfect disciples in
contrast to those who have just departed. The inclusion of both Peter
and Judas makes this an ambiguous group.

In John 11, the disciples are again characterized as resistant and
unbelieving. The disciples appear incredulous at Jesus' intention to
return to Judea on the occasion of Lazarus's death: "Rabbi, just now
the Jews were seeking to stone you, and you are going there again?"
(11:8). The disciples see the recent attempts to arrest Jesus (e.g., 10:39)
as a reason for him not to return. They seem not to have fully grasped
Jesus' teaching in the previous chapter: "I am the good shepherd, . . .
and I lay down my life for the sheep" (10:14–15). Their speech is a
misguided attempt to prevent Jesus from returning. They likewise misunderstand Jesus' intention to "awaken" Lazarus from sleep (11:11).[20]
Their response is similar to that of other characters in the chapter. Mary
and Martha seem to have expected that Jesus could have healed their
brother's illness and thus prevented his death (11:21, 32), but not that
Jesus would raise him from the dead (11:24, 39; see my discussion in
chap. 5). Yet Jesus' statement should not be beyond the comprehension
of the disciples. Jesus speaks of Lazarus having "fallen asleep" (11:11),

a conventional metaphor for death. Jesus claims not only that Lazarus is sleeping but also that he will "awaken" him. The disciples—having been with Jesus, seen his signs, and heard his previous metaphors—cannot fathom that this is also metaphorical speech and that Jesus goes to raise Lazarus from the sleep of death.

As in chapter 4, John's narration of the interaction with the disciples in chapter 11 highlights the disciples' misunderstanding. Their response to Jesus' desire to awaken Lazarus might first be read as metaphorical speech, an interaction in the mode of Nicodemus or the Samaritan woman: "Lord, if he has fallen asleep, he will recover" (11:12). The Greek word σωθήσεται (*sōthēsetai*), translated "recover," also means "be saved," which opens the possibility that these words represent a good understanding of things Jesus has previously said (as in 6:39–40). Their statement could mean, "If Lazarus is dead, he will be saved."[21] However, the narrator's voice intervenes to exclude this possibility. "Jesus had been speaking about his death, but they thought that he spoke of sleep" (11:13). The disciples give voice to a truth of this chapter—Lazarus is dead and will be saved—but they do so without knowing it, much as Caiaphas prophesies unintentionally at the end of the chapter (11:49–52). The narrative aside reinforces that the disciples have misunderstood Jesus' speech. Although the interactions with Nicodemus and the Samaritan are more ambiguous, in the disciples' speech the ambiguity is lost. They do not understand that Jesus speaks metaphorically. In each case, Jesus takes care to expound on the metaphor for the disciples. In the discussion in chapter 4, he states the metaphor more explicitly: "My food is to do the will of the one who sent me" (4:34). In the prelude to the raising of Lazarus, he again highlights what he meant by sleep: "Lazarus is dead" (11:14). Yet there is no later indication that the explanation leads to greater understanding on the disciples' part. Rather than progressive enlightenment, the narrative highlights the disciples' continued ignorance.[22]

At the Last Supper, the disciples' lack of comprehension is again striking.[23] The only indication of their understanding of the footwashing is by comparison with Peter, who repeatedly rejects Jesus' efforts (13:6–11). Jesus goes on to predict his betrayal, pointing out again that he explains this "so that when it does occur, you may believe that 'I am'" (13:19). As noted above, Jesus' words presume the disciples' future belief but imply a current lack of understanding or belief. The disciples also show a lack of comprehension in missing the meaning of

Jesus' identification of Judas (13:21–30). Although the disciple next to him poses the question to Jesus about the identity of the betrayer (see my discussion in chap. 6), the discussion of the topic began publicly, and all of the disciples are curious about who will betray Jesus (13:21–22). Nothing indicates that the others do not hear the question and answer. Yet they do not understand Jesus' words to Judas, "Do quickly what you are going to do" (verse 27). Even if the reader assumes the disciples' ignorance of the private discussion, they are characterized as being curious yet unenlightened on this important topic.

In the Farewell Discourse, the disciples' belief appears stronger, though it is still qualified. In John 16, both Jesus' and the disciples' speech also characterizes them as believing. Jesus says, "The Father himself loves you, because you have loved me and have believed that I came from God" (16:27). This is a direct indication of the disciples' prior belief. "You have believed" (πεπιστεύκατε, *pepisteukate*) indicates the disciples' prior and continuing belief in him. The disciples' next words confirm their belief: "Look, now you are speaking clearly and not in a figure of speech. Now we know that you know everything and do not need anyone to ask you. By this we believe that you came from God" (16:29–30). The disciples affirm a central theme of the Gospel's portrayal of Jesus: his divine origins. Jesus' prayer also affirms the disciples' belief: "They have believed that you sent me" (17:8). Thus, aspects of the discourse clearly point to the disciples' belief in Jesus.

Yet the discourse also suggests the disciples' misunderstanding. In chapter 16, the disciples are again characterized as both believing and misunderstanding. In 16:16–18, the disciples' speech displays a singular lack of understanding.[24] In comparison to other instances where the disciples misunderstand Jesus' metaphorical speech as literal speech, here they seem to have no reference point—even a literal one—with which to understand Jesus' words. Jesus says to them, "'A little while and you will no longer see me, and again a little while and you will see me.' Therefore his disciples said to him, 'What is this that he is saying to us: "A little while and you will not see me, and again a little while and you will see me?" and "because I am going to the Father"'? They said therefore, 'What is this that he says, "a little while"? We do not know what he is talking about'" (16:16–18). The repetition in the narrative mirrors the disciples' thought process as they reach for a way to understand Jesus' words. As in John 4, they seem reluctant to ask Jesus directly. They speak "to one another" (16:17), but the narrator indicates that they wanted to ask Jesus (16:19). Here the disciples seem at something of a low point in terms of their comprehension.

The disciples' affirmation of their belief in 16:30 simultaneously casts doubt on their belief. Jesus has just said that the disciples have believed, yet the disciples themselves claim this belief as a new thing: "Now we know" (16:30). Their words suggest a sudden change of heart, as if they now understand. Their words also may leave the reader with questions: they claim that Jesus now speaks plainly, but Jesus himself claims to have spoken in figures of speech and foretells a future time when he will speak plainly (16:25). The disciples claim to understand, but it is still not clear if they can discriminate between figures of speech and plain language. The words they claim to understand are similar to things Jesus has said before: "I have come from the Father and have come into the world; again, I am leaving the world and going to the Father" (16:28; cf. 8:42; 14:2–3). His language does not appear markedly different from before, leaving open the question of what has changed the disciples' understanding.

Jesus' speech likewise affirms and raises questions about the disciples' faith. In 16:27, he affirms, "You have believed that I came from God." But in 16:31, Jesus questions the disciples' claims about their belief: "Do you now believe?" (16:31).[25] The disciples' current belief is questionable because Jesus knows their subsequent behavior: they will "be scattered," leaving Jesus alone (16:32). At the same time that he confirms their prior belief in him, Jesus raises questions about the disciples' affirmation of that belief. The Gospel presents Jesus' words as trustworthy. His own testimony and that of others is valid (5:32–39), and his foreknowledge is confirmed by the events of the Gospel (e.g., 6:70–71; 13:1, 3). The reader is thus conditioned to understand both sentences as true: "You have believed that I came from God" (16:27) and "Do you now believe?" (16:31). The disciples have believed, they confess belief, and yet their later scattering points to their lack of belief.[26]

In summary, during the course of Jesus' life, the disciples show a marked failure to understand Jesus and his words. They do not interact with him about the terms he uses, as other characters do, and as a result the reader is not drawn further into an understanding of the metaphors through the character of the disciples. The reader learns that disciples both do and do not believe in Jesus. They understand and misunderstand. The recurrence of their misunderstanding and disbelief suggests that they do not undergo a linear progress toward belief. Belief and unbelief occur simultaneously. The disciples have believed, and at the same time they are only now coming to believe. They believe, and yet their actions will cast doubt on their belief.

ABIDING AND SCATTERING

Ambiguity in the disciples' belief may lead the reader to look for other qualifications for discipleship. To stay or "abide" with Jesus (μένω, menō) is a command of Jesus (e.g., 15:4–7). Abiding and following are, along with believing, standards against which the character of the disciples might be judged. They help to broaden the reader's view of the disciples; though they do not always believe in Jesus, they do follow him. Raymond Brown argues that the disciples' following in John 1 "means more than walking in the same direction, for 'follow' is the term par excellence for the dedication of discipleship."[27] Likewise, Alan Culpepper writes, "Abiding is the test of discipleship (cf. 8:31)."[28] Abiding with Jesus provides the reader with an additional set of standards for assessing the disciples' character.

The disciples' actions and environment characterize them as those who abide with Jesus. This is said of them explicitly (1:38; 2:12), and Jesus also abides with them: "After this Jesus and his disciples went into the Judean countryside, and he remained there with them and baptized" (3:22; cf. 11:54). Other aspects of the disciples' character reflect their presence with Jesus. In chapter 1, Jesus calls individual disciples to "follow" him (1:43; cf. 1:37) or to "come and see" (1:39; cf. 1:46), both of which are invitations "to see Jesus with the eyes of faith."[29] This corresponds to what the reader sees the disciples doing in the Gospel. Other aspects of the narration suggest the disciples' proximity to Jesus: he sits down with them (6:3), washes their feet (13:5), and is said to have met with them often in the garden where he is arrested (18:2).

Yet the disciples are not characterized in a straightforward way as those who abide with or follow Jesus. Even during the ministry of Jesus, the narrative is often silent as to their presence. Long stretches go by without any indication of the presence of the disciples (as in 4:43–5:47; 7:1–8:59).[30] The Gospel's silence regarding the disciples does not mean that they are not present. Their presence may be assumed. This seems to be the case in chapter 11, where they are present with Jesus at the beginning, indicate that they will travel with him, and then are not mentioned again until 11:54, when they travel with Jesus again. The narrative lapses with respect to the disciples may point to their silence rather than their absence.

The presence of the disciples during the trial and crucifixion of Jesus is likewise ambiguous. But here, the disciples' not being mentioned points to their absence. Jesus says to the soldiers and police, "If it is me that you seek, let them go" (18:8). Peter and another disciple "follow" Jesus (18:15) for one more leg of his journey, but since this sets up Peter's denial of Jesus, it is certainly an ambiguous act. A few of the women and the Beloved Disciple appear at the foot of the cross: these characters may be said to abide with Jesus. But "the disciples" as a corporate character are not mentioned at all. It seems likely that Jesus' words "You will be scattered" (16:32) showed foreknowledge of this time. The disciples are characterized both by following or abiding with Jesus and by scattering. They are imperfect followers of Jesus, just as they are imperfect believers.

THE FUTURE OF THE DISCIPLES

While the disciples are ambiguous believers and followers, the Gospel nonetheless points to a future time when their activity will be important. Much of this language is found in the Farewell Discourse (John 14–17). Chapters 14–16 consist largely of the words of Jesus addressed to the disciples who are present with him at the Last Supper ("you" in this section of the text is plural). Jesus says the disciples will live (14:19), testify (15:27), weep and mourn (16:20), and rejoice (16:21–22). He also indicates that others will believe through their word (17:20). These future activities are empowered by the Spirit, who will "be in you" (14:17), teach and remind (14:26), and "guide you into all truth" (16:13). Some of the language of the Farewell Discourse suggests that the promises Jesus makes are given to those who believe and follow without qualification. Fernando Segovia argues that the promises made in John 14 are offered "to those, and only those, who believe in him."[31] Jesus' promises are contingent—they are true for those who love and who keep Jesus' word:

> If you love me, you will keep my commandments; and I will ask the Father, and he will give you another advocate. (14:15–16)

> Those who love me will be loved by my Father, and I will love them and will reveal myself to them. (14:21)

> Those who love me will keep my word, and my Father will love
> them, and we will come to them and make our dwelling place
> with them. (14:23)

The language of the Farewell Discourse suggests that the disciples
of the future will be much less ambiguous than those of the present
narrative.

Some interpreters offer a narrative of progress to make sense of these
details. While the disciples are ambiguously portrayed in the course of
Jesus' lifetime, they eventually become perfect believers. Thus Meeks
argues that the disciples "are progressively enlightened and drawn
into intense intimacy with Jesus, until they, like him, are not 'of this
world.'"[32] The Gospel creates a contrast between those who are "not
of this world" and those who are "of this world," and the disciples
eventually become "not of this world."[33] Segovia also sees a progression
in the disciples' understanding. He argues that at the point when the
promises are made in chapter 14, the disciples do believe in Jesus, but
imperfectly: they do not yet accept Jesus' departure and death. This is
to be expected: "The disciples do possess correct belief in Jesus; however, at the same time it is also clear that such belief cannot be complete
or perfect until after the resurrection of Jesus."[34] Following Jesus' resurrection appearances, the disciples' "perfect" belief is expected.

Other aspects of the Gospel's language reinforce a notion of progression in the disciples' understanding. Jesus never questions the disciples'
future belief, as he does their current belief. In addition, the narrator
comments that the disciples will later remember the events of Jesus'
life and understand them in a new way in light of Jesus' resurrection
(2:22; 12:16). The narrator's asides confirm Jesus' words about the
disciples' future. Jesus also indicates that he speaks so that the disciples
may later understand (13:19; 16:4; cf. 13:7). And he promises that "the
Advocate, the Holy Spirit, whom the Father will send in my name,
will teach you everything and remind you of everything I have said to
you" (14:26). In at least one other case, the promises Jesus makes in the
Farewell Discourse are seen to come true in the course of the narrative:
the disciples' rejoice when they see the risen Jesus (20:20; cf. 16:22).
This verification of Jesus' words suggests that the others are also true—
so that the reader may well assume that, outside of the narrative time,
the disciples have come to live and to testify, and that others have come
to believe. Such language can be interpreted to imply that ambiguities
among and within the disciples will cease.

A drawback to the theory of progressive enlightenment is that the reader never sees the character reach such perfection. Not much is said of "the disciples" in John 20–21, but the hints that are present have much in common with the ambiguity the reader has seen before. Jesus appears to the disciples three times (20:19–23, 26–29; 21:4–33). In the first appearance the disciples are characterized as passive and frightened. Their "fear of the Jews" has led them to a place where the doors are locked, although even the locking of the doors is not attributed actively to the disciples (20:19). Although they have heard of Jesus' resurrection from Mary (20:18), they either have not believed her report or have not understood its implications.[35] Their one action is to "rejoice" when they see the Lord (20:20). This is an appropriate response, and one that Jesus has promised (16:22). Their rejoicing does not follow Jesus' initial appearance and greeting (20:19), but the display of his hands and side. This timing is ambiguous. It suggests that, like the story of Thomas that follows, they do not fully recognize Jesus apart from this sight.[36] The action in this story belongs to Jesus: he stands among the disciples (20:19), breathes on them (20:22) and speaks to them three times (20:19, 21, 22). Jesus' gift of the Spirit (20:22) initiates the promises of the Farewell Discourse (cf. 15:26; 16:7–14) and is often understood to initiate the mission of the church.[37] But John marks no clear change in the disciples' character. In the next scene, the disciples proclaim to Thomas, "We have seen the Lord" (20:25), words that suggest their belief in the resurrection. However, a week later they are still hidden away in the same house and with the doors locked (20:26). Whatever belief the disciples have found does not appear to be immediately transformative.[38]

Nor does the final chapter of the Gospel resolve this tension in any obvious way. Jesus "reveals himself" again to the disciples by the Sea of Tiberias (or Galilee; cf. 21:1; 6:1). Little is said here of "the disciples" as a character; individual disciples have greater prominence (see my discussion in chap. 6). However, what the reader can glean about the disciples suggests that they are still slow in their recognition of Jesus and tentative in their approach to him. Jesus appears, standing on the shore, "but the disciples did not know that it was Jesus" (21:4). As C. K. Barrett writes, "The failure of the disciples to recognize Jesus is difficult to understand if we are to suppose they had already seen him twice since the resurrection."[39] The reader may wish to give them the benefit of the doubt since it is daybreak (21:4) and perhaps dark, and there is an unstated distance between their boat and the shore. Perhaps the disciples strain to see clearly. Nevertheless, the characterization of the disciples remains ambiguous. After the great catch of fish and the recognition of Jesus by the Beloved Disciple, the disciples return to shore with the fish (21:7–9). The language of verse 12 is strange: "Jesus said to them, 'Come and eat breakfast.' And none of the disciples dared to ask him: 'Who are you?' knowing that it was the Lord." On the one hand, the disciples are said to know that it is the Lord. Yet they are described actively as "not daring to question him." The narrator's formulation of the question that they dare not ask ("Who are you?") suggests that the disciples are still wondering and not asking questions of Jesus, as they have throughout the Gospel. At the same time, their knowledge of Jesus' identity is affirmed. In John 21 the disciples both know and do not know Jesus.

The disciples' promised perfection always lies outside the narrative time of the Gospel. They are not progressively transformed into better disciples of Jesus. Instead, they are characterized both by their checkered history of belief and unbelief and by a future time when they believe fully. They are those who believe and misunderstand, who abide and scatter. And they are those who "will do greater things than these" (14:12) and "will keep [Jesus'] word" (14:23). The disciples are shaped not only by what they are and have been but also by what they will be. They are made up of their (somewhat fragmentary) past and present identities, and also of their future. Read this way, the simultaneous ambiguity and perfection of the disciples is not a problem to be solved but a dichotomy that contributes to the understanding of their character. If the reader saw the disciples' future perfection played out, then they would be characterized as progressing toward belief. Yet the disciples' future belief remains in the future. It is never played out on the pages of the Gospel.

CONCLUSION

Understanding John's disciples as progressing toward belief fits an understanding of salvation history that dominated twentieth-century interpretations of the Gospel. John's Gospel has been widely understood to proclaim a "realized eschatology," in which God's promised blessings of the end time are fulfilled in the present. By offering the believer "life," "joy," and "peace," Jesus grants promises associated with the last day to believers in the present. Interpreters recognize that

John's language includes references to the "last day" as an event of the future, but they often attribute these verses to the viewpoint of a redactor rather than the evangelist.[40] The preferred viewpoint of the Gospel is that the future promises are already realized. The interpretation of the disciples reflects this realized eschatology. Since the end-time promises are fully present in Jesus, his disciples should embody their effects. Indeed, if Jesus' gifts are to be "realized" in the present, they are in some sense dependent on the disciples' behavior. Interpreters do not deny the disciples' apparent imperfections but instead argue for their progress toward belief in the present. The progress of the disciples is also a template for later disciples, as Francis Moloney observes: "Despite the struggle of foundational characters in the Christian story to move from no faith through partial faith into unconditional belief, they stand at the beginning of a further generation of believers. The readers of the Gospel have come to belief in the resurrection of Jesus."[41] Thus the readers may understand their own growth in faith through the reading of the Gospel as a parallel to the "progress" of the disciples.

Viewing the disciples as an ambiguous character fits with a different understanding of John's view of redemption, one that maintains the tension between the "now" and "not yet" of the eschatological promises. Jesus' coming initiates the promises of the end time: "life," "judgment," and even "resurrection" are already present in Jesus (e.g., 3:16–19; 11:25–44).[42] Yet its completion lies in the future, with the expectation of the "last day" (e.g., 6:39–40; cf. 5:25–29). The now and future expectations are reflected in many ways in the Gospel's language. For example, Jesus declares, "This is the will of my Father, that those who see the Son and believe in him have eternal life, and I will raise them up on the last day" (6:40). There is a present promise of "having life," but part of the promise is for the future: "I will raise them up on the last day." Elsewhere, Jesus also speaks of an hour or time that is both coming and already present: "The hour is coming and is now here . . ." (4:23; cf. 5:25; 16:32). John's Gospel does not resolve the tension between the now and not yet in favor of the now, but instead includes both elements. Ambiguity in the disciples' character fits this view of Johannine eschatology. The disciples receive all the promises of the Farewell Discourse; at the same time the full realization of these promises remains a future event.

The disciples are an eschatological character: God's redemption is not only future but also already present in them. They clearly misunderstand Jesus, yet they are understood to be believers already. The indications of the disciples' perfect belief are statements by Jesus or the narrator that attribute such belief to them without qualification. Jesus speaks of the disciples as those who "have loved me and have believed" (16:27). This love and belief characterizes the disciples even though there is little tangible evidence of it. The faith that is expected in the end time is already attributed to the disciples. Thus the disciples become examples of belief and love despite their failings. They are an "eschatological character," shaped in the present by the same promises that God will fulfill on the last day.

This interpretation of John's disciples offers the reader a different perspective on discipleship. Read against the background of an either/or message about belief in Jesus, the disciples are failures who eventually progress toward perfect belief. The narrative of progress offers a perspective on human life that many readers will find comforting: work a little harder, aided by the Holy Spirit, and you may achieve unconditional belief as well. An ambiguous view of the disciples cannot offer a narrative of progress. The disciples remain confused and unbelieving. John nevertheless views the disciples from a standpoint of hope.[43] There is little they do or say that justifies the optimistic voice that the Gospel occasionally finds. It is only from an eschatological perspective that the disciples can be said to be "marked especially by their recognition of Jesus and belief in his claims."[44] This eschatological perspective might also shape the reader's view of discipleship. John offers a lens with which to see one's own discipleship from the viewpoint of God's future promises. Imperfect human actions become acts of belief and love, even as they fall short of these claims. The disciples' own failings are part of the narrative of redemption. They enter into the labor of the harvest (4:38) even though they have not labored. They are declared "clean" (13:10) on the eve of their scattering. They are loved by the Father as a result of having loved and believed (16:27)—even though the reader does not see them doing so. In John's portrayal the disciples have already been transformed by Jesus' inauguration of the end time. Readers of the Gospel may not have achieved perfection, but they may find themselves recipients of the grace upon grace that transforms the disciples as well.

BIBLIOGRAPHY

Barrett, C. K. *The Gospel according to St. John.* Philadelphia: Westminster Press, 1978.

Brown, Raymond. *The Gospel according to John*. 2 vols. Anchor Bible 29–29A. New York: Doubleday, 1966–70.

Bultmann, Rudolf. *The Gospel of John*. Philadelphia: Westminster Press, 1971.

———. "Ζάω." Pages 855–75 in vol. 2 of *Theological Dictionary of the New Testament*. Edited by Gerhard Kittel. Grand Rapids: Wm. B. Eerdmans Publishing Co., 1964.

Coulot, Claude. "Les figures du maître et de ses disciples dans les premiere communautés chrétiennes." *Revue des sciences religieuses* 59 (1985): 1–11.

Culpepper, R. Alan. *Anatomy of the Fourth Gospel: A Study in Literary Design*. Philadelphia: Fortress Press, 1983.

Cuvillier, Élian. "La figure des disciples en Jean 4." *New Testament Studies* 42 (1996): 245–59.

Dodd, C. H. *The Interpretation of the Fourth Gospel*. Cambridge: Cambridge University Press, 1953.

Du Rand, J. A. "Narratological Perspectives on John 13:1–38." *Hervormde teologiese studies* 46 (1990): 367–89.

Hoskyns, Edwyn Clement. *The Fourth Gospel*. Edited by F. N. Davey. London: Faber & Faber, 1947.

Hylen, Susan. *Allusion and Meaning in John 6*. Beiheifte zur Zeitschrift für die neutestamentliche Wissenschaft 137. Berlin: Walter de Gruyter, 2005.

Köstenberger, Andreas J. *John*. Grand Rapids: Baker Academic, 2004.

Meeks, Wayne A. "The Man from Heaven in Johannine Sectarianism." *Journal of Biblical Literature* 91 (1972): 44–72.

Moloney, Francis J. *The Gospel of John*. Sacra pagina 4. Collegeville, MN: Liturgical Press, 1988.

O'Day, Gail R. *The Gospel of John*. New Interpreter's Bible 9. Nashville: Abingdon Press, 1995.

———. "John 6:15–21: Jesus Walking on Water as Narrative Embodiment of Johannine Christology." Pages 149–59 in *Critical Readings of John 6*. Edited by R. Alan Culpepper. Biblical Interpretation Series 22. Leiden: E. J. Brill, 1997.

Poplutz, Uta. "Paroimia und Parabole: Gleichniskonzepte bei Johannes und Markus." Pages 103–20 in *Imagery in the Gospel of John: Terms, Forms, Themes, and Theology of Johannine Figurative Language*. Edited by Jörg Frey, Jan G. van der Watt, and Ruben Zimmerman. Wissenschaftliche Untersuchungen zum Neuen Testament 200. Tübingen: Mohr Siebeck, 2006.

Schenke, Ludger. "Das johanneische Schisma und die 'Zwölf' (Johannes 6.60–71)." *New Testament Studies* 38 (1992): 105–21.

Schnackenburg, Rudolf. *The Gospel according to St. John*. 3 vols. New York: Seabury Press, 1982–90.

Segovia, Fernando F. "'Peace I Leave with You; My Peace I Give to You': Discipleship in the Fourth Gospel." Pages 76–102 in *Discipleship in the New Testament*. Edited by Fernando F. Segovia. Minneapolis: Fortress Press, 1985.

————. "The Structure, *Tendenz*, and *Sitz im Leben* of John 13:31–14:31."
    Journal of Biblical Literature 104 (1985): 471–93.
Smith, Ted A. *The New Measures: A Theological History of Democratic Practice.*
    Cambridge: Cambridge University Press, 2007.
Thompson, Marianne Meye. "The Breath of Life: John 20:22–23 Once More."
    Pages 69–78 in *Holy Spirit and Christian Origins: Essays in Honor of James
    D. G. Dunn.* Edited by Graham N. Stanton, Bruce W. Longenecker, and
    Stephen Barton. Grand Rapids: Wm. B. Eerdmans Publishing Co., 2004.
————. *The God of the Gospel of John.* Grand Rapids: Wm. B. Eerdmans Pub-
    lishing Co., 2001.
————. "When the Ending Is Not the End." Pages 65–76 in *The Ending of
    Mark and the Ends of God.* Edited by Beverly Roberts Gaventa and Patrick D.
    Miller. Louisville, KY: Westminster John Knox Press, 2005.

5
Martha and Mary

Mary and Martha are widely viewed by readers as exemplary characters. John introduces these characters with the statement that they are loved by Jesus (11:5), and this shapes the reader's expectation that they will be positive characters. Martha's interaction with Jesus before the raising of her brother, Lazarus, leads many to conclude that she is an exemplar of faith. As Jesus returns to Bethany, Martha approaches him, saying, "Lord, if you had been here, my brother would not have died" (11:21). She and Jesus engage in a conversation that leads to Martha's confession, "Yes, Lord, I believe that you are the Messiah, the Son of God, the one coming into the world" (11:27). Sandra Schneiders argues that with these words, "Martha demonstrates true and perfect Johannine belief in the Word of Jesus."[1] Likewise, Jesus interprets Mary's act of anointing (12:1–8) as one that shows significant understanding of Jesus' death. "Mary's anointing makes her the first character in the narrative to recognize the uniqueness of Jesus' death."[2]

Mary and Martha are often described as two of the most faithful characters of John's Gospel. As with other characters, however, John's indirect characterization of Martha and Mary leads to questions about their character. As a result, some interpreters see Martha as misunderstanding more than she understands about Jesus: "Martha gets it wrong each time she articulates her beliefs," Francis Moloney observes.[3] Likewise, the characterization of Mary can leave the impression that she is anything but a firm believer, as Rudolf Schnackenburg notes: "Mary gives the impression of being nothing but a complaining woman."[4] Yet such conclusions are certainly in the minority. To a large extent, interpreters understand that what these characters do and say is applauded within the Gospel.

Ambiguity in Mary and Martha involves the sisters' awareness of the meaning of their words and actions. They appear to be exemplary characters who do not fully understand who Jesus is. Thus when Jesus requests that the stone be removed from Lazarus's tomb, Martha replies, "Lord, already it stinks, for it has been four days" (11:39). Her comment raises concerns for many interpreters because she seems not to truly understand what she confessed in verse 27. In contrast to Martha's lengthy conversation with Jesus, Mary is characterized primarily through her actions and speaks only once (verse 32), echoing Martha's words in verse 21. Because she is silent, the reader has no insight into what Mary thinks and must evaluate the meaning of her actions based on other clues. The tendency to interpret belief in John's Gospel as an either/or proposition creates a problem with these characters. If the interpreter's emphasis is on the importance of one's conscious belief in Jesus, the sisters cannot be straightforwardly good characters.

In this chapter I argue that John's characterization suggests a different emphasis. Mary and Martha are not perfect believers. Yet their imperfect faith is rendered complete within the scope of the Gospel narrative. In my reading, Jesus' own words and actions give a fullness of meaning to Martha and Mary's offerings of faith, love, and service. Exploration of the nature of their belief may lead the reader to deeper contemplation of the questions of life and death that surround the story of Lazarus and the Gospel as a whole.

MARTHA

Martha is an ambiguous character because she appears to have strong belief in Jesus yet without full comprehension of her own confession of faith. Her ambiguity is developed in her interaction with Jesus in John 11:17–27, 39–40. As in reading other characters, reading Martha as a believing character is a matter of judgment, for John's characterization of her is indirect. Two main questions shape interpretations of Martha's character: What is Martha's tone in her conversation with Jesus? How much does she understand or believe? I argue below that her appearances in John 11 show evidence of her belief in Jesus. Yet ambiguity in her character leads the reader to contemplate the meaning of Jesus' claims about himself and Martha's understanding of them.

Martha's initial words to Jesus show that she already has a well-developed belief in him: "Lord, if you had been here, my brother would not have died. But even now I know that God will give you whatever you ask" (verses 21–22). It is possible to read these words as accusatory. She does not understand why Jesus did not return in time to save Lazarus. Her grief overcomes her sense of propriety, and she expresses profound disappointment in Jesus' absence. Most interpreters recognize this possibility only in passing, however, and reject it in favor of viewing Martha's words as a statement of faith.[5] Her words express the idea that she still believes in Jesus' power to heal and knows him to be sent by God.[6] The death of Lazarus has not stemmed Martha's faith in Jesus' power to do God's work. But is the faith she expresses an adequate understanding of Jesus? Francis Moloney argues that she confesses faith only in Jesus' ability to work miracles, and such faith "falls short of true belief."[7] Moloney's argument, however, ignores the extent to which Martha's words are true within John's presentation of Jesus. If she sees him as "a rabbi from God who does wonderful signs because God is with him,"[8] then she knows a good deal about him. In the story of the blind man (John 9), the controversy with the Pharisees centers on their claim that Jesus is not from God, because he does not observe the Sabbath (9:16). Martha at least recognizes that Jesus' healing power comes from God, and that is a significant part of Jesus' identity.

A few interpreters argue that Martha's words show even greater understanding: Martha expresses disappointment in Jesus' absence, but she does so precisely because she believes in his God-given power to bring life.[9] Jesus could have healed her brother if he had been present during his illness, and Jesus still has power from God to heal. Martha's words are hardly the antithesis of faith; they are perhaps faith's deepest expression. In the midst of her sorrow, Martha cries out to God. Just as the psalmists state their knowledge of God's power and implore God to act, so Martha laments Jesus' absence and its results, even as she continues to believe in his power. This reading denies a simplistic division between faith and complaint in arguing that questioning God's absence during a time of crisis does not qualify Martha's faith.

Martha believes that Jesus has power to raise the dead, yet only on the day of resurrection. To Jesus' statement, "Your brother will rise again" (verse 23), she responds, "I know that he will rise again in the resurrection on the last day" (verse 24). Martha's view of a future resurrection represents a traditional Pharisaic view of the resurrection on the last day.[10] Many readers understand Martha's words as simply wrong. Her belief that Lazarus will rise on the last day represents a Jewish understanding of the resurrection that Jesus seeks to correct—either through his words or his action of raising Lazarus. A better reading of this conversation is that Martha's words are incomplete, but not incorrect. Jesus' words in verse 23, "Your brother will rise again," leave open the possibility of a resurrection in the distant future: Lazarus will rise, but Jesus does not say when. Actually Martha's response is not incorrect from the perspective of the Gospel. Her words confirm what Jesus has said; he will "raise them up on the last day" (6:40). Martha builds on the most obvious meaning of what Jesus has said, affirming Lazarus's participation in the resurrection on the last day.

Jesus confirms that Martha's understanding of future resurrection is at least partially correct. Martha has understood that Jesus brings resurrection on the last day. Jesus' words in 11:25b support Martha's view of her brother's future resurrection: "Those who believe in me, even though they die, will live" (11:25b). Following death, the believer will experience resurrection on the last day.

Yet this is not all Jesus has to say on the subject matter, and the rest of verses 25–26 seem to go beyond Martha's understanding. Jesus tells Martha, "I am the resurrection and the life" (11:25a). The verb tense is present: the expectations of both resurrection and life are available in the present through Jesus.[11] In addition, Jesus speaks of the believer's present situation: "And everyone who lives and believes in me . . ." (11:26). While verse 25b focuses on the effect of belief on the death of the believer, verse 26 emphasizes the effect of belief on the life of the believer.[12] Those who live and believe will (metaphorically) "never die" (verse 26). Many interpreters read the twin statements in verses 25b and 26 as virtually identical. In each case, Jesus offers heavenly life to believers following their physical deaths.[13] The believer already possesses the promise of this eternal life, but not "eternal life" itself. In this reading, "eternal life" is defined as something limited to the afterlife.[14] Yet Jesus' words point to a stronger present-tense aspect of the "life" that believers experience: it is not simply the promise of life that believers experience, but "life" itself. The life that Jesus brings is "eternal" in the sense that it is a quality belonging only to God. Metaphorically, the believer who will "never die" (verse 26) has life that is somehow like that of the divine. Jesus brings to believers a new quality of life, a life that already participates in the fullness of life with God.

Martha initially seems to understand what Jesus has told her about himself, and her confession of faith in verse 27 appears to be a valid understanding of Jesus, perhaps the most complete of any character in the Gospel: "Yes, Lord, I believe that you are the Messiah, the Son of God, the one coming into the world." She mirrors the statement of faith that the Gospel hopes to elicit in its readers: "These [signs] have been written so that you may believe that Jesus is the Christ, the Son of God" (20:31). The Gospel's narrator thus affirms that Martha's faith displays an impressive understanding of Jesus' identity. For many scholars, as Schneiders has observed, it is "the most fully developed confession of Johannine faith in the Fourth Gospel."[15]

Yet Martha's words contain some ambiguity. Only a few interpreters are critical of Martha's formulation of her faith in verse 27,[16] but even when her confession is understood in the strongest terms, it is ambiguous because of her response to Jesus at the tomb (verse 39). Coming on the heels of Jesus' declaration of himself as "the resurrection and the life," the reader may expect Martha's confession to show greater comprehension than her words at the tomb suggest. Her confession affirms what Jesus has said about the present-tense nature of the life he offers: He is the Christ, the one coming into the world. God will give him whatever he asks. Yet at the grave Martha does not want the stone removed, believing that death's hold on her brother is complete. She does not expect his resurrection.[17] A number of interpreters dismiss Martha's uncertainty, chalking it up to human nature or explaining that no one could be expected to foresee Lazarus's immediate resurrection. While that may be true, it can no longer be said that Martha's faith in verse 27 was perfect. She did not understand her own claim about Jesus in the fullest sense.

Jesus' act of raising Lazarus sheds new light on both his own words in verses 25–26 and Martha's confession in verse 27. The renewed life that Lazarus receives from Jesus is a powerful illustration of the present-tense nature of the "life" and "resurrection" Jesus offers. This life is not only a heavenly, spiritual existence but also a bodily, earthly one. The one who "lives and believes" in Jesus (verse 26) has a life that participates in the power that breathes life into a dead body, that unbinds Lazarus from his captivity to death.[18] It is a life that now imbues Lazarus's present, earthly existence. It is not limited to the life of the resurrection to come, nor is resurrection limited to the life to come. Martha's words also take on new meaning. Jesus is "the Messiah, the Son of God, the one coming into the world," and those titles or roles are illuminated by the powerful act of bringing life to Lazarus. As Jesus "comes into the world," this is what happens: the dead are raised to life. Jesus fully embodies God's power to bring life in the midst of death.

Martha shows a strong understanding of Jesus. Her confession, "You are the Messiah, the Son of God, the one coming into the world," stands as one of the most comprehensive of the Gospel. Yet in the context of John 11, Martha does not fully grasp the implications of her own faith. Perhaps the reader would not either, if it were not for Jesus' following action of raising Lazarus from the dead. The sign helps the reader to interpret Jesus' own words in verses 25–26 and lends new meaning to the language of Martha's confession. As "the one coming into the world," Jesus brings life into the midst of death. Martha expresses faith in Jesus, but it is Jesus' own actions that bring full meaning to her faith. Martha's partial understanding is made complete by Jesus' actions.

MARY

John never makes it entirely clear what Mary understands or believes, and hence she too is an ambiguous figure. The reader does not hear a confession of belief from Mary, as we do from Martha. Without such a confession, we assess Mary's character based on her actions in the story. Many interpreters also compare her to other characters (especially Martha and the Jews). I argue here that these aspects of Mary's character contribute to an ambiguous portrait. Nonetheless, Jesus' responses to Mary—in words and actions—contribute to a largely positive understanding of her character.

From the beginning, there are positive aspects to Mary's character. Mary's initial response to Jesus is positive, although it remains unclear what she believes about him. She responds when she learns that Jesus is calling for her (11:28), which the reader may associate with Jesus' words in 10:27: "My sheep hear my voice. I know them, and they follow me." Mary kneels at Jesus' feet (verse 32), suggesting a posture of devotion or worship, which may identify her as a believer. But what does Mary believe? Unlike with Martha, we have no clear statement of her faith. However, because her opening words are similar to Martha's ("Lord, if you had been here, my brother would not have died"; verse 32), some interpreters find a correspondence between the two sisters' understandings of Jesus.[19] Others understand Mary's kneeling as an indication that her faith is greater than Martha's.[20] Yet Martha's additional words in verses 22–27 also convey faith, and some argue that her conversation with Jesus is evidence of a learning process that Mary lacks.[21] While Mary's act of kneeling implies deference to Jesus, it does not identify what she believes that leads to such deference. In the end, many interpreters conclude that both sisters show devotion to Jesus in different ways.[22]

The sense of Mary's ambiguity is also tied to her relationship to the Jews. To the interpreters who read the Jews as hostile to Jesus in this chapter, she is an ambiguous character. Some interpreters view the Jews in John 11 as enemies of Jesus because of their prior responses in chapters 9 and 10 (9:18–34; 10:24–39; cf. 11:8).[23] Because Mary's character is linked with the Jews through the same act of weeping (verse 33), many also see her in a negative light. In this view, weeping is evidence of unbelief on the part of both Mary and the Jews. However, other interpreters differentiate between Mary's weeping and the Jews' hostility. They argue that Mary's quick response to Jesus and prostration at his feet suggest that she does believe, while the Jews are intruders on the scene.[24]

However, if the Jews are not hostile and unbelieving, these attributes should not be transferred to Mary. In my reading, the Jews show no hostility toward Jesus in this passage.[25] They say, "See how he loved him. And some of them said, 'Could not the one who opened the eyes of the blind man have kept this man from dying?'" (verses 36–37). These words show partial understanding: Jesus does love Lazarus (cf. 11:5). And Martha and Mary have shared a similar impression of Jesus: that he could have kept Lazarus from dying (verse 37; cf. verses 21, 32). The Jews even seem to correct their previous rejection of Jesus' healing of the blind man and now speak of Jesus as "he who opened the eyes of the blind man" (cf. 9:24–34). While this evidence does not suggest that the Jews have faith in Jesus at this point, neither is it evidence of their hostility. In John 11:45, the end of the passage, the response of many of the Jews to the resurrection of Lazarus is belief in Jesus. Their belief is not portrayed as inferior in any way; it is simple "belief," like that which is elsewhere attributed to the disciples. And the reality of their belief is indicated by the role it plays in the plot of the Gospel; the belief of many instigates the formal plan to put Jesus to death (11:48).

Scholars also assess Mary's grief for her brother in multiple ways. Some judge it in a negative sense, independent of its association with the Jews, seemingly on the assumption that believers should be beyond human emotion. If she is a believer, Moloney writes, she should be able to "transcend the human pain and sorrow generated by the death of a loved one."[26] In this view, responding to Lazarus's death with customary mourning shows significant misunderstanding of Jesus. Mary should understand that death no longer has power over human life, and she should not mourn. Therefore, her tears show unbelief. Others find no negative characterization here but rather see mourning as an appropriate response at the death of a loved one, even for people of faith.

Jesus' response to Mary's tears may be another indirect indication of her character, but interpretations vary. Some interpreters understand Jesus' distress in verse 33 as a response to Mary's tears. Most English translations render the Greek word (ἐμβριμάομαι, *embrimaomai*, verses 33, 38) in a way that sounds more like compassion than anger. For example, the NRSV translates this word as "greatly disturbed." However, most scholars recognize that the word reflects anger and agitation more than simple grief. For some interpreters, Jesus' anger represents judgment on Mary's tears.[27] Her weeping is evidence of a lack of faith. Like Martha, she does not believe that Jesus will raise her brother from the dead. In this reading, Jesus' tears should not be understood as grief: he already knows that Lazarus will rise from the dead. He has already stated that Lazarus's "illness does not end in death, but is for the glory of God, so that the Son of God may be glorified through it" (11:4). Thus, for many interpreters, Jesus' tears are a judgment against the mourning of those around him.

In my view it is a better option to read Jesus' tears as an affirmation of the human grief he finds here. I argue this for three reasons. First, the context of Lazarus's death prepares the reader to expect grief. Anger is an emotion commonly associated with grief, and thus the words may suggest that Jesus shares the experience of loss at the death of Lazarus, even though he is aware that Lazarus will rise.[28] Second, Jesus' anger is not directed at Mary or the Jews. Grammatically, *embrimaomai* is usually found with a pronoun identifying the person toward whom the anger is directed (this is true in the other NT uses of the word; see Mark 1:43; 14:5; Matt. 9:30). In John 11:33, if Jesus' anger is directed toward anyone, it is directed toward "the spirit"[29] rather than toward a person or group. Third, although some find Jesus' grief unlikely due to his knowledge that Lazarus will rise again, the same logic should apply to his grief due to their lack of faith. Jesus has no more reason to grieve over their lack of faith than he does over his beloved friend's death. Jesus' omniscience suggests that he would also know that the miracle will lead to widespread belief (cf. 11:15, 45; 12:9–11).[30] Instead, it seems more likely that Jesus' tears share in the complex human emotion of grief. His mourning recognizes that death is a powerful force in human life, even with the knowledge of resurrection. If death is simply an illusion for believers,[31] then the raising of Lazarus is not much of a miracle: Lazarus "lives" regardless of Jesus' act. But Jesus' mourning may show the reality of Lazarus's death. The reality of death is necessary if the raising of Lazarus is in any sense an illustration of Jesus' words "I am the resurrection and the life" (verse 25). The "life" Jesus brings comes in the midst of human despair.[32]

For some interpreters, any ambiguity in Mary's character is resolved in John 12, where the story centers on her anointing of Jesus. From the moment of Mary's introduction in John 11, she is characterized as "the one who anointed the Lord with perfume and wiped his feet with her hair" (11:2). Although her act of anointing Jesus is not narrated until later in the story, John's inclusion of it from the beginning may help the reader to see her first appearance at Lazarus's death in a more positive light.

John characterizes Mary positively through the act of anointing. Although Judas interprets her behavior negatively, charging that the money would be better spent on the poor (12:5),[33] readers are prepared to reject Judas's interpretation because he is identified as Jesus' betrayer (12:4; cf. 6:70–71), and is further described as a thief (12:6). In addition, Jesus rejects Judas's interpretation and explains Mary's action in positive terms as preparation for his burial (12:7). The disciples do not seem to comprehend the fact of Jesus' death, even after this point (e.g., 14:5; 16:17–18). Yet Jesus suggests that Mary knows of Jesus' death and is preparing for it already. This would be evidence for Mary's deep comprehension of the direction of Jesus' life, and for some interpreters, Mary becomes the first character in the narrative to show such awareness.[34]

Jesus' interpretation of Mary's act gives it an overtly positive connotation. But the ambiguity of her character remains. The reader is undoubtedly meant to understand Jesus' words as true, and to connect the act of anointing with Jesus' coming death. What remains ambiguous is the extent to which this characterizes Mary. There are not any direct indications of Mary's consciousness in the text, only Jesus' interpretation of her act. Given the context of what has just happened, it seems entirely possible that Mary's act is a lavish gift of thanksgiving, in celebration of Jesus' gift of her brother's life. Many interpreters see the preparation for burial as an unintended consequence of Mary's act of devotion. Some also understand her action in comparison to Caiaphas,[35] whose words "It is better for you that one man die for the

people than that the whole nation die" (11:50) express more than he
knows. His words are identified as prophetic (11:49–52), for he points
to the significance of Jesus' death for Israel. Mary's action can likewise
be read as a prophetic enactment of Jesus' pending burial, although like
Caiaphas, Mary may be initially unaware of the significance of her act.

Jesus' words, "Leave her alone so that she may keep it for the day
of my burial" (12:7), make Mary's anointing an eschatological act. On
one level, the words seem to suggest that Judas should not bother Mary
in order that she may have some of the perfume left over for a later
date. Yet this does not fit the context of the story, in which Mary's
anointing of Jesus has already occurred, and the narration of the act
in 12:3 suggests that Mary has expended the contents of the perfume,
leaving her nothing to "keep" for a future day when Jesus is buried.
Therefore, another possibility is that, although Jesus' burial will not
occur for another six days, Jesus declares that she has kept it for that
day. (This is implied by the NRSV: "Leave her alone. She bought it
so that she might keep it for the day of my burial.") Jesus' words can
be understood in relation to his own sayings about his "hour" as both
present and future. Jesus' hour "is coming and now is" (4:23; 5:25; cf.
16:32), as Dodd explains:

> At Cana, when His mother intervened, His ὥρα [hour] had not yet
> come (ii. 4); but when "He manifested His glory" in giving wine for
> water (ii. 11), it had, in some sense, come. Similarly, when Jesus was
> hiding in Galilee, His καιρός [time] was not yet present (vii. 6), but
> when at the Feast of Tabernacles He declared Himself the source of
> light and of living water it was, in some sense, present.[36]

Jesus' interpretation of Mary's act makes sense in the context of the
Gospel's understanding of his "hour," which is present even before
the events of Jesus' crucifixion and burial. John frames the events of
the Last Supper and Farewell Discourse in the context of Jesus' death
by indicating that Jesus' hour arrives at the start of these scenes (13:1),
on the day before his death. So also Jesus' words interpreting Mary's
anointing declare that in her act, the day of his burial is present.
Mary enacts the moment of Jesus' burial and therefore participates in
his hour.

Mary's ambiguity lies in the reader's inability to determine with any
certainty what she understands about her own words or actions. Yet
Jesus' words impart to Mary's actions a deep sense of his ministry and
purpose. His interpretation and the later event of his death add mean-

ing to Mary's act of anointing Jesus' feet, no matter what she understands about her actions. Mary is characterized as one whose ambiguous actions are made meaningful by Jesus' own words and actions. Like Martha's belief, Mary's actions are incomplete when viewed within the scope of her own explicit intentions. But Jesus breathes into them a life that goes beyond the limitations of her intentions. Regardless of her own intentions, Mary's actions come to embody the fullness of Jesus' action in the raising of Lazarus.

MARTHA AND MARY

Mary and Martha's actions in John 12 are also characterized by Jesus' words and actions in the events that follow (chaps. 12–13). Their acts of service are precursors of Jesus' teachings in these chapters.

Mary's anointing of Jesus takes on added significance in light of Jesus' similar action in 13:3–12. Her story is linked to Jesus' footwashing by the use of the same verb "to wipe" (ἐκμάσσω, *ekmassō*), which appears in the descriptions of Mary's act (11:2 and 12:3) and of Jesus' act (13:5).[37] After washing the disciples' feet, Jesus goes on to exhort his disciples to wash one another's feet (13:14). Mary's anointing anticipates Jesus' later actions and his instructions to the disciples. In retrospect, she appears as a model disciple, one who is already doing what the teacher expects.

Martha's service at the dinner in chapter 12 may also be read in light of Jesus' later teachings. Her actions are a fainter echo of Mary's, just as Mary's words in 11:32 echoed those of her sister in 11:21. Though Martha's service is often examined in light of possible connections to Luke's portrayal of these women, there is nothing to suggest a connection between the portrayals in the two Gospels. John makes no explicit contrast between the two women. Martha's "service" should be interpreted against the background of John's language. He uses the word "service" (διακονέω, *diakoneō*) in 12:2 to characterize Martha, and twice in 12:26 to characterize those who would be his disciples. "Whoever serves me must follow me, and where I am, there will my servant be also. Whoever serves me, the Father will honor." Like her sister, Martha enacts Jesus' instructions before he gives them.[38]

In the discussion of Mary's anointing, I argued that characterization through action created ambiguity in Mary's belief. In this case, however, the sisters could not be expected to be aware of Jesus' later words. As Gail O'Day has argued, "The power of the witness of Mary's discipleship in this story is that she knows how to respond to Jesus without being told. . . . She gives boldly of herself in love to Jesus at his hour, just as Jesus will give boldly of himself in love at his hour."[39] This is true of Mary's anointing as a precursor of the footwashing in a way that it is not true of her anointing Jesus for burial. Her extravagant act mirrors the kind of love and service Jesus identifies as a central component of discipleship.

CONCLUSION

Mary and Martha are positive but ambiguous characters. If belief in John's Gospel is an either/or decision, it is again difficult to place these characters neatly on one side of the divide or the other. Martha's belief is tainted by her lack of understanding of Jesus. Mary has no clearly stated belief, only what her actions suggest in the context of the Gospel. Yet readers of the Gospel often come away with a positive impression of the sisters. They appear at a climactic moment in Jesus' ministry, and their words and actions add something to the reader's understanding of the story of Jesus.

Ambiguity in the characters of Martha and Mary leads the reader to reflect on the meaning of life and death in the story of Lazarus. Martha confesses more than she truly understands about Jesus. Yet because her words about Jesus contrast with her attitude at the tomb, Martha's character may lead the reader to reflect on the meaning of Jesus' claim to be "the resurrection and the life." Jesus' life is not simply a future otherworldly possession for believers, like the future life Martha might well expect for her brother, but an embodied life in the present that participates in the fullness of life with God. Likewise, Mary's character leads the reader to reflect on the nature of death. First, the reader may question the human responses to death in the face of the news of life that Jesus offers. The narrative suggests that humans continue to experience death, even in the midst of the life that Jesus is known to bring. Although Lazarus's death leads to life, it is no less traumatic for those near to him. Second, Mary's character points to the present reality of Jesus' own death. In his trip to Bethany, Jesus knowingly risks his life in order to bring life to one he loves. His act results in life. But the belief it engenders also sets in motion the plans that lead to Jesus' death. Mary's anointing of Jesus is a reminder of this connection between Lazarus's life and Jesus' death. Her outpouring of gratitude is simultaneously a preparation for Jesus' burial.

The story of Lazarus is a metaphor for the resurrection and life that Jesus brings. It is a stunning sign of Jesus' identity and power: the gift of life where there was no hope of life, the return of the beloved to those who grieve. The "life" of faith is like the life that Lazarus received. It is not limited to the future or to heaven. It is not limited to the life of the mind or spirit. It is visceral and present, a life that partakes even now of the future resurrection of the dead.

Like their brother, Mary and Martha are examples of that "life." Their words and actions are on the right track, but they do not understand or believe in full. Jesus' later words and actions alter the reader's perception of their characters. The "life" Jesus offers in the present is manifest not just in Lazarus their brother, but also in the words and actions of these women. Jesus' words and actions breathe life into their own faith, such that within their faith there lives a deeper meaning and purpose. The sisters' awareness of that meaning is not itself the point. The reader may see in them the spark of life by which meager human offerings of faith, love, and service become part of the larger work of God. The abundant life that Jesus brings is poured into the women's words and actions, filling them with meaning that is beyond mere human knowledge.

BIBLIOGRAPHY

Barrett, C. K. *The Gospel according to St. John*. Philadelphia: Westminster Press, 1978.

Beasley-Murray, George R. *John*. Word Bible Commentary 36. Waco, TX: Word, 1987.

Bretherton, Donald L. "Lazarus of Bethany: Resurrection or Resuscitation?" *Expository Times* 104 (1993): 169–73.

Brown, Raymond. *The Gospel according to John*. 2 vols. Anchor Bible 29–29A. New York: Doubleday, 1966–70.

Bultmann, Rudolf. *The Gospel of John*. Philadelphia: Westminster Press, 1971.

Cadman, W. H. "The Raising of Lazarus (John 10, 40–11, 53)." Pages 423–34 in vol. 1 of *Studia evangelica*. Edited by Kurt Aland et al. Texte und Untersuchungen zur Geschichte der altchristlichen Literatur 73. Berlin: Akademie-Verlag, 1959.

Calvin, Jean. *The Gospel according to St. John 11–21 and the First Epistle of John*. Edited by David W. Torrance and Thomas F. Torrance. Translated by T. H. L. Parker. Calvin's Commentaries. Edinburgh: Oliver & Boyd, 1961.

Collins, Raymond F. "The Representative Figures of the Fourth Gospel—I." *Downside Review* 94 (1976): 26–46.

Conway, Colleen M. *Men and Women in the Fourth Gospel: Gender and Johannine Characterization.* Society of Biblical Literature Dissertation Series 167. Atlanta: Society of Biblical Literature, 1999.

Dodd, C. H. *The Interpretation of the Fourth Gospel.* Cambridge: Cambridge University Press, 1953.

Esler, Philip F., and Ronald A. Piper. *Lazarus, Mary and Martha: A Social-Scientific and Theological Reading of John.* London: SCM Press, 2006.

Hoskyns, Edwyn Clement. *The Fourth Gospel.* Edited by F. N. Davey. London: Faber & Faber, 1947.

Lindars, Barnabas. "Rebuking the Spirit: A New Analysis of the Lazarus Story of John 11." *New Testament Studies* 38 (1992): 89–104.

Martin, James P. "History and Eschatology in the Lazarus Narrative: John 11.1–44." *Scottish Journal of Theology* 17 (1964): 332–43.

Moloney, Francis J. "Can Everyone Be Wrong? A Reading of John 11.1–12.8." *New Testament Studies* 49 (2003): 505–27.

———. "The Faith of Martha and Mary: A Narrative Approach to John 11,17–40." *Biblica* 75 (1994): 471–93.

———. *The Gospel of John.* Sacra pagina 4. Collegeville, MN: Liturgical Press, 1988.

North, Wendy Sproston. "Jesus' Prayer in John 11." Pages 164–80 in *The Old Testament in the New Testament: Essays in Honour of J. L. North.* Edited by Steve Moyise. Journal for the Study of the New Testament: Supplement Series 189. Sheffield: Sheffield Academic Press, 2000.

O'Day, Gail R. *The Gospel of John.* New Interpreter's Bible 9. Nashville: Abingdon Press, 1995.

Pollard, T. E. "The Raising of Lazarus (John xi)." Pages 434–43 in vol. 6 of *Studia evangelica.* Edited by Elizabeth A. Livingstone. Texte und Untersuchungen zur Geschichte der altchristlichen Literatur 112. Berlin: Akademie-Verlag, 1973.

Reid, Barbara E. "The Cross and Cycles of Violence." *Interpretation* 58 (2004): 376–85.

Rena, John. "Women in the Gospel of John." *Église et théologie* 17 (1986): 131–47.

Rodríguez-Ruiz, Miguel. "Significado cristológico y soteriológico de Jn 11, 25–27." *Estudios bíblicos* 55 (1997): 199–222.

Schnackenburg, Rudolf. *The Gospel according to St. John.* 3 vols. New York: Seabury Press, 1982–90.

Schneiders, Sandra M. "Death in the Community of Eternal Life: History, Theology, and Spirituality in John 11." *Interpretation* 41 (1987): 44–56.

———. *Written That You May Believe: Encountering Jesus in the Fourth Gospel.* New York: Herder & Herder, 1999.

Seim, Turid Karlsen. "Roles of Women in the Gospel of John." Pages 56–73 in *Aspects on the Johannine Literature*. Edited by Lars Hartman and Birger Olsson. Coniectanea biblica: New Testament Series 18. Uppsala: Almqvist & Wiksell International, 1987.

Stibbe, Mark W. G. "A Tomb with a View: John 11:1–44 in Narrative-Critical Perspective." *New Testament Studies* 40 (1994): 38–54.

Story, Cullen I. K. "The Mental Attitude of Jesus at Bethany: John 11:33, 38." *New Testament Studies* 37 (1991): 51–66.

Thompson, Marianne Meye. *The God of the Gospel of John*. Grand Rapids: Wm. B. Eerdmans Publishing Co., 2001.

———. "When the Ending Is Not the End." Pages 65–76 in *The Ending of Mark and the Ends of God*. Edited by Beverly Roberts Gaventa and Patrick D. Miller. Louisville, KY: Westminster John Knox Press, 2005.

Yamaguchi, Satako. "Christianity and Women in Japan." *Japanese Journal of Religious Studies* 30 (2003): 315–38.

6

The Beloved Disciple

The Beloved Disciple is unique in the Gospels in several ways. Found only in John, he is an anonymous character, identified throughout the Gospel only as "the one Jesus loved." Many view him as the "ideal Christian convert," the "disciple par excellence."[1] As the one who reclines in the bosom of Jesus (13:23; 21:20), he is seen as emblematic of the close relationship with Jesus to which believers should aspire. As one who "believes" at the empty tomb (20:8), he is "paradigmatic of the faithful."[2] As the witness upon whose testimony the Gospel is based (19:35; 21:24), the Beloved Disciple is a model for the witness expected of later Christians. He becomes the premier example of discipleship to which readers of the Gospel are called.

Even the character of the Beloved Disciple, however, admits some ambiguity. Like many of the Gospel's characters, the Beloved is said to believe in Jesus during the course of the Gospel, yet it is not clear what the Beloved Disciple believes or understands. During Jesus' life and his resurrection appearances, for example, the Beloved expresses partial faith and does not witness to others. He is characterized as an intimate of Jesus and as a witness, aspects of discipleship the Gospel deems important. And the reader is led to believe that, beyond the narrative time of the Gospel, the Beloved Disciple has indeed become a faithful witness.

I argue below that the Beloved Disciple is both exemplary and imperfect. His primary identity is as one whom Jesus loves, yet he

92

remains an ambiguous character. And I show that John portrays the Beloved Disciple as one whose faith is genuine yet partial, and as one whose faith and understanding depend and build upon the faith and understanding of others.

IDENTIFYING THE BELOVED DISCIPLE

The character of the Beloved Disciple has always raised a number of significant questions for interpreters. Simply trying to determine which passages of the Gospel refer to the Beloved Disciple is a difficult task. Many scholars have also tried to identify him more precisely as a historical figure, with varying results. Those who are content to leave the Beloved's identity anonymous, as the Gospel does, are nevertheless confronted with questions about why he is anonymous, or how the anonymity functions for his character. Each of these questions creates some ambiguity for the Beloved Disciple from the outset.

John's characterization of the Beloved Disciple creates a number of questions regarding his identity. Even the literary identity of this character is somewhat obscure. Determining which passages of the Gospel include the Beloved is itself a difficult matter. References to "the disciple Jesus loved" appear in John 13:23–25; 19:26–27; 20:2–10; and 21:7, 20–24. Some interpreters also conclude that the Beloved is the unnamed disciple who appears with Andrew in 1:35–42,[3] and others identify him as the "other disciple" of 18:15–16.[4] John's characterization of the Beloved leaves all such conclusions within the realm of the possible, for there is no conclusive evidence to either confirm or deny these hypotheses. From a literary standpoint, it is relevant that unnamed disciples appear elsewhere in the narrative (e.g., 21:2), and that "the disciples" are often an unnamed and unnumbered group.

Given this general uncertainty, in treating the Beloved as a character I rely only on the passages in which he is clearly identified. As a character in the Gospel, the "disciple Jesus loves" appears for the first time in 13:23. Yet even in this initial appearance, he has an established relationship with Jesus, which suggests his presence in the narrative before this time. The Gospel never narrates details of his relationship with Jesus. Thus his identity and experience remain ambiguous.

The Beloved's historical identity is even more obscure. Some interpreters understand him to be representative of a historical group in the life of the Johannine community. One common assessment is that the

Beloved represents Gentile Christianity (distinguishing it from Jewish Christianity). Through the characterization of the Beloved in relation to Peter, interpreters conclude that Jewish Christianity is absorbed into Gentile Christianity.[5] An alternative argument is that the Beloved represents all Christians (as distinguished from Jews).[6] Still others look for a historical person behind the character.

Although some ancient interpreters identify the disciple as John, son of Zebedee, this possibility is not well supported by the Gospel itself, whose title, "The Gospel according to John," is not found in early manuscripts of the text, which appear to be anonymous. (While I refer to the work as "John" throughout this book, I mean this by way of convention rather than an assertion about the authorship of the Gospel.) The "sons of Zebedee" appear in the fishing expedition of seven disciples in 21:2, although neither is given a first name. While the Beloved Disciple is later named as one of these seven disciples, he could easily be one of the two unnamed disciples mentioned as well. John actually gives no details by which the reader might connect the Beloved with either of the sons of Zebedee. Because of this, the traditional identification of the Beloved Disciple as John, son of Zebedee, is no longer widely accepted, although some scholars continue to support the hypothesis.[7]

Others look for the identity of the Beloved Disciple by comparing what the Gospel says about the Beloved to what it says about other named characters. These interpreters arrive at different conclusions. Sometimes interpreters identify the Beloved as Lazarus, whom Jesus is also said to love (11:3, 5). Others select Mary Magdalene, because of her appearance alongside Jesus' mother at the foot of the cross (19:25). According to these scholars, this scene suggests that the Beloved Disciple and Mary Magdalene are the same person. Still others choose Thomas. In his wish to place his hand in Jesus' side (20:25), Thomas seems to know that Jesus' side has been pierced, which is something the Beloved Disciple has witnessed (19:34–35).[8] In each case, the interpreter reads the character of the Beloved Disciple in parallel with other named characters, and argues that the parallel suggests a correspondence in their identities. None of these conclusions has garnered a consensus. Nonetheless the existence of multiple, well-developed theories of the identity of the Beloved Disciple suggests an underlying ambiguity in his characterization: his identity is unknown.

Anonymity is part of the Beloved Disciple's character and can function in a variety of ways in a literary work. Many interpreters conclude that anonymity functions to make the Beloved an ideal character. Yet anonymity is not the deciding factor in the creation of an ideal character; other characters in the Gospel also remain anonymous (e.g., the Samaritan woman of chap. 4, the blind man of chap. 9) without necessarily being ideal. These characters may serve as examples for the reader of different things, but interpreters do not present them as the "ideal disciple." But the creation of an ideal character is only one possibility among many.[9] As I noted above, many readers have taken the lack of a name as an invitation to search for the Beloved's true identity. Anonymity may also reinforce the stylized nature of the character. The lack of a name leads the reader to emphasize elements of the Beloved's characterization—especially his identification as the "one Jesus loved," which often comes to serve in place of his name. Although the Beloved Disciple is singled out as the "one Jesus loved," John does not consign him to a class by himself. Jesus also loves other characters (cf. 11:3, 5, 36; 13:1, 34; 15:12). While the Beloved is not necessarily a perfect character, he is ideal in the sense that he is an example of one who is loved by Jesus.

In a number of instances, John's language creates opportunities to connect this disciple with other characters of the Gospel. Many interpreters arrive at their understanding of the Beloved's ideal nature by comparing his character with the words and actions of others. The comparison with Peter is common; the two often appear together in the narrative (13:21–30; 20:1–10; 21:1–25). Such comparisons, however, continue to suggest ambiguity in characterization. For example, some interpreters argue for the Beloved's clear superiority over Peter, yet others see Peter as maintaining a distinct and important role. The comparison itself raises the further question of whether the two are intentionally set in contrast to each other—in which case most interpreters assert that the Beloved Disciple comes off looking superior—or whether they appear as different examples of valid discipleship. While the comparison with Peter seems important, the Beloved is also portrayed in comparison to the disciples, Jesus' mother, Mary Magdalene, and the first-person voice of the narrator (i.e., the "we" of 21:24).

Below I emphasize these aspects of characterization to create a fuller picture of the Beloved Disciple. The various comparisons make the Beloved appear less ideal as a character, but also present a picture of discipleship as a relational process. Viewed in this way, the Beloved Disciple is not only in a relationship with Jesus, but also comes to believe and understand and testify as he does because of the belief, understanding, and witness of others.

THE BELOVED DISCIPLE
AT THE LAST SUPPER (JOHN 13)

This disciple is first introduced in John 13 as "the one Jesus loved" (13:23; cf. 19:26; 20:2; 21:7, 20). At the Last Supper, he appears "reclining in the bosom of Jesus" or "reclining next to Jesus" (13:23). The position next to Jesus suggests a place of honor at the meal, and the language is similar to what has been said of Jesus' own position: he "is in the bosom of the Father" (1:18). Thus the description of the Beloved Disciple in relationship to Jesus characterizes him as one in a position of intimacy with and proximity to Jesus. Gail O'Day concludes: "The Beloved Disciple has only one role: to embody the love and intimacy with Jesus that is the goal of discipleship in John."[10] While his intimacy to Jesus is clearly an important aspect of his character, chapter 13 presents a striking ambiguity in a character so close to Jesus: he does not clearly believe in Jesus or understand his words.

The Beloved Disciple's relationship to Peter also yields ambiguous results. John 13 is the first of three appearances where he and Peter appear as primary characters in the scene. The Beloved Disciple and Peter both appear at supper with Jesus and other disciples. In verses 21–30, they engage one another and Jesus regarding Jesus' indication that a disciple will betray him. Many interpreters understand the Beloved Disciple to be portrayed in a favorable light in comparison with Peter.[11] He is introduced as "the one Jesus loved," and as reclining in his bosom (verse 23). Being positioned next to Jesus, he appears to have a privileged place at the dinner table. Peter communicates with the disciple by motioning to him, which suggests that Peter is seated elsewhere and therefore is lower in status or importance. Others, however, read Peter in a more favorable light. They argue that he is portrayed as the active character, curious to understand Jesus' words, while the Beloved Disciple only acts at Peter's instigation. Upon Jesus' declaration of his betrayal by one of those gathered with him at supper (13:21), Peter motions to the Beloved Disciple, who reclines next to Jesus, to ask which of the disciples he means (13:23–24). The Beloved Disciple asks, and Jesus replies, "It is the one to whom I will give the bread I dip in the dish" (verse 26). He proceeds to dip the bread and give it to Judas. Although the Beloved Disciple is in a position to ask, Peter is the director of the scene. Few interpret Peter as superior to the Beloved Disciple in these verses, but many scholars emphasize that both are important figures and that there is no denigration of Peter in John 13.[12]

Though the comparison with Peter creates a certain level of ambiguity in the characterization of the Beloved Disciple, comparison to another character—the disciples—raises the important question of how much the Beloved understands. Following Jesus' prediction of his betrayal, the disciples first appear as a corporate character in verse 22: "The disciples looked at one another, uncertain of whom he was speaking." Then the Beloved is introduced as "one of his disciples, who reclined in Jesus' bosom" (verse 23). Thus the Beloved Disciple is one of them and not distinct from the gathering of disciples. After he speaks, he fades back into the crowd. Jesus gives the bread to Judas and says to him, "Do quickly what you are going to do" (verse 27). The following statement, "No one who was reclining knew why he had said this to him" (verse 28), includes the Beloved Disciple. The sense of the story demands that the Beloved Disciple is still present; it is Judas alone who leaves in verse 30. In verse 28 the repetition of the word "reclining," the same word used to identify the Beloved Disciple, also suggests that he is among those who do not understand Jesus' words about Judas, though he of all the disciples is in the best position to do so.

For many interpreters, the notion that the Beloved Disciple would not understand is unthinkable. C. K. Barrett charges that it would make him an "imbecile."[13] Indeed, it is difficult for the reader to understand how any of the disciples can miss the import of what Jesus says, but especially the one who initially asked the question and was most likely to hear Jesus' answer clearly. However, as one of "the disciples," the behavior of the Beloved does not seem out of place. They have previously misunderstood some of Jesus' rather obvious statements (e.g., 4:31–33; 11:11–12). Though their inclusion at this dinner places all of the disciples in a privileged position in relation to Jesus, he has also indicated that their belief in him is something he expects in the future: "I say this to you now, before it happens, so that when it does happen you may believe that I am" (13:19). Jesus' words imply that his disciples do not fully believe in him but will come to understand more later on.[14]

Based on his inclusion in the disciples, the Beloved Disciple appears to be an ambiguous character in the same way the disciples were ambiguous (see chap. 4). He is a positive character who will come to believe in Jesus, but at the moment he does not understand even Jesus' blunt identification of his betrayer.

THE BELOVED DISCIPLE
AT THE CRUCIFIXION (JOHN 19)

John's characterization of the Beloved Disciple at the crucifixion scene is positive but also highly ambiguous. He is characterized as part of Jesus' family, yet John leaves the significance of his presence at the crucifixion open to interpretation. The Beloved is portrayed as testifying to the events of the crucifixion. Though the role of the witness is very important to John, the Beloved's act of testimony lies outside the narrative framework. His present understanding or belief is not identified as part of the crucifixion narrative.

Indirect characterization at the crucifixion suggests a positive view of the Beloved Disciple. John's description of the scene is unique and appears stylized for a particular effect. In Matthew and Mark, only women are present at the crucifixion, and they stand at a distance (Matt. 27:55–56; Mark 15:40–41). Luke's language is similar to Matthew's and Mark's, but the scene includes male acquaintances of Jesus along with the women (Luke 23:49). John introduces the women first[15] but goes on to indicate the presence of the Beloved Disciple (John 19:25–26). All of them "stand near the cross of Jesus" (19:25), close enough to hear Jesus' words. The Beloved's inclusion in the scene seems to heighten his importance among the disciples. As elsewhere, the author does not characterize the Beloved Disciple's actions explicitly, but readers may use Jesus' words elsewhere in John to judge the actions attributed to this character. For example, the Beloved's presence at the cross may be evidence that he and the women "abide" with Jesus (cf. 15:4) and have not been "scattered, each to his own home," leaving Jesus alone (16:32). As one who responds to Jesus' words, "Behold your mother," it is possible that John characterizes the Beloved as one who keeps the command of Jesus. Based on what is said elsewhere in the Gospel of those who keep Jesus' commands, the Beloved Disciple might then be interpreted as one who loves Jesus (14:21), abides in his love (15:10), and is Jesus' friend (15:14). All such decisions are judgments made by the reader, associating the values that the Gospel presents with the behaviors of the characters at the foot of the cross.

John also characterizes the Beloved Disciple as part of Jesus' family. Jesus' words to his mother and the Beloved Disciple from the cross create a parent-child relationship between the two: "Woman, behold your son. . . . Behold your mother" (19:26–27). Jesus' words obligate both his mother and the Beloved Disciple to a relationship with each other.

The creation of familial ties echoes language elsewhere in the Gospel. John suggests that Jesus' followers will become children of God (1:12) and that they share in the relationship that Jesus has to his Father (e.g., 14:20–21; 17:21; 20:17). The connection forged between the Beloved Disciple and Jesus' mother may be emblematic of such shared familial ties.

Many interpreters find symbolic or allegorical meaning in the union of Jesus' mother and the Beloved. The event is most frequently interpreted as the unity of the church, or the reception and assimilation of Jewish Christianity (Mary) into Gentile Christianity (the Beloved).[16] While each of these possibilities resonates with aspects of Christian tradition and conventional interpretations of John, neither shows strong evidence from the Gospel itself. In interpreting the crucifixion scene this way, interpreters draw upon knowledge that is certainly likely to have been available in the late first century—the notion of Mary as a metaphor for the church, for example, or the rise of Gentile Christianity. If these ideas were supported elsewhere by the language of John, especially in reference to these characters, such interpretive moves would be much stronger. Although many understand the Beloved Disciple as representative of believers, he is not clearly portrayed in ways that associate him with Gentiles, nor is Jesus' mother associated with either the future church or Jewish Christianity. Many possible interpretations were available to early readers of the Gospel about the significance of these characters, and John does not clearly indicate a preference for one set of meanings for these characters and their actions.

This kind of openness in the Beloved Disciple's character suggests a different kind of ambiguity than what I have suggested about other characters. Ambiguity comes in the case of the Beloved Disciple not from a lack of specificity about whether he believes (see my discussion of Nicodemus in chap. 2, above) or from questions about what he believes (see my discussion about Martha in chap. 5), but from an openness in what his speech and actions mean. John's language in this section seems figurative—Jesus' words and the events of the crucifixion are presented in relationship to Scripture (e.g., 19:24, 28, 36–37), suggesting that their meaning goes beyond the simple recording of the events themselves. Yet the meaning is left open. Many of the features highlighted in the crucifixion scene are some of the most difficult for interpreters of the Gospel: the importance of the hyssop (19:29),[17] the significance of the blood and water (verse 34),[18] as well as the connection forged between the Beloved and Jesus' mother. The Beloved's character is clearly shaped by his inclusion in this crucial moment of the narrative, but its precise meaning is left open.

John 19 also characterizes the Beloved Disciple as a future witness to the events of the crucifixion. The narrator verifies his testimony: "The one who saw has witnessed, and his testimony is true, and that one knows that he tells the truth" (19:35).[19] Yet although the Beloved Disciple is characterized as having witnessed, this activity is not narrated within the time frame of the Gospel. Instead, the narrator steps aside to point to activities of the Beloved Disciple that exist outside of the Gospel story. The Beloved Disciple is thus characterized as one with a future that lies outside of the narrative time of the Gospel, much like the disciples as a whole (see chap. 4, above). This is also true in the interaction at the cross between the Beloved, Jesus, and his mother. In that case, the narrator has inserted a comment pointing to the future relationship of the Disciple and Jesus' mother: "From that hour he took her into his home" (19:27). This verse does not indicate that the two characters depart immediately (which would make the Beloved Disciple absent between verses 27 and 35). Rather, as C. H. Dodd notes, the episode "breaks the unities of time and place, since we are obliged for the moment to leave the scene of Golgotha on Good Friday afternoon and place ourselves at the home of the Beloved Disciple in the time following."[20] In doing so, John characterizes the Beloved Disciple as one whose future is shaped by his experience at the cross of Jesus. The relationship created there endures beyond the time frame of the Gospel, as does the Disciple's testimony to what he has seen there.

THE BELOVED DISCIPLE
AT THE EMPTY TOMB (JOHN 20)

John's portrayal of the Beloved Disciple at Jesus' empty tomb is a primary text for those who see this character as the ideal exemplar of faith. The Beloved enters the tomb, sees, and believes (20:8). Sandra Schneiders argues that the Beloved's belief at the empty tomb is "genuine paschal faith." "The response of the Beloved Disciple, 'He both saw and believed,' is the perfect response and precisely that which is evoked by the 'signs' throughout the fourth gospel."[21] The Beloved Disciple understands who Jesus is and what the empty tomb means. In Alan Culpepper's view, "He is unlike the other Johannine characters only in that he is the ideal disciple, the paradigm of discipleship. He has no misunderstandings."[22] For many interpreters, the faith and understanding of this disciple are typical of what is expected of later believers.[23]

The Beloved's belief at the tomb is important. In John's rhetoric, all such belief is to be taken seriously as part of the Gospel's aim, and the Beloved's belief at this important moment in the narrative is significant. Yet it is not without ambiguity. As some interpreters observe, the content of his belief is unstated. Some argue that he simply believes Mary Magdalene's report: "They have taken the Lord out of the tomb, and we do not know where they have laid him" (verse 2), others that he believes Jesus is alive.[24] While each of these suggestions is logically possible in the flow of the narrative, the use of the word "believe" in the Fourth Gospel is likely to prepare the reader to understand the Beloved Disciple in a straightforwardly positive light: he does what Jesus has been calling disciples to do (e.g., 11:15; 13:19).[25] Even so, the characterization of the Beloved leaves the content of his belief an open question.

Verse 9 raises further questions by characterizing the Beloved Disciple as misunderstanding. Both he and Peter are included in the statement that immediately follows his belief: "For they did not yet understand the scripture, that he must rise from the dead" (verse 9). For some interpreters, this verse does not qualify the Beloved Disciple's belief. Sandra Schneiders argues that the Beloved Disciple believes that Jesus, like Moses, has ascended to God; only later does he come to understand that "Jesus has also returned to take up his abode in them,"[26] something that is confirmed by the resurrection appearances. A number of commentators understand verse 9 positively, suggesting that the Beloved believes before he sees Jesus in the resurrection appearances.[27] The Beloved Disciple thus becomes a model of those who believe without seeing (cf. 20:29), a paradigm for later believers. Yet the juxtaposition of believing and not understanding in verses 8–9 rightly creates questions for interpreters of the Gospel. The sense of verse 9 is not simply that the disciples do not understand the Scriptures, but that as a result they do not understand that Jesus will rise from the dead. Although the Beloved Disciple's belief is notable, it is not complete.[28]

Finally, it is not clear that the Beloved Disciple is characterized as superior to the other characters of the scene in his response. Comparisons with Peter's actions again play strongly in arguments for the ideal role of the Beloved. For many scholars the details of the Beloved Disciple reaching the tomb first and believing first suggest his primacy over

Peter.[29] He outruns Peter (verse 4); though he does not immediately enter the tomb, when he does, the Gospel explicitly narrates his belief (verse 8). Peter may eventually come to understand and to believe in Jesus, but here he is not characterized as believing, while the Beloved Disciple is. However, the actions of the Beloved Disciple in this passage again seem highly dependent on others. Throughout the scene, the two disciples alternate in taking incremental steps toward the tomb. The Beloved Disciple runs ahead and reaches the tomb first, looks in and sees the burial cloths, but does not enter (verses 4–5). Peter then enters the tomb and sees not only the burial cloths but also the headcloth, lying in a separate place (verses 6–7). Only then does the Beloved enter, see, and believe (verse 8).

Mary Magdalene's role may also be compared to the Beloved's. She first informs the disciples about Jesus' absence from the tomb, returns with them, and unlike Peter or the Beloved, stays at the tomb. Mary does not look into the tomb until verses 11–12, and she sees the addition of two angels, who speak with her. Jesus appears first to Mary (verses 14–17), who proclaims his resurrection to the disciples ("I have seen the Lord!" verse 18). Mary might also be described as an ambiguous character: she is slow to understand the situation, fails to recognize Jesus, and perhaps seeks to cling to him. Yet her continued presence at the tomb and her active response to Jesus' appearance also contrast with that of the Beloved Disciple, who does not share his belief with others.[30]

John characterizes the Beloved Disciple at the tomb as one who both believes and does not fully understand. His belief is significant although its content is unclear. He is portrayed in relationship to Mary Magdalene and to Peter. All three disciples take alternating steps toward the revelation of Jesus' resurrection. The Beloved Disciple is ultimately dependent on the faithful actions of these others.

THE BELOVED DISCIPLE
IN THE RESURRECTION (JOHN 21)

In the Gospel's final chapter, the Beloved Disciple is once again a positive figure. He recognizes Jesus and is characterized as a witness. Yet the certainty of his belief is not resolved, and his witness remains a future event. Both belief and witness are intertwined with and complement that of other followers of Jesus.

In the fishing scene (21:1–14), the Beloved Disciple's understanding of Jesus remains somewhat unclear. He is first to recognize Jesus: "It is the Lord!" (verse 7). As a result, Schneiders writes: "It is the Beloved Disciple who recognizes him with perfect clarity and proclaims him authoritatively."[31] However, as in John 13, the Beloved Disciple's understanding is qualified by his inclusion with the disciples. Jesus invites the disciples to eat breakfast, and the narrator adds: "And none of the disciples dared to question him, 'Who are you?' knowing that it was the Lord" (verse 12). This is a curious statement, as I noted in chapter 4 (above). It confirms that the disciples know who Jesus is, yet at the same time it formulates the question they do not dare to ask, a question suggesting that they do not know who he is. It characterizes the disciples as being caught somewhere in the tension between these two: they are uncertain about Jesus and afraid to ask him questions, and they also know who he is. The Beloved Disciple is included in this group. Although he also has recognized Jesus, he is part of the group of disciples who do not dare to ask.

Here the Beloved Disciple is again characterized in relation to Peter. The Beloved Disciple identifies Jesus, and Peter responds enthusiastically (21:7). Peter is instructed to take on a pastoral role in relation to Jesus' sheep (verses 15–17), while the Beloved is described as a witness (21:24). Each disciple's death is discussed (21:18–19, 20–23). The parallels between the two disciples in this chapter seem to invite comparison, but the results of such comparison in terms of the characterization of the Beloved are ambiguous.

The ambiguity in this implicit characterization is seen in the variety of conclusions that interpreters reach. Some see the chapters as establishing Peter's preeminence among the disciples, a reading based largely on verses 15–19, which focus on Peter alone.[32] Peter's pastoral role mirrors Jesus' own (verses 15–17). Jesus indicates that Peter will die in a way that glorifies God (verses 18–19), a likely reference to traditions that Peter becomes a martyr for the faith. The description in these verses and Jesus' command to "follow" indicate that his death is linked to Jesus' own in an important way.[33] In Raymond Brown's view, "A major pastoral role is being assigned to [Peter]—indeed a role that in Johannine theology is highly unexpected."[34] In this reading the Beloved Disciple, in contrast to Peter, takes on none of these important roles, and so Peter rises to a status above that of the Beloved Disciple.

In contrast, others interpret the Beloved Disciple as superior to Peter. The Beloved Disciple's introduction as following Peter and Jesus (verse

20) indicates that he does not need Jesus to command him to follow, as Jesus commands Peter in verses 19 and 22, for the Beloved Disciple is already following.[35] What is more, Jesus indicates the Beloved will "abide," a word previously used in the Gospel to indicate an important role of the disciple (cf. 6:56; 8:31; 15:4–7, 9–10).[36] Thus Hoskyns argues, "The reader is meant to understand that the perfect discipleship of which the Beloved Disciple is the type and origin will never fail the Church."[37] The Beloved Disciple also has an important representative role in these verses, that of witness. His testimony becomes the basis of the Gospel itself (21:24). Though supporters of this argument often recognize Peter's role as a shepherd, they understand his role to be less important than that of the Beloved.[38]

Yet another perspective identifies the roles of Peter and the Beloved as distinct but of similar importance. For some, Peter remains a representative of the important pastoral function of later leaders of the church, but without eclipsing the importance of the Beloved Disciple. Many of these interpreters understand the two as leaders of different groups of Christians: the Beloved Disciple of Johannine Christians, Peter of "apostolic Christians."[39] For others, Peter embodies "active service" while the Beloved Disciple represents "perceptive witness."[40] Although the Beloved Disciple and Peter are characterized in relationship to each other, John gives no explicit valuation of one over the other in the pages of the Gospel.

The final verses of the Gospel characterize the Beloved Disciple as a witness. The Gospel points to a time between the narrative time of the Gospel and the writing of the Gospel in which the Beloved Disciple has testified. His role as witness is not explicitly narrated in the Gospel. If the Beloved has understood Jesus' response about Judas in chapter 13, he is not said to share this knowledge with others.[41] Neither does John narrate the proclamation of his belief in 20:8. If the Beloved Disciple becomes the perfect witness to Jesus, it is only in the time that lies outside of the boundaries of the narrative, a time to which the final verses point the reader.[42]

In the final verses, the witness of the Beloved Disciple includes others who share in the witness of the Gospel. The incursion of the narrator's voice in verse 24 identifies the Beloved Disciple as the one "who is testifying to these things and has written them, and we know that his testimony is true." On the one hand, this verse identifies the Beloved Disciple as one who testifies or witnesses. (These English words translate related Greek forms: the verb μαρτυρέω, *martyreō*; and the noun μαρτυρία, *martyria*.) On the other hand, the inclusion of the first-person "we" adds a layer of complexity to the Gospel's claims about this witness.[43] Many interpreters understand the "we" as the voice of the author, representing his community, and tying the Gospel's authenticity to the earlier witness of this unnamed disciple.[44] Most agree that the Beloved Disciple is not the author of the Gospel of John as it stands; rather, the Gospel writer claims this disciple as the authoritative source of its tradition.[45] As a character in the Gospel, the Beloved Disciple witnesses important events of the life of Jesus and passes on his testimony to others. Many interpreters point to this important function as this disciple's ideal quality.[46] Understood to be trustworthy (21:24), he is characterized as one who authenticates the Gospel's witness. Yet in terms of the characterization of the Beloved Disciple, the addition of the first-person voice also characterizes the Beloved in relationship with other characters. His witness relies on the "we" for verification and possibly also passing that witness along in a written form.

CONCLUSION

Is the Beloved Disciple an ideal character? As I have argued in previous chapters, many characters provide examples of ideal qualities the Gospel upholds. Perhaps another way to pose the question would be, Is he more ideal than other characters of the Gospel?

Of all the Beloved Disciple's characteristics, the one that seems least to qualify him as ideal is his intimate relationship with Jesus. True, his identification as "the one Jesus loved" is constant throughout his appearances, and his position of reclining in Jesus' bosom appears at the first and last introduction of this character (13:23 and 21:20). Yet Jesus' love and acceptance of him cannot be tied to his actions or faith. It appears as suddenly as the Beloved Disciple himself does on the scene in the Last Supper; with no prior knowledge of him, the reader is simply told of the "one Jesus loves." Jesus' love for his followers should not surprise the reader at this point. John also describes Mary, Martha, and Lazarus as loved by Jesus (11:5). As in the case of those three characters, Jesus' love for the Beloved Disciple is not explained as deserved or earned through perfect faith or witness; it is simply part of the description with which John characterizes him. If the Beloved Disciple is an ideal character, he is ideal in being one who is loved rather than because he has achieved perfection. Like the Beloved, others may understand themselves as one whom Jesus loves, who through that love are some-how enabled to become faithful witnesses.

As a witness, the Beloved Disciple may also be an ideal character in that he verifies the future faithfulness of Jesus' disciples. He is a con-crete example of one who is known to have followed through (eventu-ally) with what Jesus asks of disciples. I argued in chapter 4 that "the disciples" are an eschatological character; they are shaped by a future known only to Jesus. This is also true of Peter and the Beloved as they are characterized in John 21. Yet each of their cases points the reader to a concrete fulfillment of the requirements of discipleship: the tradition of Peter's martyrdom is well known to early Christians, and the Gos-pel itself serves as a confirmation that the Beloved "witnesses to these things and has written them" (21:24). As a whole, the disciples remain a group whose later belief and testimony are confirmed by Jesus' words. The Beloved and Peter provide evidence that this expectation is carried out. Thus the Beloved Disciple is an exemplary character, although not more or less so than Peter. They both go on to provide examples of a disciple's faith and testimony.

If the Beloved's witness is exemplary, perhaps the open-ended nature of his witness should be understood as exemplary as well. The Beloved Disciple and his witness set out certain events or data for the reader without predetermining what they mean. He is characterized as a witness to the events of Jesus' crucifixion, but not as determining their meaning for others. Though he plays a crucial role in the way the Gospel portrays its own authority, he does not assume an author-ity to interpret these events. Instead, he invites readers into their own encounters with the meaning of Jesus' life, death, and resurrection.

The Beloved Disciple is exemplary but not perfect. In his imper-fections, the modern reader may catch a glimpse of an aspect of dis-cipleship that is somewhat foreign to us: he shows the importance of relational discipleship. In each appearance the Beloved's actions are enmeshed with those of other characters. He and Peter act in concert, and they both join with Mary Magdalene to reach knowl-edge of Jesus' resurrection. Modern readers often seem to interpret the Beloved Disciple with the assumption that belief and disciple-ship are solitary affairs, that individuals come to faith or do not come to faith on their own. But the Beloved Disciple—and his faith and understanding in particular—are intertwined with what others believe and do.

BIBLIOGRAPHY

Barrett, C. K. *The Gospel according to St. John.* Philadelphia: Westminster Press, 1978.

Bauckham, Richard. "The Beloved Disciple as Ideal Author." *Journal for the Study of the New Testament* 49 (1993): 21–44.

———. "The Martyrdom of Peter in Early Christian Literature." Pages 539–95 in *Principat*, 26.1, of *Aufstieg und Niedergang der römischen Welt.* Edited by H. Temporini and W. Haase. Berlin: Walter de Gruyter, 1992.

Beck, David R. *The Discipleship Paradigm: Readers and Anonymous Characters in the Fourth Gospel.* Biblical Interpretation Series 27. Leiden: E. J. Brill, 1997.

Beetham, F. G., and P. A. Beetham. "A Note on John 19:29." *Journal of Theological Studies* 44 (1993): 162–69.

Booth, Wayne C. *The Rhetoric of Fiction.* Chicago: University of Chicago Press, 1961.

Brown, Raymond. *The Gospel according to John.* 2 vols. Anchor Bible 29–29A. New York: Doubleday, 1966–70.

———. "The Resurrection in John 21: Missionary and Pastoral Directives for the Church." *Worship* 64 (1990): 433–45.

Bultmann, Rudolf. *The Gospel of John.* Philadelphia: Westminster Press, 1971.

Busse, Ulrich. "The Beloved Disciple." *Skrif en kerk* 15, no. 2 (1994): 219–27.

Byrne, Brendan. "The Faith of the Beloved Disciple and the Community in John 20." *Journal for the Study of the New Testament* 23 (1985): 83–97.

Charlesworth, James H. *The Beloved Disciple: Whose Witness Validates the Gospel of John?* Valley Forge, PA: Trinity Press International, 1995.

Conway, Colleen M. *Men and Women in the Fourth Gospel: Gender and Johannine Characterization.* Society of Biblical Literature Dissertation Series 167. Atlanta: Society of Biblical Literature, 1999.

Culpepper, R. Alan. *Anatomy of the Fourth Gospel: A Study in Literary Design.* Philadelphia: Fortress Press, 1983.

De Boer, Esther A. "Mary Magdalene and the Disciple Jesus Loved." *Lectio difficilior: European Electronic Journal for Feminist Exegesis* 1 (2000): 1–17.

Dodd, C. H. *Historical Tradition in the Fourth Gospel.* Cambridge: Cambridge University Press, 1963.

Dunderberg, Ismo. "The Beloved Disciple in John: Ideal Figure in an Early Christian Controversy." Pages 243–69 in *Fair Play.* Edited by Heikki Räisänen et al. Leiden: E. J. Brill, 2002.

Franzmann, Majella, and Michael Klinger. "The Call Stories of John 1 and John 21." *St. Vladimir's Theological Quarterly* 36 (1992): 7–15.

Garcia, Hugues. "Lazare, du mort vivant au disciple bien-aimé: Le cycle et la trajectoire narrative de Lazare dans le quatrième évangile." *Revue des sciences religieuses* 73 (1999): 259–92.

Gunther, John J. "The Relation of the Beloved Disciple to the Twelve." *Theologische Zeitschrift* 37 (1981): 129–48.

Hakola, Raimo. "A Character Resurrected: Lazarus in the Fourth Gospel and Afterwards." Pages 223–63 in *Characterization in the Gospels: Reconceiving Narrative Criticism*. Edited by David Rhoads and Kari Syreeni. Sheffield: Sheffield Academic Press, 1999.

Hawkin, David J. "The Function of the Beloved Disciple Motif in the Johannine Redaction." *Laval théologique et philosophique* 33 (1977): 135–50.

Hoskyns, Edwyn Clement. *The Fourth Gospel*. Edited by F. N. Davey. London: Faber & Faber, 1947.

Koester, Craig. "Hearing, Seeing, and Believing in the Gospel of John." *Biblica* 70 (1989): 327–48.

Lagrange, M.-J. *Évangile selon St. Jean*. Edited by J. Gabalda. 5th ed. Études bibliques. Paris: Librairie Lecoffre, 1936.

Lindars, Barnabas. *The Gospel of John*. New Century Bible. London: Oliphants, 1972.

Loisy, A. *Le quatrième évangile*. Paris: Nourry, 1921.

Mahoney, Robert. *Two Disciples at the Tomb: The Background and Message of John 20.1–10*. Theologie und Wirklichkeit 6. Bern: Herbert Lang, 1974.

Maynard, Arthur H. "The Role of Peter in the Fourth Gospel." *New Testament Studies* 30 (1984): 531–48.

Meyer, Eduard. "Sinn und Tendenz der Schlusszene am Kreuz im Johannesevangelium." Pages 157–62 in *Sitzungsberichte der Preussischen Akademie der Wissenschaften*. Berlin: Verlag der Akademie der Wissenschaften, 1924.

Minear, Paul Sevier. "The Beloved Disciple in the Gospel of John." *Novum Testamentum* 19 (1977): 105–23.

———. "We Don't Know Where, John 20:2." *Interpretation* 30 (1976): 125–39.

Moloney, Francis J. *The Gospel of John*. Sacra pagina 4. Collegeville, MN: Liturgical Press, 1988.

Neirynck, Frans. "John 21." *New Testament Studies* 36 (1990): 321–36.

O'Brien, Kelli S. "Written That You May Believe: John 20 and Narrative Rhetoric." *Catholic Biblical Quarterly* 67 (2005): 284–302.

O'Day, Gail R. *The Gospel of John*. New Interpreter's Bible 9. Nashville: Abingdon Press, 1995.

Pamment, Margaret. "The Fourth Gospel's Beloved Disciple." *Expository Times* 94 (1983): 363–67.

Quast, Kevin. *Peter and the Beloved Disciple: Figures for a Community in Crisis*. Journal for the Study of the New Testament: Supplement Series 32. Sheffield: Sheffield Academic Press, 1989.

Reinhartz, Adele. *Why Ask My Name? Anonymity and Identity in Biblical Narrative*. New York: Oxford University Press, 1998.

Sava, A. F. "The Wound in the Side of Christ." *Catholic Biblical Quarterly* 19 (1957): 343–46.

Schnackenburg, Rudolf. *The Gospel according to St. John.* 3 vols. New York: Seabury Press, 1982–90.

Schneiders, Sandra M. "The Face Veil: A Johannine Sign (John 20:1–10)." *Biblical Theology Bulletin* 13 (1983): 94–97.

———. "John 21:1–14." *Interpretation* 43 (1989): 70–75.

———. *Written That You May Believe: Encountering Jesus in the Fourth Gospel.* New York: Herder & Herder, 1999.

Scott, E. F. *The Fourth Gospel: Its Purpose and Theology.* 2nd ed. Edinburgh: T&T Clark, 1908.

Snyder, Graydon F. "John 13:16 and the Anti-Petrinism of the Johannine Tradition." *Biblical Research* 16 (1971): 5–15.

Strachan, R. H. *The Fourth Gospel: Its Significance and Environment.* London: SCM Press, 1941.

Thornecroft, John K. "The Redactor and the 'Beloved' in John." *Expository Times* 98 (1987): 135–39.

Thurian, Max. *Mary: Mother of All Christians.* New York: Herder & Herder, 1963.

———. "The Ministry of Unity of the Bishop of Rome to the Whole Church." *Centro pro Unione Bulletin* 29 (1986): 9–14.

Tolmie, Donald François. "John 21:24–25." *Skrif en kerk* 17 (1996): 420–26.

Van Tilborg, Sjef. *Imaginative Love in John.* Leiden: E. J. Brill, 1993.

Vanhoozer, Kevin J. "The Hermeneutics of I-Witness Testimony: John 21:20–24 and the 'Death' of the 'Author.'" Pages 366–87 in *Understanding Poets and Prophets.* Edited by George W. Anderson and A. Graeme Auld. Sheffield: JSOT Press, 1993.

PART 2

7
The Jews

The Jews in John's Gospel are widely viewed as an unambiguously negative character. They are seen as "representatives of disbelief" and enemies of Jesus.[1] Because of this, John's Gospel is often viewed as anti-Jewish. Although the Gospel clearly draws on Jewish imagery to understand Jesus, interpreters see the author's perspective as one of harsh criticism of Jewish thought. In this chapter I explore the usefulness of indirect characterization and ambiguity with regard to the characterization of the Jews. I argue that even the Jews may be read as an ambiguous character. My hope in approaching the Jews as a character is to open up some new interpretive possibilities and conversation on the subject of the Jews.

Scholarly treatments of the Jews begin with their hostility toward Jesus. While the Jews may show some openness to Jesus, this is seen as brief and insincere; rather, they are understood to be overtly hostile to him and are ultimately responsible for his death.[2] For example, John Ashton summarizes three questions that scholars ask about the Jews: "The first asks who they are, the second what role or function they fulfill, the third why the evangelist regards them with such hostility."[3] While there is disagreement regarding all three of the questions Ashton identifies, there is consensus regarding their formulation. No one asks the more open-ended question "Does the evangelist regard the Jews with hostility?" for there is general agreement that in John the Jews are enemies of Jesus.

Underlying this consensus are three important points of agreement. First, most scholars define John's use of the Greek term *hoi Ioudaioi* (οἱ Ἰουδαῖοι) as referring not to all Jews, but to Jewish authorities who persecuted the Christians of John's community.[4] Second, John's negative portrayal of the Jews is understood as an "attack . . . against the religious position of Judaism,"[5] following a hostile separation of Christians from the synagogue. The language of the Gospel reflects John's community's experience of this hostility. Third, John has a strongly dualistic worldview. When the choices presented are "belief versus unbelief" and "darkness versus light," the Jews appear on the side of "darkness" and "unbelief"; as a result, they come to be seen as an irretrievably negative character.

Scholars who advocate the above three points often recognize that John's language does not entirely support their conclusions. In defining the Jews as "the authorities," scholars respond to (1) John's portrayal of the Jews as a group that is undertaking coordinated action, and (2) the way John uses "the Jews" interchangeably with "the Pharisees" (e.g., 9:13–23) or "the chief priests" (19:13–16).[6] Most scholars also recognize that the relationship between the Jews and the authorities is not carried out systematically throughout the Gospel. In 11:46 some of the Jews report to the Pharisees, suggesting that the two groups are not identical. In other instances there is no clear distinction between the Jews and the crowd. During the crowd's conversation with Jesus in 6:41 the narrator suddenly refers to them as the Jews (cf. 6:24–25). The interpreter's choice to equate the Jews with the Jewish authorities may minimize the inconsistencies in John's portrayal to the greatest extent possible, but the inconsistencies still remain.

Finally, most interpreters recognize that John's portrayal of the Jews is not uniformly negative, and that the Jews are not always hostile to Jesus. It is true that on a number of occasions they "persecute Jesus" and "seek to kill him" (5:16, 18), and this behavior is clearly important to their character (cf. 7:1; 8:59; 10:31). Yet at other times the Jews "believe in him" (8:31; 11:45; 12:11). The belief of large numbers of Jews in response to the raising of Lazarus leads directly to the concerted effort to execute Jesus (11:45–53; cf. 12:10–11). And in 10:19, the Jews are portrayed as "divided again because of [Jesus'] words." The word "again" suggests a recurring division, although this is the first time the Jews have been characterized as divided. In addition to these more positive portrayals are cases where *hoi Ioudaioi* is used simply to describe a festival or tradition as "Jewish" (e.g., "the Passover, the festival of the Jews, was near," 6:4; cf. 2:6, 13; 5:1; 7:2; 11:55; 19:42). In these instances the Jews appear neither hostile nor accepting of Jesus.

Scholars have long recognized this variety in John's language regarding the Jews and disagree only about how to understand it. Some explain the discrepancies by establishing different ways John uses the term *hoi Ioudaioi*: there are "neutral" uses, as when John says "the Passover of the Jews was near"; and there are "Johannine" uses, which are the hostile characterizations of the Jews. The decision to categorize John's language as neutral or Johannine is peculiar in that it implies that "neutral" uses of *hoi Ioudaioi* are not "Johannine." Indeed, in his classic essay Urban von Wahlde argues that the neutral use includes "references to people who are termed 'Jews' but who clearly do not exhibit the hostility characteristic of the Johannine Jews."[7] Clearly, what von Wahlde understands to be "characteristically Johannine" are the references indicating hostility. From a literary perspective, however, all of John's language is "Johannine."[8] The decision to categorize some of John's language as "Johannine"—and by implication, other parts as "non-Johannine"—imposes the interpreter's own criteria on the language of the Gospel. Some scholars define different uses of the term "the Jews" and identify each with a separate stage in the Gospel's editing.[9] Others suggest that the belief that the Jews are said to have is not to be taken seriously, or that it represents a lesser form of belief that the Gospel disparages.[10] Some argue that a subset of the Jews believe in Jesus, based on the indication that "many of the Jews" believed in Jesus (11:45; 12:11).[11] Although at the outset these interpreters acknowledge a great deal of variety, they explain much of that variety away, and the hostile subgroup of the Jews takes center stage as the "Johannine" view of Judaism.

The discussion of John's characterization of the Jews is complicated by the need to counter contemporary anti-Jewish biases,[12] in addition to the need to consider many textual factors. The Gospel of John presents some of the harshest rhetoric against a group called the Jews: including the language of 8:44, "You are of your father the devil," which has been interpreted to suggest that all Jews are Satan's spawn. John's language has long been appropriated by Christians to support and inflame prejudice against Jews, most notably and recently in the Holocaust. This has led some recent scholarship to identify the hostility in John's language and to account for it in some way. Thus one explanation draws on the notion that the Gospel speaks on two different levels: the story of Jesus and the story of the Johannine community. These interpreters agree that John's hostile portrayal of the Jews was generated by the context in which the Gospel was written and reflects anger among Christians at their expulsion from the synagogue by their Jewish neighbors.

As a way of addressing modern anti-Judaism, understanding John's context like this distances the Gospel from the negative impact of its language on modern readers. One implication of this view is that John's harsh portrayal of the Jews is culturally bound to that context in a way other aspects of John's language are not. As Colleen Conway observes, "The historical context is to help make clear that such anti-Jewish language is no longer relevant to our context, but its presence in the Gospel is understandable. Understanding why such language is in this canonical text enables us to preserve the authority and relevance of other more palatable parts of the Gospel."[13] Placing John's language within a history of the separation of Christianity from Judaism helps to explain why such language would appear in the Bible, but it also allows the interpreter to leave it behind. John's rhetoric addressed its own context but is not appropriate to ours. This move allows the interpreter to "rescue" other aspects of the Gospel so that they remain useful to modern Christians. However, as Conway points out, interpreters can easily shift from using John's context to explain the language about the Jews, to then using the context to justify John's rhetoric, as if a difficult situation somehow exonerates the Gospel's perspective. When this happens, scholars make little headway in addressing modern anti-Judaism.

An additional problem is that in seeking to correct for John's anti-Jewish tendencies, interpreters have reinscribed the stark separation between John's perspective and that of the Jews.[14] In assessing the Jews as Jesus' enemies, the reader identifies with the believers of John's community in opposition to the unbelieving Jews. Invited to view the world from John's perspective, the reader is necessarily aligned in opposition to the Jews. Many interpreters ultimately suggest that the reader should leave behind John's negative view, which was shaped by his context. Yet in some sense the message remains: believers and Jews form opposite poles of a spectrum. An additional consequence of reading the Jews as simple enemies of Jesus has been that the Jews have little role in the Gospel message. Interpreters may leave behind the disturbing language characterizing the Jews when speaking and writing for contemporary audiences. But at the same time, the Jews do not contribute anything to the message of the Gospel that can be deemed relevant for today.

THE JEWS AS A CHARACTER

Reading the Jews as a character in the Gospel opens up new ways of seeing the Jews. In this chapter I apply the same method of analyzing John's modes of characterization that I have used in the previous chapters. Because of the limited space available, this is neither a full treatment of the texts in which the Jews appear nor of the issues involved in the question of John's anti-Judaism. However, I hope that approaching the Jews as a character may open up some interpretive possibilities that could be useful within the context I have described above.

1. First, reading the Jews as a character in the Gospel provides a different framework for interpretation. The Jews can be read much as I have read "the disciples," as a corporate character that John portrays in a particular way. From the outset of the Gospel, John introduces the Jews as a group acting in concert. They appear in the narrative immediately following the prologue: "The Jews sent priests and Levites from Jerusalem to ask [John the Baptist], 'Who are you?'" (1:19). Their joint action encourages the reader to see them collectively as a character.[15] The later descriptive references (e.g., "a festival of the Jews," 5:1; "salvation is from the Jews," 4:22) reinforce the corporate nature of this character. Instead of understanding the Jews as a group with internal divisions (i.e., some who believe and some who do not), the notion of a corporate character suggests that the division itself may be part of the Jews' character: as a group, they both believe and disbelieve.

2. Second, approaching the Jews as a character means that the connections between them and other characters can be read as one of John's indirect modes of characterization, comparison of characters. As we have seen, John's characters are sometimes defined in comparison to one another. The stories of Nicodemus and the Samaritan woman are narrated in ways that highlight their differences. Their responses to Jesus can also be compared to that of the disciples. In the same way, the Jews may be compared to other corporate characters in the Gospel: in particular, the Pharisees, the chief priests, the crowd, and the disciples. One of the main reasons why the Jews appear to be authority figures is that John slips back and forth between referring to them as *hoi Ioudaioi* and as recognizable authorities. So in John 9:13, the Pharisees are questioning the blind man, when suddenly in verse 18 John calls them "the Jews." There is no apparent change in the people who make up the group of questioners; in fact, the continuity of the conversation suggests that the groups

are identical. Scholars who equate the Jews with the authorities understand the two designations as synonyms: the same character is called by
different names. This interpretive strategy makes sense in chapter 9 but
not in other parts of the Gospel; John's language undercuts any simple
identification of the Jews with the authorities by switching terminology and referring to the Jews as "the crowd." In chapter 6 the crowd
that appears in conversation with Jesus (6:24–25) is later called "the
Jews" (6:41, 52). Limiting the definition of "the Jews" to the Jewish
authorities can explain only the shifts between the terms "the Jews" and
"the Pharisees," but it does not explain all of the shifts in John's characterization of the Jews. Reading the Jews as a character requires the
reader to step back and consider this feature of John's portrayal: sometimes the Jews appear to be authorities; sometimes they are the masses.
Instead of choosing one of these over the others, each instance may be
characterizing the Jews by comparing them with another character of
the Gospel. These comparisons may each add something distinctive to
a complex portrait.

3. Finally, when the Jews are viewed as a character, the so-called
neutral and "Johannine" uses of the term *hoi Ioudaioi* may also appear
as different aspects of the Jews' character. Instead of assigning positive
and negative character traits to distinct references or redactional layers,
the interpreter asks how the various modes of characterization contribute to the Jews as a character. What does it mean, for example, for John
to speak of "the festival of the Jews" (6:4), to indicate that "the Jews
were seeking . . . to kill him" (5:18), while also saying that "many of the
Jews . . . believed in him" (11:45)? When we read the Jews as a character, each of these statements points to a different aspect of the Jews'
character. In the discussion that follows, I argue that the Jews' mixed
actions—both belief in Jesus and attempts to take his life—point to a
contradiction within the character. On the basis of the characterization
through their actions, the Jews may be seen as divided in their response
to Jesus, rather than simply hostile toward him. This division is not
among the Jews, but *within* the Jews as a character. The portrayal of the
Jews suggests a conflicted or divided character, perhaps even a contradictory character, one who believes in Jesus and also seeks to kill him.

I explore this approach through two test cases, John 6 and John 8.
Although this exploration is preliminary, it points to two possibilities.
The first possibility is that the Jews are an ambiguous character: they
both believe and disbelieve in Jesus. They understand and accept some
of his claims while rejecting others. The second possibility is that the

characterization of the Jews is ironic. Irony allows the reader to see how the Jews' rejection of Jesus is simultaneously also a rejection of religious principles they hold dear. Through his portrayal of the Jews, John makes important theological claims about Jesus, while affirming Jesus' continuity with Judaism. Neither of these possibilities has the power to solve the problems of anti-Jewish interpretations of John, but they have some potential to reframe the way contemporary Christian readers view themselves in relation to Judaism.

THE JEWS AS A CONFLICTED CHARACTER

In John 6 the Jews are characterized as both believing and unbelieving. Their belief in Jesus is implied through their association with the crowd, whose response to the feeding miracle (6:1–12) was to call Jesus a prophet (6:14), seek to make him king (6:15), and cross the lake looking for him (6:24). In a later request for a sign like the manna (6:30–31), they affirm Jesus' ability to give bread, which suggests that they may see Jesus as a "second Moses." The switch in terminology from "the crowd" to "the Jews" in verse 41 aligns the Jews with this previous group: in effect, the crowd becomes the Jews. Although they have not been mentioned since the crowd crossed the lake, the Jews speak as those who have been listening to Jesus all along, and their response shows considerable understanding of Jesus' words. First, they are said to "grumble" at his words "I am the bread that came down from heaven" (6:41). Jesus has not said exactly these words, but they capture the meaning of his speech very well (cf. verses 33, 35, 38), for he has interpreted the Scripture "He gave them bread from heaven to eat" (verse 31) in relationship to himself as bread. The Jews are similarly characterized in verse 52: they "fought against one another, saying, 'How can this man give us his flesh to eat?'" In this verse the Jews' question again shows that they follow Jesus' interpretation of Scripture. Their words echo the initial text and substitute the terms Jesus offered in his interpretation: "He gave them bread from heaven to eat" has become "This man gives us his flesh to eat."[16] John characterizes the Jews as understanding Jesus' interpretation.

Their paraphrase shows that the Jews comprehend Jesus' teaching, yet they also reject certain aspects of it. They do not question Jesus' ability to give this bread, but they do question whether he can be manna. In verse 41, then, they grumble because he interprets the manna story by saying, "I am the bread that came down from heaven." Why is Jesus' claim to "be manna" so problematic to the Jews? Their objection makes sense in the context of Jewish tradition, in which manna was associated with God's word. Because of the instructions regarding its collection, eating manna was associated with adherence to God's command. The manna story is recalled this way in Deuteronomy: "[God] afflicted you by causing you hunger, then by feeding you with manna . . . in order to make you understand that one does not live by bread alone, but by every word that comes forth from the mouth of the LORD" (Deut. 8:4; cf. Wis. 16:26). Jesus' claim to be manna builds on this conventional association of manna and God's word or wisdom,[17] and he ascribes to himself the life-giving functions of God's word. The Jews' speech indicates that, while they might accept Jesus' ability to work signs like Moses, his claim to be God's word is unacceptable.

The Jews' "grumbling" characterizes them as wavering and contradictory. I argued in chapter 4 that the disciples' "grumbling" (cf. 6:61) characterizes them by comparison to the Israelites of the exodus story, who grumbled against Moses and God in the wilderness (e.g., Exod. 16:7). The same is true of the Jews. Along with their grumbling, John attributes a second verb to the Jews, "fought with one another" (6:52; ἐμάχοντο, emachonto), which may also recall the quarreling of the Israelites (LXX: Exod. 17:2; Num. 20:3, 13). The Jews are thus characterized as similar to the Israelites. But as I suggested with the disciples, this characterization is not simply negative. According to Exodus, the Israelites believed God (Exod. 14:31) and still grumbled, a strange reaction for those who have just experienced God's salvation in the crossing of the Red Sea. The allusion in John 6 characterizes the Jews by means of the same contradictory behavior.

This similarity in the portrayal of the Jews and the Israelites has three implications for the character of the Jews. First, the Jews' response is not necessarily hostile here. They are seen as questioning Jesus, but with the style of interpretation exhibited in John 6:31–58, such questioning can be seen as normal and even faithful rather than simply hostile. Their questions are exploratory and show significant understanding of Jesus' words.

Second, the Jews are not simply a negative character. Their response to Jesus is the same response that the Israelites had to God's salvation in the wilderness. They may waver, they may perhaps be fickle, but all in a way that parallels the behavior of those whom God previously claimed as God's people. Nor does their grumbling preclude belief, for the Israelites believe and also grumble. So do the Jews and the disciples in John. The comparison of the Jews' behavior to that of the disciples is an important element of their characterization in John 6. Their grumbling suggests a rejection of Jesus' claims, yet that rejection characterizes not just the Jews but also the disciples. In this case the Jews' behavior does not prove them to be enemies of Jesus, for his disciples have the same response.

Third, the contradiction seen here is not that of a division between individual Jews, some of whom believe and some do not. John 6 suggests a division internal to the corporate character of the Jews. In behaving like the Israelites, the Jews both believe and grumble.

BEHAVIOR AND BELIEF IN CONFLICT

John 8 is preeminent among texts in which the Jews are characterized as Jesus' enemies. Jesus says they seek to kill him (8:37) and that they do not believe (8:45). The exchange between Jesus and the Jews in 8:31–59 is one of the most acrimonious of the Gospel, with both sides trading insults. Jesus says they are from their father the devil (8:44), and the Jews respond that he is a Samaritan and has a demon (8:48). The passage ends with the Jews picking up stones to throw at Jesus and Jesus' subsequent escape. Although the Jews do appear as Jesus' opponents in this passage, they are not simply characterized as his enemies. As in chapter 6, John continues to portray them as conflicted about Jesus. They believe in him, yet they also understand Jesus' claims as contradicting elements of their faith. As a result, they reject important aspects of his message, and John characterizes this rejection of Jesus as unfaithful to the Scripture and tradition the Jews claim to uphold.

Many aspects of the Jews' portrait in John 8 lead interpreters to deny any positive attributes to their character.[18] First, Jesus characterizes the Jews as "from below" (8:23); they do not have the same origin as Jesus, who is "from above." Second, Jesus' response to their question "Who are you?" (8:25) characterizes the Jews as slow to understand. The rest of verse 25 can be translated two ways: either "Why do I speak to you at all?" (NRSV), or "What I have told you from the beginning."[19] Both translations express the idea that the Jews have what they need to understand who Jesus is and need not have asked the question, although the tone of the first translation makes Jesus sound more exasperated. Against this background, their subsequent belief (verses

30–31) is unexpected. The narrative that follows 8:30–31 also contradicts the belief of the Jews. As noted above, they seek to kill him (verses 37, 40) and do not believe (verse 45).

Yet verses 30–31 are an important indication that John also characterizes the Jews as believing. The belief in these verses is attributed to the Jews by the narrator, whose perspective is meant to be reliable: the statement of their belief functions in the same way as the statement of the disciples' belief in 2:11. While in 8:30 John first indicates simply that "many" believed, verse 31 attributes this belief to the Jews: "Therefore Jesus said to the Jews who had believed in him . . ."[20] At the opening of this conversation, then, the Jews are characterized as believing in Jesus, although the rest of the conversation between the Jews and Jesus highlights an inconsistency in the Jews' character: their behavior contradicts their belief.[21] This does not necessarily render their belief invalid, but it does suggest a complex character: they believe in Jesus and they seek to kill him.

The Jews' belief parallels that of the disciples in other ways as well. Though the statement of the Jews' belief may be surprising, it is no more unexpected than the disciples' belief. As I argued in chapter 4, given the disciples' consistent misunderstandings, their sudden confession in 16:30 also sounds hollow. In addition, the belief that is attributed to the disciples is often something that is assumed about their future, not something for which the reader finds clear evidence in their present. Similar language is found in reference to the future of the Jews in John 8:28, when Jesus says to them: "When you have lifted up the Son of Man, then you will know that I am, and I do nothing on my own, but I speak these things as the Father has taught me." Jesus' words indicate that the Jews will understand following his crucifixion and ascension, much as the disciples will (e.g., 13:19). The Gospel never narrates the Jews' later understanding, just as the disciples' perfect belief always remains in the future.

Assertions about the Jews' parentage in John 8:31–59 continue the portrayal of the Jews' behavior as conflicting with their belief. Interpreters tend to focus on Jesus' words connecting the Jews with "your father the devil" (verse 44). While this is clearly part of their characterization, it is also important that Jesus twice identifies the Jews as being exactly what they claim to be, "children of Abraham." One such statement occurs early in the conversation (8:37), and one toward the end (8:56).[22] How can the Jews be children of both Abraham and of their father the devil? These statements reinforce the metaphorical nature of 8:44: Jesus is not claiming a literal relationship between the Jews and the devil, but a metaphorical and rhetorical one. He uses the phrase to describe their rejection of his claims and characterizes their actions and words through the metaphor of paternity: they "should do that which they have heard from the Father" (8:38), or should do "what Abraham did" (8:39). If God were their Father, Jesus says, they would love Jesus (8:42). But they do not accept his word (8:43) and they seek to kill him. Therefore, while the Jews clearly stand in the line of Abraham as inheritors of the promises of Israel, their behavior toward Jesus aligns them not with God but the devil. John characterizes them as both faithful and unfaithful to the God of Israel.

The Jews in John 8 are characterized as being in disagreement with Jesus. The language does not point to an existential rift between them, but it does indicate a serious dispute. The conversation continues the discussion of Jesus' origins from John 7. The question of Jesus' origins is used metaphorically to describe his identity: he "comes from heaven," is "sent by God," is "from above," is "God's son."[23] This origin is evident in his actions (7:23) and words (7:16–17). The conversation in John 8 draws on the same principles as the one about Jesus' origins: Jesus' identity is apparent through his actions and words, and so is that of the Jews. The accusations fly back and forth. According to Jesus, their actions toward him are not from God. Jesus calls the Jews "of your father the devil" (8:44; cf. 8:41) and they respond, "Are we not right in saying that you are a Samaritan and have a demon?" (8:48; cf. 8:52). While the language may sound harsh, it was common to first-century disagreements.[24] The rhetoric need not indicate an unbridgeable gap between Jesus and Judaism, but points instead to a disagreement between Jesus and the Jews about whose words and actions are most akin to God's will.

Rather than seeing the Jews as simple enemies of Jesus, my analysis of John 8 suggests that the Jews believe in Jesus but reject certain aspects of his claims. John characterizes them in ways that parallel the disciples: their belief comes as something of a surprise, yet it is stated in a straightforward manner, and their further understanding is expected in the future. Yet John wants the reader to see how the Jews' behavior is in conflict with their belief and also conflicts with their own intentions of fidelity to God. Their actions suggest that they are in line with the devil rather than with God's will.

IRONY IN THE CHARACTER OF THE JEWS

Though difficult to define, irony usually includes the reader's perception of two levels of meaning within the text; an incongruity or contradiction between the two levels, and a character or characters who operate on one level of meaning and are unaware of the other.[25] As Allan Rodway notes, although two levels of meaning are in play, "irony is not merely a matter of seeing a 'true' meaning beneath a 'false,' but of seeing a double exposure . . . on one plate."[26] The incongruity in meaning draws the reader toward a new understanding of the situation, one that is not explicitly stated in the literary work.

John's portrayal of the Jews is often ironic. Many interpreters see irony in the characterization of the Jews in John 8. Jesus says, "If you abide in my word, you are truly my disciples, and you will know the truth, and the truth will set you free" (8:31–32). The Jews respond, "We are children of Abraham and have never been slaves to anyone. Why do you say, 'you will become free'?" (8:33). This response has more than one meaning. On the literal level, the Jews are probably accurate in reporting that they have never been slaves. However, Jesus' words "the truth will set you free" (verse 32) are easily recognizable as metaphor. "Slavery" and "freedom" are common metaphors in antiquity, in a religious or philosophical sense (in the New Testament, e.g., Matt. 6:24; Rom. 6:6, 19–20; Gal. 5:13). Being a "servant" or "slave" of God suggests one's ultimate devotion to God. Understood in this light, the Jews' words, "We are children of Abraham and have never been slaves to anyone," may be an assertion of their fidelity to the God of Israel.[27] They present themselves as those who are devoted to God alone, as Abraham was. However, in context, their statement may also be read ironically.[28] John 7–8 is set in the temple during the Festival of Booths (7:2).[29] The Festival of Booths (Lev. 23:39–43) is a reminder of the literal enslavement of the Israelites and the wilderness period following their release, in which their devotion to God was tested. The statement "we have never been slaves" distances the speakers from the history they are meant to remember in the Festival. Thus, the Jews' objection to Jesus may be said to enact a misunderstanding of their own Scripture and tradition.

A similar pattern occurs in John 18:1–19:16, in the portrayal of the Jews and the chief priests in the trial narrative. In this passage the Jews appear interchangeable with the Jewish religious authorities who converse with Pilate. The authorities are called "the Jews" a number of times (18:31, 38; 19:12, 14) and are characterized primarily through their conversation with Pilate. One of the main topics of their conversation is Jesus' identity as "King of the Jews" (18:33, 39; 19:3, 14, 19, 21). This title characterizes Jesus yet also characterizes the Jews by associating them with this king. In calling for Jesus' crucifixion, the Jews pledge allegiance to Caesar, denying Jesus' kingship. The irony of this declaration is situational: they declare allegiance to Caesar at the moment that the Passover lambs are being sacrificed in the temple at the opening of the Passover festival (19:14–15).[30] As Wayne Meeks has pointed out, the affirmation of God's kingship over Israel was likely a well-known theme of the Passover celebration.[31] Thus John tells his story in such a way that the reader familiar with Jewish tradition is prepared to see what the Jews do not: their rejection of Jesus is also a rejection of the kingship of God as known in the exodus.

John's irony may also be served by the so-called "neutral" uses of *hoi Ioudaioi* (as when John speaks of "the Passover of the Jews," 6:4; 11:55). On a literary level, this language connects the Jews as a character to the festival settings. As I have discussed above, the festival settings often contribute to John's irony by creating a context in which the Jews' words take on an additional level of meaning. The Passover setting of John 6 is one of the first of many allusions in that chapter to the exodus story.[32] It forms a backdrop against which the Jews reject Jesus' metaphorical assertion that he can be understood as manna. Likewise, the festival setting in John 7 sets the stage for the Jews' renunciation of their history as slaves in Egypt. And the Passover setting of the trial narrative forms the backdrop against which the Jews reject not only Jesus' kingship but also God's. In these cases, language of "the festival of the Jews" may function ironically to underscore whose traditions these are. The Jews are the people who know the stories of the exodus, who stand in their lineage, and whose behavior mirrors that of their ancestors. They are in the best position to understand who Jesus is, and they do understand a good deal, but they also reject key claims that Jesus makes identifying himself with God and God's word.

When we read these texts this way, through the lens of irony, the incongruity between the Jews' understanding and misunderstanding points the reader to a deeper understanding of Jesus. In John 6, the grumbling of the Jews reinforces Jesus' identity as the bread from heaven. Their response is to be expected: the Israelites did the same thing. Because the Jews are characterized in relationship to the Israelites, their questions become evidence of their lack of faith in God rather than remaining as troubling questions for the reader. Likewise, in John 8 the Jews' perception of Jesus is flawed by their misunderstanding of their own tradition, found in their claim that they "have never been slaves to anyone." Because they deny their history of slavery and consequently of God's salvation, their rejection of Jesus and his role in bringing freedom is shown to be based on an inadequate understanding of their own tradition. Because of their mistake, the Gospel's perspective is reaffirmed: when the tradition is properly understood, Jesus is seen as the faithful extension of God's acts of deliverance and promises to Israel. The ironic characterization of the Jews contributes to John's message about Jesus.

The literary function of the Jews' character is ironic in these examples. Every time they respond to Jesus in defense of religious principles, they miss something important. My understanding of John's irony is similar to that of other interpreters in understanding irony to align the reader's perspective with that of the Gospel. The reader knows something that the character does not and shares this understanding with the narrator's viewpoint.[33] However, my reading of John's irony points to a slightly different function for the Jews' character. When read as enemies of Jesus, the Jews understand little about Jesus and are simple "victims" of John's irony.[34] By contrast, when they are seen as an ambiguous character, we see that the Jews understand a good deal about Jesus. They understand Jesus' claim to be a giver of bread and his claim to be that bread. They understand that his words in John 8 represent a claim to unity with God. Furthermore, John agrees with much of their perspective. He shares their commitment to the worship of one God, and he advocates following God's word and seeking God's will. What the reader learns by means of John's irony is not that these principles are wrong, but that the Jews' rejection of Jesus betrays these principles. Jesus' claims about himself are true and not blasphemy. Following him is following God's word. John's irony suggests that the Gospel is not attacking Jewish religion, but presenting itself as the faithful proponent of Jewish Scripture and tradition.

AMBIGUITY IN THE CHARACTER OF THE JEWS

Reading the Jews as an ambiguous character does not render them exemplary believers, nor does it solve, once and for all, the question of John's anti-Judaism. However, it does suggest some new possibilities for looking at this complex set of issues. The main opening it creates is that the Jews no longer exist only on the wrong side of a deep dualistic divide, as the exemplars of Jesus' opponents. When we read the Jews as a flat character, we have no option but to interpret the Jews negatively. In a Gospel that calls for belief in Jesus, they represent those who disbelieve. As an ambiguous character, however, the Jews are much like all the rest. Like the disciples, they both believe and disbelieve. Like Martha, they understand a great deal and yet deeply misunderstand at what seems to be the crucial moment. If their behavior does not match their stated intentions, it is not any more or less so than with the rest of humanity.

Interpreting the Jews in this way requires a different way of understanding the first-century context in which John wrote, one in which John may even self-identify as Jewish. The weight of scholarship in support of the argument that John's community has already broken ties with Judaism makes this point difficult to argue, especially in the limited space I have here. However, as a starting point for a new conversation on the subject, I make the following three suggestions. First, although John's use of *hoi Ioudaioi* as a designation is often seen as evidence of his distance from Judaism, suggesting that "the Jews" are a group that he distinguishes as *Other*, this is not necessarily the case. I can imagine, for example, that I might write a creative work that was highly critical of a group I called "the Americans." The use of the term does not preclude me from being myself a U.S. citizen, or even from considering myself a faithful or patriotic American. Likewise, John's creation of a character called "the Jews" does not tell us anything positive or negative about his relationship to that group.

Second, when the Jews are seen as ambiguous, it becomes possible to suggest that John's intended reader would self-identify as Jewish. When belief and unbelief are an either/or option for John, then any criticism of a character can relegate them to the side of "those who walk in darkness." But if characters can be ambiguous, then criticism is possible. Judaism has a long tradition of self-criticism: the authors of Exodus, Numbers, and Isaiah are sometimes harsh in their assessment of Israel's faithfulness.[35] John draws on these traditions explicitly in expressing the difficulties that people encounter in believing in Jesus. Though John's language is certainly critical of the character "the Jews," it may not be so different from other biblical self-criticism.

Third, reading John as having separated from Judaism goes hand in hand with an understanding of the Gospel that is supersessionist. By "supersessionist," I mean the understanding that Jesus fulfills the traditions and Scriptures in a way that replaces (and thereby nullifies) them. This is a common Christian understanding in which Jesus is often contrasted with elements of the culture around him. Many popular as well as scholarly works suggest that Jesus offered an alternative to Judaism that was more spiritual, ethical, and/or liberating than the Judaism of his day.[36] From this viewpoint, there is necessarily something deficient about first-century Judaism that Jesus comes to "fix," either by repairing it or replacing it with something else entirely. The Gospel of John has often been understood in these terms, as rejecting the Jewish imagery it uses and offering something new in its place. It is difficult to see this point of view as Jewish in anything but a nominal way.

In the end, the text of John does not give us sufficient information with which to make a historical determination about John's community location, although scholarly interpreters of John try to situate the language of the Gospel in a context in which it makes sense. In arguing that John may self-identify as Jewish, I am not trying to make a historical argument about the separation of Christianity from Judaism, but to hypothesize a context in which it makes sense to read the Jews as an ambiguous character. John does not simply disagree with the Jews. He shares many of their values. When John does take issue with the Jews, it is regarding specific aspects of Jesus' identity. The Jews understand Jesus' claims as blasphemy, as putting himself on par with God. John agrees that blasphemy is wrong, but he wants the reader to see how, in Jesus' case, his claims are true and therefore not blasphemy. In other cases, as I discussed above, John tries to show how, in their rejection of Jesus, the Jews have not been faithful to their own tradition. In my reading, John does not view Judaism as deficient, nor understand Jesus as replacing Judaism. When he differs with the Jews, it is regarding specific questions of Jesus' identity. As I discuss in the next chapter, John understands Jesus as one who faithfully carries forward the word of God to God's own people—the Jews.

Reading John in a way that is not supersessionist offers a different way of addressing anti-Jewish prejudice in contemporary preaching and scholarship. Many Christians are unconscious of anti-Jewish rhetoric in their own sermons or exegesis. In reading John's language as anti-Jewish, some interpreters hope to make modern readers aware that they should not simply reproduce such sentiments in their own writing and speech. My reading of John takes a different approach, by pointing out how much John's viewpoint shares with and affirms Judaism. If John does not view Judaism as deficient, neither should the modern interpreter.

By itself, neither the negative reading of the Jews nor my alternative ambiguous portrait will cure the modern reader of anti-Jewish biases. Such prejudice does not come from the text of John by itself; instead, it is found there by readers who import their assumptions about Judaism and Christianity. Identifying John as anti-Jewish does not solve the problem of modern anti-Judaism, because the way John's rhetoric against the Jews is described is so overwhelmingly negative that few modern Christians would identify their own words as similarly offensive. John's bias can be explained and relegated to the past, while modern manifestations of anti-Judaism persist. However, my own approach runs the risk of letting modern prejudice go unexamined. If John's language is not anti-Jewish, there is no reason to explore the problems in Christian rhetoric about the Jews.

While reading the Jews as an ambiguous character will not by itself change anti-Jewish interpretation, it may have a positive effect on the contemporary context. If the Jews are in some ways similar to the disciples as a character, then it also becomes more likely that the modern reader might understand them as an example. Just as the disciples convey a message about what it means to believe or follow Jesus, so also the Jews may serve a similar function. Like the disciples, the Jews are a mixed bag. They believe in Jesus in large numbers, yet they also seek to kill him. They see their rejection of him as faithfulness toward God, but John invites the reader to see how they have misunderstood. Their attempt to be faithful is ironically portrayed as a betrayal of their traditions and of God. As they do with other characters, Christian readers of the Gospel might hold this example up as a parallel for their own lives.[37]

Imagining oneself in parallel with the Jews has some potential to transform Christian anti-Jewish thinking. To ask modern Christians to identify with John's Jews seems to be a daunting task. The gap in our imaginations is wide, and both historical and interpretive factors contribute to its depth. Perhaps because of this, reading the Jews as an ambiguous character may be useful in countering anti-Judaism simply because it asks the reader to make an imaginative leap: to envision oneself as Jewish. To do so, the Jews can no longer be viewed as the negative Other, and the reader would need to attend to the points of continuity between Jewish and Christian traditions. However, drawing connections with the Jews as a character is not a cure-all for Christian anti-Judaism. A drawback to this reading is that it leaves openings for the reader's own anti-Jewish sentiments to creep back in. If the Jews are allowed to be held up as an example, but only a negative one, then comparing modern Christians to the Jews will not help to lessen the reader's anti-Judaism. The interpreter would also need to portray the Jews in a positive light, to underscore their similarities to the disciples, and to show the many ways in which John agrees with them. Understanding the Jews as an ambiguous character means coming to grips with John's strongly positive assessment of their motivations and of the traditions this character defends.

BIBLIOGRAPHY

Ashton, John. "The Identity and Function of the 'ΙΟΥΔΑΙΟΙ in the Fourth Gospel." *Novum Testamentum* 27 (1985): 40–75.

Augenstein, Jörg. "'Euer Gesetz'—Ein Pronomen und die johanneische Haltung zum Gesetz." *Zeitschrift für die neutestamentliche Wissenschaft* 88 (1997): 311–13.

Barbe, Katharina. *Irony in Context*. Pragmatics and Beyond, New Series. Amsterdam: John Benjamins Publishing Co., 1995.

Barrett, C. K. *The Gospel according to St. John*. Philadelphia: Westminster Press, 1978.

———. *The Gospel of John and Judaism*. London: SPCK, 1975.

Bauer, W., F. W. Danker, W. F. Arndt, and F. W. Gingrich [BDAG]. "'Ιουδαῖος." Pages 478–79 in *A Greek-English Lexicon of the New Testament and Other Early Christian Literature*. 3rd ed. Chicago: University of Chicago Press, 2000.

Baum, Gregory. *The Jews and the Gospel: A Re-examination of the New Testament*. Westminster, MD: Newman Press, 1961.

Bieringer, Reimund, Didier Pollefeyt, and Frederique Vandecasteele-Vanneuville. "Wrestling with Johannine Anti-Judaism: A Hermeneutical Framework for the Analysis of the Current Debate." Pages 3–37 in *Anti-Judaism and the Fourth Gospel*. Edited by Reimund Bieringer, Didier Pollefeyt, and Frederique Vandecasteele-Vanneuville. Louisville, KY: Westminster John Knox Press, 2001.

Borgen, Peder. *Bread from Heaven: An Exegetical Study of the Concept of Manna in the Gospel of John and the Writings of Philo*. Novum Testamentum Supplement 10. Leiden: E. J. Brill, 1965.

Brown, Raymond. *The Community of the Beloved Disciple*. New York: Paulist Press, 1979.

———. *The Gospel according to John*. 2 vols. Anchor Bible 29–29A. New York: Doubleday, 1966–70.

Bultmann, Rudolf. *The Gospel of John*. Philadelphia: Westminster Press, 1971.

———. *Theology of the New Testament*. 2 vols. New York: Scribner, 1951–55.

Callaway, Mary C. "A Hammer That Breaks Rock in Pieces: Prophetic Critique in the Hebrew Bible." Pages 21–38 in *Anti-Semitism and Early Christianity*. Edited by Craig A. Evans and Donald Alfred Hagner. Minneapolis: Fortress Press, 1993.

Charlesworth, James H. "The Gospel of John: Exclusivism Caused by a Social Setting Different from That of Jesus." Pages 247–78 in *Anti-Judaism and the Fourth Gospel*. Edited by Reimund Bieringer, Didier Pollefeyt, and Frederique Vandecasteele-Vanneuville. Louisville, KY: Westminster John Knox Press, 2001.

Colebrook, Claire. *Irony*. The New Critical Idiom. New York: Routledge, 2004.

Conway, Colleen. "The Production of the Johannine Community: A New Historicist Perspective." *Journal of Biblical Literature* 121 (2002): 479–95.

Culpepper, R. Alan. *Anatomy of the Fourth Gospel: A Study in Literary Design*. Philadelphia: Fortress Press, 1983.

———. "Anti-Judaism in the Fourth Gospel as a Theological Problem for Christian Interpreters." Pages 61–82 in *Anti-Judaism and the Fourth Gospel*. Edited by Reimund Bieringer, Didier Pollefeyt, and Frederique Vandecasteele-Vanneuville. Louisville, KY: Westminster John Knox Press, 2001.

———. "The Gospel of John and the Jews." *Review and Expositor* 84 (1987): 273–88.

Cuming, G. J. "The Jews in the Fourth Gospel." *Expository Times* 60 (1948–49): 290–92.

Darr, John A. *On Character Building: The Reader and the Rhetoric of Characterization in Luke-Acts*. Louisville, KY: Westminster/John Knox Press, 1992.

Davies, W. D. "Reflections on Aspects of the Jewish Background of the Gospel of John." Pages 43–64 in *Exploring the Gospel of John: In Honor of D. Moody Smith*. Edited by R. Alan Culpepper and C. Clifton Black. Louisville, KY: Westminster John Knox Press, 1996.

De Boer, Martinus C. "The Depiction of the Jews in John's Gospel: Matters of Behavior and Identity." Pages 141–57 in *Anti-Judaism and the Fourth Gospel*. Edited by Reimund Bieringer, Didier Pollefeyt, and Frederique Vandecasteele-Vanneuville. Louisville, KY: Westminster John Knox Press, 2001.

Dodd, Charles Harold. "Behind a Johannine Dialogue." Pages 41–57 in *More New Testament Studies*. Grand Rapids: Wm. B. Eerdmans Publishing Co., 1968.

———. *Historical Tradition in the Fourth Gospel*. Cambridge: Cambridge University Press, 1963.

Duke, Paul D. *Irony in the Fourth Gospel*. Atlanta: John Knox Press, 1985.

Dunn, James D. G. "The Embarrassment of History: Reflections on the Problem of 'Anti-Judaism' in the Fourth Gospel." Pages 41–60 in *Anti-Judaism and the Fourth Gospel*. Edited by Reimund Bieringer, Didier Pollefeyt, and Frederique Vandecasteele-Vanneuville. Louisville, KY: Westminster John Knox Press, 2001.

Egenter, Richard. "Joh. 8, 31 f. im christlichen Lebensbewusstein." Pages 1583–1605 in *Wahrheit und Verkündigung*. Edited by Leo Scheffczyk, Werner Dettloff, and Richard Heinzmann. Munich: Verlag Ferdinand Schöningh, 1967.

Haenchen, Ernst. *John*. 2 vols. Hermeneia. Philadelphia: Fortress Press, 1984.

Hoskyns, Edwyn Clement. *The Fourth Gospel*. Edited by F. N. Davey. London: Faber & Faber, 1947.

Hunn, Debbie. "Who Are 'They' in John 8:33?" *Catholic Biblical Quarterly* 66 (2004): 387–99.

Hylen, Susan. *Allusion and Meaning in John 6*. Beiheifte zur Zeitschrift für die neutestamentliche Wissenschaft 137. Berlin: Walter de Gruyter, 2005.

Johnson, Luke Timothy. "The New Testament's Anti-Jewish Slander and the Conventions of Ancient Polemic." *Journal of Biblical Literature* 108 (1989): 419–41.

Katz, Steven T. "Issues in the Separation of Judaism and Christianity after 70 C.E.: A Reconsideration." *Journal of Biblical Literature* 103 (1984): 43–76.

Kierspel, Lars. *The Jews and the World in the Fourth Gospel*. Tübingen: Mohr Siebeck, 2006.

Kimelman, Reuven. "Birkat Ha-Minim and the Lack of Evidence for an Anti-Christian Jewish Prayer in Late Antiquity." Pages 226–44 in *Jewish and Christian Self-Definition*. Vol. 2. Edited by E. P. Sanders. Philadelphia: Fortress Press, 1981.

Leistner, Reinhold. *Antijudaismus im Johannesevangelium? Darstellung des Problems in der neueren Auslegungsgeschichte und Untersuchung der Leidensgeschichte*. Theologie und Wirklichkeit 3. Bern: Herbert Lang, 1974.

Levine, Amy-Jill. "The Disease of Postcolonial New Testament Studies and the Hermeneutics of Healing." *Journal of Feminist Studies in Religion* 20 (2004): 91–99.

———. *The Misunderstood Jew: The Church and the Scandal of the Jewish Jesus*. San Francisco: Harper, 2006.

Lindars, Barnabas. *The Gospel of John*. New Century Bible. London: Oliphants, 1972.

Lowe, Malcolm. "Who Were the 'ΙΟΥΔΑΙΟΙ?" *Novum Testamentum* 18 (1976): 101–30.

Martyn, J. Louis. "A Gentile Mission That Replaced an Earlier Jewish Mission?" Pages 124–44 in *Exploring the Gospel of John: In Honor of D. Moody Smith*. Edited by R. Alan Culpepper and C. Clifton Black. Louisville, KY: Westminster John Knox Press, 1996.

———. *History and Theology in the Fourth Gospel*. 3rd ed. Louisville, KY: Westminster John Knox Press, 2003.

Meeks, Wayne A. "'Am I a Jew?' Johannine Christianity and Judaism." Pages 163–86 in *Christianity, Judaism and Other Greco-Roman Cults: Studies for Morton Smith at Sixty*. Edited by Jacob Neusner. Studies in Judaism in Late Antiquity 12. Leiden: E. J. Brill, 1975.

———. *The Prophet-King*. Supplements to Novum Testamentum 14. Leiden: E. J. Brill, 1967.

Michael, J. Hugh. "The Jews in the Fourth Gospel." *Expository Times* 60 (1948–49): 290–92.

Morris, Leon. *The Gospel according to John*. Grand Rapids: Wm. B. Eerdmans Publishing Co., 1971.

Muecke, Douglas Colin. *The Compass of Irony*. London: Methuen & Co., 1969.

O'Day, Gail R. *The Gospel of John*. New Interpreter's Bible 9. Nashville: Abingdon Press, 1995.

———. *Revelation in the Fourth Gospel*. Philadelphia: Fortress Press, 1986.

———. "'Show Us the Father and We Will Be Satisfied' (John 14:8)." *Semeia* 85 (1999): 11–17.

Perri, Carmela. "On Alluding." *Poetics* 7 (1978): 289–307.

Reinhartz, Adele. *Befriending the Beloved Disciple: A Jewish Reading of the Gospel of John*. New York: Continuum, 2001.

———. "Introduction: 'Father' as Metaphor in the Fourth Gospel." *Semeia* 85 (1999): 1–10.

———. "The Johannine Community and Its Jewish Neighbors: A Reappraisal." Pages 111–38 in *What Is John? II, Literary and Social Readings of the Fourth Gospel*. Edited by Fernando F. Segovia. Atlanta: Scholars Press, 1998.

———. "John 8:31–59 from a Jewish Perspective." Pages 787–97 in vol. 2 of *Remembering for the Future: The Holocaust in an Age of Genocide*. 3 vols. Edited by John K. Roth and Elisabeth Maxwell. New York: Palgrave, 2001.

Rensberger, David. "The Politics of John: The Trial of Jesus in the Fourth Gospel." *Journal of Biblical Literature* 103 (1984): 395–411.

Rodway, Allan. "Terms for Comedy." *Renaissance and Modern Studies* 6 (1962): 102–24.

Sanders, E. P. "Jesus, Ancient Judaism, and Modern Christianity: The Quest Continues." Pages 31–55 in *Jesus, Judaism, and Christian Anti-Judaism*. Edited by Paula Fredriksen and Adele Reinhartz. Louisville, KY: Westminster John Knox Press, 2002.

Schnackenburg, Rudolf. *The Gospel According to St. John*. 3 vols. New York: Seabury Press, 1982–90.

Smith, D. Moody. *John*. Abingdon New Testament Commentaries. Nashville: Abingdon Press, 1999.

Swetnam, James. "The Meaning of πεπιστευκότας in John 8, 31." *Biblica* 61 (1980): 106–9.

Thompson, Marianne Meye. *The God of the Gospel of John*. Grand Rapids: Wm. B. Eerdmans Publishing Co., 2001.

Tyson, Joseph B. "Anti-Judaism in the Critical Study of the Gospels." Pages 216–51 in *Anti-Judaism and the Gospels*. Edited by William R. Farmer. Harrisburg, PA: Trinity Press International, 1999.

Von Wahlde, Urban C. "The Johannine 'Jews': A Critical Survey." *New Testament Studies* 28 (1982): 33–60.

———. "Literary Structure and Theological Argument in Three Discourses with the Jews in the Fourth Gospel." *Journal of Biblical Literature* 103 (1984): 575–84.

White, Martin Christopher. *The Identity and Function of the Jews and Related Terms in the Fourth Gospel.* Ann Arbor, MI: University Microfilms, 1972.

Wróbel, Miroslaw Stanislaw. *Who Are the Father and His Children in Jn 8:44? A Literary, Historical and Theological Analysis of Jn 8:44 and Its Context.* Cahiers de la Revue biblique 63. Paris: J. Gabalda et Cie Éditeurs, 2005.

8

Jesus

Jesus is the least ambiguous of all John's characters. He is sent from the Father to perform God's works (e.g., 4:34; 5:36). He brings light and life to those who believe (e.g., 1:3–5; 8:12). The entire Gospel seems to be crafted in order to lead the reader toward greater comprehension of these features of Jesus' identity. When the Gospel sets up clear contrasts—being "from above" versus "from below," or "of the world" versus "not of the world" (8:23)—Jesus is the one character who clearly falls within the preferred category. Although it is difficult for readers to miss the importance of the figure of Jesus, nonetheless many elements of John's characterization make him appear mysterious and elusive. Even with this most important character, John's language is not straightforward, and elements of indirect characterization lead to ambiguity in the character of Jesus. In this chapter, I explore one important aspect of John's indirect characterization of Jesus: his use of metaphor.

No one disputes John's use of metaphorical language in reference to Jesus, and John's metaphors have always been a rich source for understanding his character. The "I am" sayings (e.g., "I am the bread of life," 6:35; "I am the true vine," 15:1), which are unique to John's Gospel, have enriched the liturgy, art, and theological understanding of Christians throughout the centuries. Interpreters locate metaphors in all aspects of the Gospel's characterization of Jesus. They find them in Jesus' speech ("I am the gate for the sheep," 10:7) and in speech about him by others ("Behold, the lamb of God," 1:36). Metaphors are

found in Jesus' actions, as in his washing of the disciples' feet as a metaphor for cleansing or service (13:10, 15–16). Metaphors are commonly
noted in Jesus' environment, especially in the festival settings that form
the backdrop to Jesus' words and actions (e.g., 7:2; 13:1). And metaphors are found in the characterization of Jesus through comparison
with other characters, as when the interaction between Pilate and Jesus
in John 18–19 leads readers to reflect on who is truly "king."

Metaphors that relate to Jesus' character draw on familiar concepts—usually from Jewish Scripture and tradition—to shed light on
the person of Jesus. "The essence of metaphor is understanding and
experiencing one kind of thing in terms of another."[1] When Jesus says,
"I am the bread of life" (6:35), he draws on conventions associated
with God's gift of manna in the wilderness. Manna is named in the
Scripture reference of 6:30–31. Jesus goes on to interpret the manna
in relation to himself. His words claiming to "be bread" create a relationship between Jesus and the manna that sustained Israel those forty
years in the desert. In the language of conceptual metaphor theory,
readers draw on aspects of the "source domain," manna, to understand
the "target," Jesus.[2] When Jesus says, "The bread of God is that which
comes down from heaven and gives life to the world" (6:33), his words
apply equally well to the manna and himself.[3] The language asks readers to enter into a way of imagining Jesus: he is life-giving, miraculous
sustenance meant to sustain God's grumbling people.[4]

At first glance, what I am claiming here about John's metaphors
for Jesus may not seem surprising or different from what others have
argued. Yet reading John's language as metaphor carries a number of
implications that differ from the more common approach of reading
it as symbol. A symbol is defined broadly as "something that stands
for something else," or more specifically in regard to John, as "an
image, an action, or a person that is understood to have transcendent
significance."[5] A symbol points to a truth that lies beyond or outside
of conventional understanding of the source domain. An example is
the image of Jesus as shepherd in John 10. In a symbolic reading, the
shepherd image reveals a transcendent truth about the person of Jesus:
"Shepherding in the world is only an image and pointer to the true,
proper shepherding which is shown in the rule of the Revealer."[6]

A metaphor, in contrast, uses the conventions of shepherding to
understand Jesus. These conventions are drawn from practices of shepherding that were common in that day, and they also reflect the language of Scripture, where shepherding is already a metaphor for God's

care for Israel or the care of a leader God sends (e.g., Isa. 40:11; Jer.
23:2–4; Ezek. 34). Read metaphorically, Jesus' words make a claim
about his identity in relation to this scriptural background. He is to
be understood as the one whom God sends to act on God's behalf
as the caretaker and guardian of the people, or even as one fulfilling
God's promise to shepherd the sheep directly. These are certainly theological claims, but in a metaphorical reading there is no transcendent
truth that lies outside of the metaphorical meaning. Instead, meaning is
found as the reader tries to understand Jesus in terms of the Old Testament shepherding imagery.

The symbolic view of John has two immediate advantages. First, it
draws the reader toward John's theological meaning. The reader rightly
perceives that "I am the vine" (15:5) is not literal language characterizing Jesus but is meant to express something deeper, with theological
content. In conceiving of John's language as symbol, interpreters understand themselves to be accessing a transcendent and divine truth through
the medium of human language. "Symbol can be seen paradoxically as
the limited expression of a reality that transcends anything that human
speech or imagination can articulate."[7] The symbols that surround Jesus
communicate pieces of a divine mystery, a world otherwise inaccessible
to humans, as Sandra Schneiders has observed: "It is only in terms of
symbol, correctly understood, that we can grasp John's presentation of
the incarnation as salvation."[8] The expectation created by this description of John's language is that symbols correspond to doctrinal truths
about Jesus. Symbols use human language but speak of "transcendent
realities," which are otherwise difficult for humans to access.

The second advantage of a symbolic view of John's language is
that it facilitates a unified understanding of John's Gospel as a whole.
Though the metaphors of the Gospel are diverse and varied, reading
them symbolically allows the reader to arrive at a unified understanding. This is in part because the symbols are all understood to point to
the same transcendent reality. In Bultmann's view, for example, John
presents Jesus as the Revealer. Each of John's symbols, properly understood, expresses a different aspect of this overarching truth. "I am the
gate" (10:7) points to "the exclusiveness and the absoluteness of the
revelation." "I am the bread of life" (6:35) contains "the whole paradox
of the revelation. . . . Whoever approaches [Jesus] with the desire for
the gift of life must learn that Jesus is *himself* the gift he really wants."[9]
Each image, gate and bread, illumines aspects of the overall identity of
Jesus as Revealer.

Although the symbolic approach sets out to provide a unified, theological truth, it is not clear that symbolic interpretations accomplish this goal. As I discuss below, interpreters who claim to expound on John's eternal truths usually end up speaking in terms of John's metaphors rather than in language of transcendent truths. Nor do interpreters agree on a single unified truth to be found within the Gospel. In this chapter I argue that understanding John's language as metaphor rather than symbol helps to explain these failures of the symbolic approach. In addition, a metaphorical view of John's language has several distinct advantages over a symbolic understanding. First, when metaphors are translated into transcendent truths, much of the specific content of the metaphor is lost or minimized. The images of the Gospel are a rich source for theological contemplation—not of eternal doctrinal truths, but of the concrete ways that certain subjects (shepherd, manna, water, vine) shed light on the character of Jesus. Second, attempts to unify John's metaphors under one theme also forfeit much of the rich diversity of John's language. Reading the Gospel's imagery as metaphor provides a way of retaining the complexity of Jesus' character. This complexity comes with its own form of ambiguity, ambiguity that may challenge some readers of the Gospel, but that is also a potential resource for deepening theological understanding.

METAPHORICAL MEANING
AND THE CHARACTER OF JESUS

Given the promises that interpreters make in describing Johannine symbolism, the result should be just such abstract, theological language. Most twentieth-century Western readers would expect that meaning pointing to transcendent truths would be expressed literally—as a relationship between the words of the text and objective reality, as Mark Johnson has observed: "To give the meaning of a particular utterance is to give the conditions under which it would be true."[10] Though such a description of meaning seems natural to many expressions that we understand as literal, when metaphor is involved, this quest for meaning becomes murky.[11] How is one to define the conditions under which the words "Jesus is bread" can be said to be "true" in an objective sense? Understanding the imagery as symbol is one way of addressing the translation of literary imagery to literal language. A symbol like water conveys an idea or point, such as "spiritual sustenance," that can then be employed as literal language. However, symbolic readings of the Gospel rarely result in doctrinal language. When they do, a great deal of the richness of John's language is lost. Below I discuss how understanding John's language as metaphor accounts for each of these difficulties.

Symbolic interpreters of the Gospel often express meaning not in abstract, propositional language but as metaphor. In her discussion of the vine imagery of John 15, Dorothy Lee elaborates on the various attributes of the vine, the vinegrower, and the branches. Her expression of the meaning of the passage remains within its metaphorical framework: "This vineyard will no longer fall into disrepair or be uprooted."[12] Lee is not translating the metaphor into a transcendent truth; instead, she is elaborating the metaphor. Likewise, John Painter's expression of "light" metaphors remains metaphorical: John "9.4–5, 39–41 together make the point that all men are in fact blind and in the darkness."[13] Here, though Painter claims to express the "point" of the passage, the meaning is metaphorical. He is not claiming that all people are literally blind. Such examples show an implicit recognition that expressing the meaning of metaphors like "I am the vine" or "I am the light of the world" is not a matter of translating the metaphorical language into transcendent truths. The interpreter expresses meaning by elaborating the terms of the metaphors John employs.

Such symbolic interpretations make sense when John's language is viewed as metaphor. From the perspective of conceptual metaphor, meaning is not limited to propositional language. Meaning can be metaphorical. In many cases, metaphors are not easily translated into propositional statements. For example, when the metaphor "Sally is a block of ice" is converted to the statement "Sally is cold," the meaning of the sentence remains metaphorical.[14] The metaphor expresses something about Sally's emotional availability, not her temperature. The translation of John's bread metaphor to "spiritual sustenance" displays the same effect. "Sustenance" is still metaphorical when understood in reference to the spiritual realm. The interpreter restates the metaphor in different terms, but the meaning is metaphorical rather than literal.

In maintaining metaphorical meaning, interpreters may implicitly recognize that the translation to doctrinal language would actually be damaging. Important aspects of meaning may be lost in the attempt to convert metaphorical meaning into literal language. This is because metaphors have conceptual content that their literal "equivalent" lacks. As an example, Mark Johnson uses the statement "Babe Ruth's home run threw the crowd into a frenzy":

> If we say "Babe Ruth's home run caused the crowd to get emotion-
> ally excited," we lose the key semantic details expressed by *threw*.
> "Caused to get excited" does *not* capture the *manner* of the causa-
> tion, which is rapid initial "force" followed by an extended trajec-
> tory after the initial event.[15]

In other words, the full meaning of the metaphor is not contained
within the literal statement. This is true of John's metaphors. Translating the metaphors to literal terms does not capture the metaphorical
meaning.

Examples of particular metaphors that have been translated into
propositional language provide evidence of what may be lost in a symbolic reading. For example, the metaphor of eating Jesus' "bread" in
John 6 is often translated as "belief in him." When Jesus says, "Those
who eat my flesh and drink my blood have eternal life" (6:54), eating
Jesus' flesh may be understood as a symbol for believing in him. Understood this way, the specific bread references of John 6 are a jumping-off
point for an abstract notion of "food" that Jesus provides. If Jesus is
bread and eating means believing in him, the metaphor "I am the bread
of life" really points to the necessity of faith in Jesus.[16] The specific
content of the bread metaphor is lost in this interpretation. Yet the
source domain of the metaphor could provide "key semantic details"
for understanding the character of Jesus. Jesus is not just any bread,
but manna. In understanding a metaphor, readers draw on their cultural knowledge of the source domain (e.g., bread) to understand the
target (Jesus). This means that whatever "bread" means in relation to
Jesus should be understood within the cultural context of John's initial
readers. The Gospel gives the reader clues as to what kind of bread
is meant: the crowd mentions manna and quotes Scripture about the
manna story: "He gave them bread from heaven to eat" (6:31).[17]

It is in this context that Jesus goes on to identify himself as "bread."
In doing so, the language of John reflects existing cultural conventions
about the manna story. In Jewish tradition, manna came to be associated with God's wisdom or God's law. The instructions that God gave
regarding the collection of the manna (see Exod. 16:16–30) are used in
Scripture metaphorically, such that eating manna is associated with following God's word, as in Deuteronomy 8:3: God fed you with manna,
"in order to make you understand that one does not live by bread alone,
but by every word from the mouth of the LORD." Later traditions associate the manna story with walking in God's wisdom (e.g., Wis. 16:20–

26).[18] Understood against this background, "I am the bread of life," relates Jesus not only to the life-giving function of the manna as food for the hungry Israelites, but also to the life-giving function of God's wisdom and law (see Prov. 8:35–36; 9:6; Sir. 17:11; 45:5). In John 6, language about teaching and learning (6:45) may be read in this context. Jesus is manna; those who partake learn God's wisdom.

By contrast, symbolic readings of the Gospel may separate the symbol from its context. A symbol points to a transcendent truth, and it is that truth, not the human context of the symbol, that provides the most important information for the reader's understanding. In many cases, John's symbolism is understood not as continuous with but in contrast to its Jewish background. Thus Painter argues that, although Jewish tradition made the Torah the earthly referent for the symbol of the divine light, John uses this same symbol in reference to Jesus. Painter writes, "By using the same symbols, and referring them to Jesus, the evangelist attacked the Jewish self-understanding and offered a new understanding. The meaning of the symbols is transformed by the new point of reference, Jesus."[19] In this reading, light is an independent symbol that can be applied to either Jesus or Torah. In my view, if "the Torah is light" already exists as a metaphor in John's context, then John's metaphor expresses an association between Jesus and the light of God's word as found in the Torah. In other words, the language associates Jesus with the Torah rather than distancing him from it.

Understood in this way, the context becomes a great theological resource for exploring the character of Jesus. John is not portraying Jesus in abstract terms as "light," but specifically as the same light God has provided Israel in the gift of the Torah. The positive associations of God's word are equally true of Jesus. Likewise, the characterization of Jesus as "bread of life" evokes the richness and theological depth of the exodus story of manna. John's language employs not only the concept of manna but many of its attributes from the exodus story. Jesus can be understood as miraculous food that God provides, a food that brings "life" to those who eat of it. The life the manna provided is both physical and spiritual sustenance. Likewise, Jesus brings physical life (e.g., in the prior feeding miracle [6:1–14] and in the raising of Lazarus [11:38–44]) and takes on the life-giving attributes of God's word. The cultural context for the metaphor is incorporated into its meaning, rather than discarded.

Converting John's metaphors for Jesus to doctrinal language is possible but unsatisfactory. I do not mean to say that interpretations offered by symbolic readings of the Gospel are all wrong. In many cases I agree with the broad outlines of their conclusions, such as the notion that John's Gospel underscores the importance of belief in Jesus. But the metaphorical meaning that is lost in the process has great potential for understanding the character of Jesus. John's emphasis on belief need not be lost in a metaphorical reading. Belief is also an integral part of the story of the manna. The Israelites' grumbling against God and Moses was a sign of their continued disbelief, even in the face of the signs and wonders they had witnessed. The manna is presented as a means to reinforce their knowledge of God: "At twilight you shall eat meat, and in the morning you shall have your fill of bread; then you shall know that I am the LORD your God" (Exod. 16:12). The manna is also a test "whether they will follow my instruction or not" (16:4). The relationships between eating and belief are illumined by the manna story. Those who trusted God followed God's command and were fed with manna; their meal becomes further evidence for their continued belief in God. A metaphorical reading of John 6 deepens the connections between eating and belief in ways that the symbolic reading misses. "Continued processes of abstraction—however well they serve various purposes of inquiry, and however revealing and necessary they may be—do not always bring us closer to the fullness of a situation; they may take us farther from its full meaning."[20] The metaphorical meaning offers important theological resources not contained in the "transcendent truths" that are the goal of a symbolic reading.

Because metaphorical meaning is built on existing cultural understandings, John's metaphors maintain deep connections between the character of Jesus and Jewish tradition. This continuity with Jewish tradition agrees with what John says elsewhere. The Gospel never intimates that God's word revealed to Israel is no longer valid. Instead, those who understand God's word understand Jesus as its logical extension (e.g., 5:45–47). Yet many contemporary readings of John posit a separation between John and its Jewish roots. John 6 thus represents a rejection of Jewish tradition in favor of the "bread" that Jesus offers. Jesus, not the manna, now supplies sustenance.[21] Painter's work on John 9 provides a clear example of how this occurs. He writes, "By asserting that the true light is to be found in Jesus, the evangelist has taken a symbol from the world of common experience, which came to him through the tradition of Judaism, and has interpreted it in a new way by giving it a new point of reference in Jesus."[22] By separating the symbol from its context, the use of Jewish symbols becomes an attack on Judaism. Jesus provides a new light that replaces the former Jewish light.

Reading John metaphorically involves recognizing positive associations between Jesus and Judaism.[23] Using Painter's example of the light metaphor, Jesus does not replace the Old Testament light but is its logical extension. This is expressed through John's use of conventional metaphors. In first-century Jewish culture, the law and God's wisdom were already understood as a light that illumines one's path (e.g., Job 24:13; Ps. 119:105, 130). In portraying Jesus as "the light of the world," John creates a relationship between Jesus and God's law and wisdom. God's wisdom and law still are sources of light. However, the light that Israel has known through the Torah is now available in Jesus. Later Christians will come to reject the Torah as a path to God, but this view is not expressed in the pages of this Gospel. The same is true in reading John's bread metaphor: the manna still maintains its function as life-giving food. Jesus' association with the manna does not make the manna less important. Instead, the reader draws on the meaning of the manna story to understand who Jesus is. Jesus does not replace manna; he becomes a continuation of the manna story. Manna—both as the life-giving food that God once gave to Israel and as the sustenance that God continues to give through God's word—is now available in Jesus.

JESUS AS A COMPLEX AND AMBIGUOUS CHARACTER

John uses diverse imagery to characterize Jesus. A symbolic reading helps the interpreter to arrive at a unified picture of Jesus' character. Many approaches achieve unity by prioritizing one set of imagery over others. Some interpreters determine which set has priority by assigning John's imagery to different sources or redactors. J. Louis Martyn attributes the language that associates Jesus with the expected "prophet like Moses" to the Signs Source, an earlier stage in the Gospel's composition history that reflects its Jewish roots. He argues that in its final editing, the evangelist moved away from this understanding and toward that of the "Son of Man," a more mature christological reflection born out of the experience of expulsion from the synagogue.[24] Other scholars arrive at different conclusions, but from the same framework: different christological viewpoints within the Gospel represent different historical layers of the Johannine community.[25] Each of these approaches implies that the earlier source or metaphor is not really useful for understanding the character of Jesus. The reader should either disregard it or at least subordinate it to the later metaphor. In doing so, the inconsistencies that are generated by multiple images, while still present in the text, are minimized within the interpretation.

A more recent approach to John's diverse imagery, which coordinates the imagery under one dominant metaphor,[26] has a similar effect. In Jan van der Watt's work *Family of the King*, Jesus' character is defined primarily through the familial language of the Gospel. He is the Son of the Father, and through relationship with him, believers are incorporated into this familial relationship.[27] The specific content of other metaphors in John is minimized, since all contribute to the overarching family metaphor; for example, the bread metaphor of John 6 is interpreted generally in terms of sustaining life.[28] The presence of "Father" imagery in 6:57 places all of this imagery within the familial context: "Family conventions of antiquity provide the socio-cultural ecology for understanding the impact of these metaphors."[29] Similarly, Mary Coloe's work on household imagery coordinates John's imagery under the framework of the household. Her discussion of Nicodemus is framed as a story of "Life in the Household,"[30] although the Gospel does not explicitly identify the Nicodemus story as one of a household. While both of these works can help readers to explore the richness of the imagery that is present in the Gospel, by emphasizing one or two metaphors, van der Watt and Coloe risk overinterpreting other elements of John.

Reading John metaphorically offers an alternative to this forced unity: each of John's metaphors contributes its own particular content to the character of Jesus. The Gospel portrays Jesus against a rich background of Jewish Scripture and tradition: he is the good shepherd, the true vine, the king of the Jews, the Passover offering. Each of these metaphors has a great deal to offer the reader in terms of the theological meaning that the metaphor creates. Studies like those of Coloe and van der Watt suggest the fruitfulness of exploring a single metaphor in relation to Jesus' character.[31] Though each of these metaphors is worthy of its own in-depth exploration with regard to Jesus' character, I find it fruitful to focus on the sheer variety and quantity of metaphors the Gospel uses to characterize Jesus.

The fact of this variety creates a certain kind of ambiguity in the character of Jesus. It is not the same kind of ambiguity I have observed in other of John's characters. Jesus is not like Nicodemus, whose ambiguity lies in the difficulty of discerning whether and to what extent he ever does believe. Jesus is not ambiguous in the way Martha is: her words and actions leave the reader to wonder how much she understands of her own claim to believe that Jesus is "the Messiah, the Son of God, the one coming into the world" (11:27). The ambiguities of many of John's characters suggest an uncertainty in being able to determine how the reader should understand them according to the ideals of the Gospel, such as belief in Jesus, abiding in him, or witnessing to him. Such ambiguities reflect one definition of "ambiguity" as "uncertain, open to more than one interpretation, of doubtful position."[32] This kind of ambiguity does not fit well with the character of Jesus as John portrays him. The reader is not left to doubt whether Jesus fulfills the stated metaphorical terms.

John's variety of metaphors causes a different kind of ambiguity. Each metaphor creates its own worldview. It asks the reader to comprehend Jesus in specific—and distinct—metaphorical terms. Because John's metaphors are so different, each one requires the reader to understand Jesus differently. JESUS IS MANNA evokes one set of ideas about Jesus' character, while JESUS IS A SHEPHERD evokes another. As Semir Zeki has observed regarding ambiguity in visual art, the ambiguity involved "is not uncertainty, but certainty—the certainty of many equally plausible interpretations, each one of which is sovereign when it occupies the conscious stage."[33] In characterizing Jesus, John asks the reader to hold together multiple, distinct ways of understanding who he is. The metaphors cannot be collapsed into a simple list of character traits, yet their coexistence may lead to a rich and complex understanding of Jesus.

John's use of multiple metaphors to characterize Jesus reflects the ways that humans often use multiple metaphors to express understanding of complex concepts like time, love, or death.[34] For example, one set of metaphors for time expresses the idea that TIME MOVES (e.g., "time flies"; "the deadline is approaching"). Another set expresses TIME IS MONEY (e.g., "I'm saving time"; "That mistake cost me an hour"). In the first set, time is mobile and somewhat ethereal; in the second, it is more concrete, like money stored in a vault for later use. The two metaphorical conceptions are not entirely consistent with each other, yet each expresses something important about modern Western conceptions of time.

Metaphors provide us with important but partial ways of understanding complex notions like time. The concept TIME is partially

structured by the source domain MONEY. The source domain highlights
certain aspects of time while hiding others. TIME IS MONEY highlights
the value human beings assign to time and how, in a modern economy,
we experience time and money as exchangeable through practices like
the payment of an hourly wage. The metaphor also hides aspects of
the concept of time—such as not being able to store time for our later
use as we can money. "The metaphorical structuring involved here is
partial, not total. If it were total, one concept would actually *be* the
other, not merely be understood in terms of it."[35] The many common
metaphors for a concept like time are useful because, as Lakoff and
Johnson note:

> When we try to conceptualize the wealth of our experiences of these
> domains, no single, consistent structuring of that experience is pos-
> sible; instead we need to import structure from a wide variety of
> source domains if we are to characterize anything approaching the
> full richness of the target domains.[36]

Each metaphor illumines a piece of our understanding and experience
of time, but no single metaphor encompasses it.

In arguing for a metaphorical interpretation of John, I am suggesting
that John presents Jesus as a complex character. Any single metaphor
cannot encompass the scope of John's understanding of Jesus. In presenting multiple metaphors, the language of the Gospel suggests that
readers need a variety of metaphors to understand the character of Jesus.
The reader is not asked to choose between the various metaphors or
even to prioritize one over another. Each metaphor adds something to
the reader's understanding of a complex concept.[37] Each expresses something about Jesus that John wants the reader to understand as true.

The partial structuring of each metaphor leads to ambiguity in the
character of Jesus. In some cases, John's metaphors are not only distinct
but also somewhat divergent. The metaphors create ambiguity in the
character of Jesus when the terms of different metaphors conflict with
one another. In John 6, the reader who enters into the metaphorical
understanding of Jesus as manna comes to see Jesus as a gift that God
gave to the Israelites, through the assistance of Moses. Yet the story also
presents Jesus as Moses: like Moses, Jesus is sent by God (6:38–39, 44,
57), performs signs (6:2), ascends a mountain (6:3), and facilitates a
miraculous meal (6:10–12). In the intervening story of the disciples'
crossing the sea and Jesus' walking on water, Jesus is neither Moses
nor manna. Instead, the disciples experience Jesus as God: he is the

one with power over the waters, who comes to them as "I AM" (6:20), toward whom the disciples rightly respond with fear (6:19).[38]

On one level, this combination of metaphors does not make sense. In the exodus story, manna, Moses, and God are distinct narrative elements, and the distinctions between them are important to the story. How can Jesus be the manna that God gives and also be God, the giver of manna? Understood metaphorically, each image characterizes Jesus in a different way. Jesus is Moses, one sent by God to provide for God's people in their time of need. He mediates God's word to the people. Jesus is God, whose power over the waters in the crossing of the Red Sea is present also in Jesus. Jesus is manna, a gift of God to sustain those who follow in God's ways. Partial structuring of metaphors means that the connection forged between the two terms of the metaphor is partial, not total. Jesus is not equated with Moses or manna or God; he "is" each of these things in some ways but not in others.

Some of the Gospel's most contradictory language about Jesus makes sense as metaphor. Jesus says both "The Father and I are one" (10:30) and also "the Father is greater than I" (14:28). Read on a literal level, the statements seem to be contradictory. Metaphorically, both statements can be understood to be true of the character Jesus. Jesus is one with the Father and distinct from him at the same time. As such, John's metaphors have the important theological function of preserving monotheistic belief: "The figurative classification of Jesus makes it possible . . . to express an intrinsic bond between God and Jesus without risking a blasphemous violation of the principal commandment."[39] As doctrine, the two statements end up being only confusing. But as metaphor, each conveys something important about Jesus' character.

By interpreting John in this way, I do not mean to refute Christian understandings of Jesus as divine. However, I do mean to argue that the language of John is not the language of the creeds, and that reading the Gospel as such runs the risk of missing much that John has to offer. When metaphors are assumed to offer nothing outside of traditional creedal formulations of Jesus' divinity, the reader will miss the ways in which the character of Jesus is distinct from the character of God. Many of the metaphors point to such distinctions in Jesus' role. As vine, Jesus is distinct from "the vinegrower," who undertakes the pruning of the vine (15:1–2). As "Son," Jesus is sent by God to save the world (3:17). As manna, Jesus does the will of the Father: he gives life (6:40). As such, these metaphors provide opportunities for the reader to explore the character of Jesus' relationship to God in a way that may

not presume doctrinal orthodoxy, but that may also bear fruit in terms
of the reader's theological understanding.

Reading John metaphorically has the advantage of giving each metaphor its own voice. It also results in a complex and ambiguous picture
of Jesus. Prioritizing one metaphor allows the interpreter to draw a clear
conclusion about the character of Jesus. But if each of John's metaphors
has something distinctive to contribute to the reader's understanding of
Jesus, such summary statements become difficult or impossible. John's
many metaphors for Jesus create a complex character.

DISCERNING THE CHARACTER OF JESUS

Symbolic readings promise the reader a "truth" about Jesus that corresponds to "transcendent reality." What does a metaphorical reading
have to offer? If John's metaphors are "true," they are true metaphorically: if the readers perceive their situation in such a way that the terms
the metaphor provides make sense, then the metaphor is understood
to be "true." Using the example of the conventional metaphor LIFE IS A
STORY, George Lakoff and Mark Johnson observe how we humans construct our lives in terms of stories: thus in telling your own "life story,"
you would likely employ various conventions of storytelling. You might
suggest how people you have encountered have played various "roles."
You might present events in a linear sequence. There are likely to be
particular settings and stages—perhaps even a climax—to the story.

> If you tell such a story and then say, "That is the story of my life,"
> you will legitimately see yourself as telling the truth if you do, in
> fact, view the highlighted participants and events as the significant
> ones and do, in fact, perceive them as fitting together coherently
> in the way specified by the structure of the narrative. The issue of
> truth in this case is whether the coherence provided by the narrative
> matches the coherence you see in your life.[40]

The metaphorical "truth" is not one of expressing a preexisting reality
but of enabling us to structure our conception of "reality."

The power of the Gospel's metaphors is to harness conventional
metaphorical thinking in order to create the possibility of new meaning.
Extending their discussion of the metaphor LIFE IS A STORY, Lakoff and
Johnson discuss Shakespeare's novel extension of this metaphor, "Life's

. . . a tale told by an idiot, full of sound and fury, signifying nothing."
This metaphor breaks the boundaries of conventional understandings
of stories. If it makes sense to us, it is because parts of our lives do not
conform to the conventions of storytelling. We understand the metaphor
because we are deeply familiar with the concept of life as a story. But to
ask, "Is Shakespeare's metaphor 'true' in an objective sense?" misses the
point.

> The real significance of the metaphor LIFE'S . . . A TALE TOLD BY AN
> IDIOT is that, in getting us to try to understand how it could be true,
> it makes possible a new understanding of our lives. It highlights
> the fact that we are constantly functioning under the expectation
> of being able to fit our lives into some coherent life story but that
> this expectation may be constantly frustrated when the most salient
> experiences in our lives, those full of sound and fury, do not fit any
> coherent whole and, therefore, signify nothing.[41]

The power of Shakespeare's metaphor is that it harnesses a conventional way in which we understand life; at the same time it may cause
us to see something new about our lives.

Reading John metaphorically asks the reader to look for a different
kind of significance within the Gospel's pages. It is not the significance of an eternal transcendent truth. It is, rather, the significance of
new understanding made possible by conceiving of Jesus as manna,
shepherd, or vine. In getting us to understand how it could be true,
the Gospel's metaphors make possible a new understanding of our
lives. For example, John 6:51–58 is an extension of Jesus' discussion
of the manna and is best read in relation to the manna story. Here
Jesus claims that manna is God's gift not only in the present but also
in the future. He points to a later eating that Christian readers of the
Gospel will likely hear as a reference to the Eucharist. By connecting
this later bread with Jesus' self-identification as manna, John associates the eating of eucharistic bread with manna. The extension of the
metaphor suggests a layer of meaning that is often lost in Christian
celebrations of the Eucharist: Jesus is present in the eucharistic meal as
manna. When manna is used to understand Jesus and the Eucharist,
the Christian meal becomes the wilderness meal, and the believer steps
into the shoes of the Israelites, those freed by God yet encountering the
challenges and frustrations of surviving in the wilderness. Eating this

bread suggests reliance on God for life; it is a means by which people learn to follow God's commands.

In using multiple metaphors to characterize Jesus, John invites the reader into an act of imagination. The reader enters into John's worldview and begins to conceive of Jesus in the various terms John offers. The metaphors also bring the reader into a relationship with the character of Jesus. John asks us to see ourselves as the wandering Israelites, grumbling against a God who has delivered us, fed by that same God when we follow Jesus' word. John asks us to see ourselves as sheep, for whom many perils and enemies exist, but to whom God sends (and is) a shepherd who will guide us to good pasture. John asks us to see ourselves as branches, organically united with Jesus the vine and pruned by the vinegrower so that we may produce good fruit. And the list goes on. By using many metaphors, John ensures that the character of Jesus will not be easily defined or narrowed to a single point. John's metaphors shape both an understanding of Jesus and a self-understanding that readers may explore and deepen with each reading of the Gospel. The outcome is not a firm doctrinal truth, but a relationship to the stories of Jesus and the stories of Israel that can enrich the life of faith.

BIBLIOGRAPHY

Anderson, Paul N. *The Christology of the Fourth Gospel: Its Unity and Disunity in the Light of John 6.* Tübingen: J. C. B. Mohr, 1996.

Attridge, Harold W. "The Cubist Principle in Johannine Imagery: John and the Reading of Images in Contemporary Platonism." Pages 47–60 in *Imagery in the Gospel of John: Terms, Forms, Themes, and Theology of Johannine Figurative Language.* Edited by Jörg Frey, Jan G. van der Watt, and Ruben Zimmerman. Wissenschaftliche Untersuchungen zum Neuen Testament 200. Tübingen: Mohr Siebeck, 2006.

Boismard, Marie-Émile. *Moses or Jesus: An Essay in Johannine Christology.* Translated by B. T. Viviano. Minneapolis: Fortress Press, 1993.

Borgen, Peder. *Bread from Heaven: An Exegetical Study of the Concept of Manna in the Gospel of John and the Writings of Philo.* Novum Testamentum Supplement 10. Leiden: E. J. Brill, 1965.

Brown, Raymond. *The Community of the Beloved Disciple.* New York: Paulist Press, 1979.

Bultmann, Rudolf. *The Gospel of John.* Philadelphia: Westminster Press, 1971.

Coloe, Mary L. *Dwelling in the Household of God: Johannine Ecclesiology and Spirituality.* Collegeville, MN: Liturgical Press, 2007.

———. *God Dwells with Us: Temple Symbolism in the Fourth Gospel*. Collegeville, MN: Liturgical Press, 2001.

Cullmann, Oscar. *The Johannine Circle*. Translated by J. Bowden. London: SCM Press, 1976.

Culpepper, R. Alan. *Anatomy of the Fourth Gospel: A Study in Literary Design*. Philadelphia: Fortress Press, 1983.

De May, Mark. "Mastering Ambiguity." Pages 271–304 in *The Artful Mind: Cognitive Science and the Riddle of Human Creativity*. Edited by Mark Turner. Oxford: Oxford University Press, 2006.

Fauconnier, Gilles, and Mark Turner. *The Way We Think: Conceptual Blending and the Mind's Hidden Complexities*. New York: Basic Books, 2002.

Gibbs, Raymond W. *The Poetics of Mind: Figurative Thought, Language, and Understanding*. Cambridge: Cambridge University Press, 1994.

Haenchen, Ernst. *John*. 2 vols. Hermeneia. Philadelphia: Fortress Press, 1984.

Harstine, Stan. *Moses as a Character in the Fourth Gospel: A Study of Ancient Reading Techniques*. Journal for the Study of the New Testament: Supplement Series 229. Sheffield: Sheffield Academic Press, 2002.

Hylen, Susan. *Allusion and Meaning in John 6*. Beiheifte zur Zeitschrift für die neutestamentliche Wissenschaft 137. Berlin: Walter de Gruyter, 2005.

Johnson, Mark. *The Body in the Mind: The Bodily Basis of Meaning, Imagination, and Reason*. Chicago: University of Chicago Press, 1987.

———. *The Meaning of the Body: Aesthetics of Human Understanding*. Chicago: University of Chicago Press, 2007.

Jones, Larry Paul. *The Symbol of Water in the Gospel of John*. Journal for the Study of the New Testament: Supplement Series 145. Sheffield: Sheffield Academic Press, 1997.

Koester, Craig R. *Symbolism in the Fourth Gospel: Meaning, Mystery, Community*. 2nd ed. Minneapolis: Fortress Press, 2003.

Lakoff, George, and Mark Johnson. *Metaphors We Live By*. Chicago: University of Chicago Press, 1980.

Lakoff, George, and Mark Turner. *More Than Cool Reason: A Field Guide to Poetic Metaphor*. Chicago: University of Chicago Press, 1989.

Lee, Dorothy A. *Flesh and Glory: Symbolism, Gender, and Theology in the Gospel of John*. New York: Crossroad, 2002.

Martyn, J. Louis. *History and Theology in the Fourth Gospel*. 3rd ed. Louisville, KY: Westminster John Knox Press, 2003.

Painter, John. "Johannine Symbols: A Case Study in Epistemology." *Journal of Theology for Southern Africa* 27 (1979): 26–41.

Schneiders, Sandra M. *Written That You May Believe: Encountering Jesus in the Fourth Gospel*. New York: Herder & Herder, 1999.

Thompson, Marianne Meye. "'Every Picture Tells a Story': Imagery for God in the Gospel of John." Pages 259–77 in *Imagery in the Gospel of John: Terms, Forms, Themes, and Theology of Johannine Figurative Language*. Edited by Jörg

Frey, Jan G. van der Watt, and Ruben Zimmerman. Wissenschaftliche Untersuchungen zum Neuen Testament 200. Tübingen: Mohr Siebeck, 2006.

Turner, Mark. *The Artful Mind: Cognitive Science and the Riddle of Human Creativity*. Oxford: Oxford University Press, 2006.

———. *The Literary Mind*. New York: Oxford University Press, 1996.

Van der Watt, Jan G. *Family of the King: Dynamics of Metaphor in the Gospel
according to John*. Biblical Interpretation 47. Leiden: E. J. Brill, 2000.

Zeki, Semir. "The Neurology of Ambiguity." Pages 243–70 in *The Artful Mind:
Cognitive Science and the Riddle of Human Creativity*. Edited by Mark Turner.
Oxford: Oxford University Press, 2006.

Zimmerman, Ruben. *Christologie der Bilder im Johannesevangelium: Die Christopoetik des vierten Evangeliums unter besonderer Berücksichtigung von Joh 10*.
Edited by Jörg Frey. Wissenschaftliche Untersuchungen zum Neuen Testament 171. Tübingen: Mohr Siebeck, 2004.

———. "Imagery in John: Opening Up Paths into the Tangled Thicket of
John's Figurative World." Pages 1–43 in *Imagery in the Gospel of John: Terms,
Forms, Themes, and Theology of Johannine Figurative Language*. Edited by
Jörg Frey, Jan G. van der Watt, and Ruben Zimmerman. Wissenschaftliche
Untersuchungen zum Neuen Testament 200. Tübingen: Mohr Siebeck,
2006.

9

Conclusion

I have argued that John's characters display ambiguity of different kinds. With certain characters, it is difficult for the reader to determine whether the character believes in Jesus or not. Nicodemus is one such character. Although many details suggest Nicodemus's belief, John does not give the reader clear-enough signals to decide. A second and more prominent ambiguity is that of characters who believe in Jesus and at the same time disbelieve or misunderstand a good deal about him. The Samaritan woman, Martha, the Beloved Disciple, the disciples, and even the Jews are such ambiguous characters. In addition, the Beloved Disciple's character is ambiguous in the sense that it is open to interpretation. John's language suggests that aspects of the character are metaphorical without clearly defining what conclusions the interpreter should reach. Finally, Jesus' character displays a different kind of ambiguity, one created by the many metaphors that characterize him. Jesus' character is unambiguously positive, yet the multiple metaphors John employs create an elusive character. The reader must simultaneously hold together multiple views of Jesus, some of which seem mutually exclusive or contradictory. These competing claims are all in some way possible and are necessary to understand his identity.

Although the ambiguities of these characters are somewhat different, each seems to function in similar ways. Ambiguities draw the reader into deeper understanding of Jesus' own character and of the role of the disciple of Jesus. Thus in assessing Martha's character, the reader discerns whether her understanding of Jesus is a good one from the perspective of the Gospel. Are her words and actions those of a faithful character? What does she understand about Jesus' words? What does it mean to be a faithful disciple when confronted by the death of a loved one? What does it mean for Jesus to be "the resurrection and the life"? Likewise, the characterization of the Jews in John 8 points to a key aspect of discipleship, the importance of one's own actions. Religious identity is not defined by birthright, but by doing the will of God, which in John's view includes loving Jesus and accepting his word (8:42–43). Ambiguity in the Jews' character also leads the reader toward deeper understanding of Jesus. The reader who perceives irony in John's portrayal of the Jews sees how their rejection of Jesus undermines their claims to follow God's word. Their misunderstanding leads them to deny their heritage as slaves and God's subsequent redemption (8:33), and their demands for Jesus' death lead them to declare allegiance to Caesar rather than God (19:15). In recognizing their misperceptions, the reader comes to see Jesus as the faithful continuation of the Jews' own ideals.

Ambiguity in Jesus' character may also lead the reader into deeper understanding of him. Each of John's metaphors involves the reader in an act of imagination, putting the character of Jesus into a relationship with an aspect of Jewish tradition. As the metaphors accumulate, the reader may come to see Jesus from various angles, each of which offers a distinct perspective. Many of the Gospel's metaphors also involve the reader, as one who eats Jesus' bread or is a branch connected to him. Ambiguity in the character of Jesus involves the reader in a theological task that does not end when the Gospel closes, but deepens as the reader returns again and again to understand different aspects of his character.

In conclusion, I discuss four implications of my reading of John's characters for some of the traditional scholarly questions surrounding the Gospel. Here I briefly identify four of these: the historical context in which the Gospel was produced, the theological content of belief in Jesus, the function of John's dualistic language, and the question of the ethics implied by the Gospel.

THE GOSPEL IN ITS ANCIENT CONTEXT

Literary methods like characterization do not provide a means of identifying a specific historical context for John. John's portrayal of individual characters may serve a number of purposes, but treating them as literary characters involves recognizing that they are constructed by the author for a purpose rather than reflective of actual historical persons or groups. The Samaritan woman does not represent a group of Samaritan believers or a certain type of believer, but is a character through whom the reader may encounter Jesus' gift of living water, and come to understand the importance of being a witness.

Although characters cannot be said to specify John's location, the reader can read the language of the Gospel within a plausible ancient context. It is still possible to ask: "What kind of community would produce such a writing?" "For whom would these characters make sense?" The picture of John's community that emerges from reading characters ambiguously differs strongly with other interpretations on one issue: John's relationship to Judaism. John's language is usually seen as marking a sharp break with Judaism. Having been placed on the negative side of the dualistic divide, the Jews are wholly separate from the Johannine community. In my interpretation, the Jews both believe and disbelieve (see chap. 7, above). As ambiguous characters, they are not altogether different from the disciples and other individual characters. Instead of rendering Judaism a separate and negative entity, the characterization of the Jews serves to heighten the irony of the Gospel. Each denial of Jesus brings evidence of the Jews' misunderstanding or rejection of their own tradition. This portrayal helps the reader to see how belief in Jesus is a faithful continuation of Judaism. The Gospel makes an argument for followers of Jesus as being central to Jewish tradition, not as distinct from and superior to it. Such characterization fits within a context in which John's community has not fully separated from other forms of Judaism. There is division among Jews over the role and identity of Jesus. But the argument of the Gospel is that those who understand the Jewish law and tradition embrace Jesus as Messiah.

The portrayal of other characters reinforces the importance of Jewish tradition. Jesus is characterized with a series of metaphors that put him into relationship with many important aspects of Jewish tradition. The reader who understands how Jesus "is" each of these things—word, vine, shepherd, and so forth—explores the importance of each image to Jewish tradition and enters into an act of creative comprehension in seeing Jesus as the extension of each. The characterization of Jesus suggests a Jewish-Christian community searching for ways to express new meaning within the framework of a tradition they affirm and draw upon. Other characters' interactions with Jesus are often centered around conventional metaphors like the spiritual "food" that God provides or being born as God's "child." Although they do it with mixed results, the characters are portrayed as doing what John also expects the reader to do: to draw on the images of Judaism to understand both the person of Jesus and the task of discipleship.

Viewed within a Jewish framework, the Gospel displays a remarkable feat of creative comprehension. John calls on readers to believe "that Jesus is the Messiah, the Son of God" (20:31). Yet what do these terms mean? An answer like this seems obvious to many Christians looking back at John's Gospel through two thousand years of doctrine and confession. But the answers that seem so natural to us—such as the notion that the Messiah was to be born of a virgin (citing Isa. 7:14) and suffer for people's sins (e.g., Isa. 53:3–4)—were not readily available to the author of the Gospel. This particular interpretation and combination of Scriptures did not exist before Jesus' death and resurrection. The Gospel of John shows evidence that first-century Jewish people might reasonably differ over what to look for in a Messiah (e.g., John 7:27, 41–42). Identifying Scriptures like the two from Isaiah and applying them to what they had seen and heard was an act of theological imagination by early Christians. I use the word "imagination" here in a positive sense, not to say that belief in Jesus as the Messiah is a figment of someone's imagination, but to indicate that the act of comprehension of this new religious experience was creative. For early Christians, the life, death, and resurrection of Jesus required new ways of using language to express new meaning. John cites neither Isaiah passage but draws on a great variety of images as a way of voicing a new religious understanding, one that he understands as faithful to its Jewish roots. As he does so, the reader catches a glimpse of this creative process.

THE MEANING OF BELIEF

Throughout the book, I have contrasted my reading with a common view of John's characters as "flat": characters either believe in Jesus or do not, and this response determines everything. Theologically, this reading of John serves to highlight the importance of belief and to present belief in Jesus as an either-or proposition for the reader as well. In engaging in this process of reading John's characters, readers are formed as a particular type of disciple. They are positioned to understand the message of the Gospel and to judge others accordingly. As such, readers are situated as "insiders." They are led to believe that "outsiders" can be easily identified.

When John's characters are viewed ambiguously, a different picture of the Gospel's message emerges. Belief and unbelief are still important categories for the reader to have in mind, and belief is the stated goal. But if belief is viewed only as complete belief along with perfect understanding of Jesus, none of the characters of the Gospel qualifies as a believer. For the Gospel's ambiguous characters to function as examples for the reader requires a different understanding of what it means to believe.

The ambiguity in John's characters suggests that belief is a process or spectrum rather than an all-or-nothing affair. Belief mingles with disbelief and misunderstanding through the Gospel. The Samaritan woman is an effective witness without clearly formed belief. Martha does not understand her own confession. The disciples are said to believe, yet many aspects of the narrative show disbelief and misunderstanding mixed in with their belief. Full understanding remains a future possibility.

Nor is belief confined to an identifiable moment within the Gospel story. There is not a singular, defining event for each character, after which everything falls neatly into place. Even the high moments that occur—Martha's confession in 11:27, the Beloved Disciple's belief at the tomb—are followed by qualifications suggesting that belief is not over. Both characters learn a great deal more about Jesus in the verses that follow. There is more for the disciple to discover and understand. Belief, then, appears partial and piecemeal rather than as a singular event.

The way that John characterizes Jesus through metaphor makes it difficult to imagine belief as a singular event. Each metaphor invites the reader into an act of creative comprehension, unfolding layers of meaning within the image and as a result understanding Jesus in a new way. The multiple metaphors of the Gospel provide further impetus for readers to return to the Gospel again and again, finding new meaning and belief. The characterization of Jesus reinforces the notion that belief is an ongoing process for the disciple.

Reading John's characters as ambiguous also highlights the content of the belief to which the reader is called. Bultmann's statement that I discussed in the introduction, "Jesus reveals nothing but that he is the Revealer,"[1] makes sense when characters are flat. They largely do not understand Jesus' words and appear on the scene only long enough to set up Jesus' self-revelation. In contrast, in my reading the characters of the Gospel show some comprehension of Jesus' words, and it is often in their attempts to understand certain aspects of Jesus' character that the reader is drawn further into the content of belief. The Samaritan woman, for example, has a lengthy conversation about many aspects of Jesus' identity. At the outset, he offers her "living water" (4:10). What does this offer involve? The Samaritan woman is curious enough to engage Jesus in a conversation on the matter. What she understands (or misunderstands) in that conversation may help the reader shed light on the offer of living water. As the reader interacts with the characters, belief in Jesus takes on content as belief in one who offers living water, or belief in one who is the bread of life. In each case, the content of belief is metaphorical, not doctrinal, but it is nonetheless a rich resource that John offers for theological reflection.

THE LANGUAGE OF CONTRASTS

In conventional wisdom, John's contrasting pairs function as descriptions of the world. There is "above" and "below," and nothing else. Characters must therefore be placed in one category or the other. In order to fit in the preferred category—being from above, walking in the light, believing in Jesus—the character must attain a standard of perfect belief. Ambiguity in a character's response to Jesus is simply evidence of being "from below" or "walking in darkness." John's language positions the reader to understand what the characters may not, creating a solidarity among readers as "insiders."

The Gospel does present contrasting categories for understanding responses to Jesus, but I have argued that the characters of the Gospel serve to blur rather than to reinforce these distinctions. Which of John's characters can be said to "walk in the light"? Which is "born from above"? If either of these phrases refers to a complete spiritual identity forged by belief in Jesus, then none of John's characters is a strong candidate for such designations. Yet at the same time the characters do not clearly fit the standards, they are upheld as exemplars for the reader. Early on, the disciples "believe in him" (2:11), an unqualified good. The Samaritan woman acts as a witness, a role to which all disciples are called (15:27). Martha's statement of faith in 11:27 corresponds closely to the Gospel's stated aim in 20:30–31. The presentation of exemplary characters who nonetheless do not fit the rhetoric of the Gospel suggests that the contrasts represent ideals rather than strict expectations for all who would follow Jesus.

Thus the language of contrasts may be read as a rhetorical framework rather than as a worldview. John's indirect characterization draws the reader into a process of discernment. John gives no explicit instructions for evaluating characters, nor is there one simple solution for each. Readers may arrive at different understandings of individual characters or may place emphasis on different aspects of the character of Jesus. John leaves these possibilities open. In this context, the framework of contrasts serves a useful purpose. There is a clear framework of standards, communicated metaphorically as "above and below," "light and darkness." Entering into the Gospel's worldview involves trying to understand how the characters of the Gospel should be understood and evaluating them according to the criteria John sets forth. John invites the reader into a process of discernment, asking questions like these: What does it mean to believe in Jesus? What does it look like to abide with Jesus and to love one another? The Gospel becomes a training ground for those who would seek understanding and belief. The act of reading John's characters draws the reader deeper into understanding the norms that the Gospel upholds.

THE ETHICS OF THE GOSPEL'S PERSPECTIVE

John's Gospel raises serious questions for readers who seek to understand what Christians should actually do in the world.[2] Yet it is true that the Gospel's language focuses much attention on Jesus while leaving the reader with little practical advice for everyday behavior. John contains few of the ethical commands of Jesus found in the Synoptic Gospels: there is no parallel in John to the exhortations of Matthew's Sermon on the Mount (Matt. 5–7). Yet a number of scholars point out that, though John does not provide many moral teachings, nevertheless the Gospel does create a worldview with ethical implications. So Richard Hays writes, John's "story of a 'man from heaven' who comes to reveal God's truth to an unbelieving world is fraught with ethical implications for the community that accepts the message and finds itself rejected by the world."[3] As some have argued, John has an ethos rather than an ethic.[4]

This approach to John has been fruitful. Interpreters have identified how the Gospel's language contributes to the formation of readers who are shaped by its outlook on the world. Wayne A. Meeks describes the Gospel's voice as "sharply sectarian, and culturally and politically subversive."[5] With other scholars, Meeks points to countercultural aspects of John's ethos. As Fernando F. Segovia argues, John's worldview is one in which "all powers-that-be as well as all human beings in the this-world lie and should lie under the ultimate and supreme power of the Word."[6] Jey Kanagaraj and Jan van der Watt discuss the Gospel's ethos as sharing the moral vision of the Decalogue, which would then shape the behavior of John's readers.[7] Gail R. O'Day explores the vocabulary of friendship in John, concluding that "friendship is one of the ways in which the revelation of God in Jesus is extended beyond the work of Jesus to the work of the disciples."[8] These approaches to the Gospel do not limit "ethics" to a search for moral teaching and hence can consider the broad implications of various aspects of John's language.

Even when the ethos of the Gospel is under consideration, the common reading of John's characters as flat may still leave the reader with questions about whether John's worldview is ethical. When John is read as having a sharply dualistic perspective, the application of the Gospel's standards to its characters may appear random or unfair. As Meeks notes, "The disciples do not understand any better than the others; they are saved, not because they are clever or right, but because they are chosen."[9] Characters are consigned to "walking in darkness" because of common human flaws. The standards of the Gospel seem unattainable, and the consequences of being deemed imperfect are severe. A further implication of this view is that the implied reader is meant to categorize people in dualistic terms. Determining whether characters are believers or unbelievers encourages readers to stereotype: the complexity of a character is lost in the attempt to assess characters simply as believers or unbelievers.

A related question is that the one exhortation with obvious ethical content, "Love one another" (John 13:34–35; cf. 15:12–17), commands love only toward those within the community. If love is central to the Gospel's teaching but is aimed only toward those inside John's community, then the ethos of the Gospel is parochial at best. However, recent scholarship emphasizes that the Gospel does not encourage believers to hate others; hatred is only identified as something that believers experience at the hands of others (15:18). In addition, Gail O'Day points out that following the command to love one another can in many cases be as difficult a task as loving one's enemies.[10] O'Day also argues that the inclusion of Judas in Jesus' act of footwashing, which serves as an example of love and service for Jesus' followers, suggests that the Gospel casts a wider net in terms of who is loved.[11]

My reading of John's characters suggests that in many cases it is difficult to tell who is an insider or outsider. If the reader's task is to divide characters into two categories, believers and unbelievers, the language of the Gospel makes such distinctions difficult. Is Nicodemus an outsider or an insider? John does not provide a single, clear answer. Readers of John have superior knowledge to characters in the Gospel, but this only leaves them with the task of discerning what to do with that knowledge. The reader is left to judge the sometimes quite vague words and actions of characters according to the standards the Gospel sets forth. Has Nicodemus "come to the light"? Does he understand the validity of Jesus' self-testimony? Does he believe that Jesus is King of the Jews, even in his death? There are not clear answers to these questions, but asking them forms the reader's judgment according to the standards of the Gospel. In chapter 3, John's language sets up standards by which Nicodemus may be judged: belief in Jesus (3:15–16, 18), coming to the light, and doing what is true (3:18–21). The standards are clear. It is the act of judgment that is complex. The reader may decide that positive and negative aspects of Nicodemus coexist. A reader may see Nicodemus's witness to Jesus through his burial as a good understanding of Jesus' identity, yet also understand that in the Gospel's worldview public testimony to Jesus is more faithful than private or secret testimony. This reader learns that a life of discipleship involves more than simple either/or judgments that place people inside or outside the community of God's faithful.

John's ambiguous characters assist in the formation of readers, but not readers as "insiders" with complete knowledge who judge others in black-and-white terms. Interpreting characters of the Gospel draws readers into a process of discernment. The rhetoric of the Gospel does set up ideal categories, but the fact that no one meets them suggests that it may not be wise or necessary to categorize people in these terms. "Walking in the light" serves as a metaphor to help the reader understand what it means to follow Jesus and the benefits of doing so, rather than as a shorthand for identifying insiders. Seeing the ways in which characters of the Gospel both meet these ideals and ultimately fall short may function as a mirror for the reader's own behavior. If even Jesus' disciples do not perfectly understand him, perhaps the reader is not expected to achieve perfect understanding either. John's readers may come to understand themselves as ambiguous characters.

BIBLIOGRAPHY

Bultmann, Rudolf. *Theology of the New Testament.* Translated by K. Grobel. New York: Charles Scribner's Sons, 1951–55.

Hays, Richard B. *The Moral Vision of the New Testament: A Contemporary Introduction to New Testament Ethics.* San Francisco: Harper Collins, 1996.

Kanagaraj, Jey J. "The Implied Ethics of the Fourth Gospel: A Reinterpretation of the Decalogue." *Tyndale Bulletin* 52 (2001): 33–60.

Matera, Frank J. *New Testament Ethics: The Legacies of Jesus and Paul.* Louisville, KY: Westminster John Knox Press, 1996.

Meeks, Wayne A. "The Ethics of the Fourth Evangelist." Pages 317–26 in *Exploring the Gospel of John: In Honor of D. Moody Smith.* Edited by R. Alan Culpepper and C. Clifton Black. Louisville, KY: Westminster John Knox Press, 1996.

Nissen, Johannes. "Community and Ethics in the Gospel of John." Pages 194–212 in *New Readings in John: Literary and Theological Perspectives.* Edited by Johannes Nissen and Sigfred Pedersen. Journal for the Study of the New Testament: Supplement Series 182. Sheffield: Sheffield Academic Press, 1999.

O'Day, Gail R. *The Gospel of John.* New Interpreter's Bible 9. Nashville: Abingdon Press, 1995.

———. "Jesus as Friend in the Gospel of John." *Interpretation* 58 (2004): 144–57.

Segovia, Fernando F. "The Gospel of John." Pages 156–93 in *A Postcolonial Commentary on the New Testament Writings.* Edited by Fernando F. Segovia and R. S. Sugirtharajah. New York: T&T Clark, 2007.

Van der Watt, Jan G. "Ethics and Ethos in the Gospel according to John." *Zeitschrift für die neutestamentliche Wissenschaft und die Kunde der älteren Kirche* 97 (2006): 147–76.

Notes

Chapter 1: Introduction

1. R. Alan Culpepper, *Anatomy of the Fourth Gospel: A Study in Literary Design* (Philadelphia: Fortress Press, 1983), 102.

2. Ibid., 104.

3. For this interpretation of Nicodemus, see, e.g., Wayne A. Meeks, "The Man from Heaven in Johannine Sectarianism," *JBL* 91 (1972): 54–55. On the Samaritan woman, see Peter F. Lockwood, "The Woman at the Well: Does the Traditional Reading Still Hold Water?" *LTJ* 36 (2002): 15; Sandra M. Schneiders, "Feminist Hermeneutics," in *Hearing the New Testament: Strategies for Interpretation* (ed. Joel B. Green; Grand Rapids: Wm. B. Eerdmans Publishing Co., 1995), 358. On the disciples and the Jews, e.g., see Culpepper, *Anatomy*, 115, 129; Craig R. Koester, *Symbolism in the Fourth Gospel: Meaning, Mystery, Community* (2nd ed.; Minneapolis: Fortress Press, 2003), 58, 62.

4. Colleen M. Conway, "Speaking through Ambiguity: Minor Characters in the Fourth Gospel," *BibInt* 10 (2002): 328. Cf. Marianne Meye Thompson, "When the Ending Is Not the End," in *The Ending of Mark and the Ends of God* (ed. Beverly Roberts Gaventa and Patrick D. Miller; Louisville, KY: Westminster John Knox Press, 2005), 69–72.

5. Culpepper, *Anatomy*, 115.

6. Although Nicodemus represents a group of people who misunderstand Jesus based on his signs, the overall point of the story is that "Jesus is incomprehensible" to Nicodemus. Meeks, "Man from Heaven," 57.

7. Ibid., 54.

8. Robert Scholes and Robert Kellogg, *The Nature of Narrative* (New York: Oxford University Press, 1966), 164. Cf. 123, 160–67. Scholes and Kellogg argue for a difference between Greek and Hebrew characters, noting that biblical characters often show change or development. For the application of this approach, see Culpepper, *Anatomy*, 103; David H. Johnson, "The Characterization of Jesus in Mark," *Did* 10 (1999): 3; David Rhoads, Joanna Dewey, and Donald Michie, *Mark as Story: An Introduction to the Narrative of a Gospel* (2nd ed.; Minneapolis: Fortress Press, 1999), 100–101.

9. See Aristotle, *Poetics* 6.7–21; 9.1–10. For this interpretation of Aristotle, see, e.g., John Jones, *On Aristotle and Greek Tragedy* (New York: Oxford University Press, 1962), 32–33. Aristotle's understanding of *ethos* (usually translated

as "character") is extended by Seymour Chatman, *Story and Discourse: Narrative Structure in Fiction and Film* (Ithaca, NY: Cornell University Press, 1978), 108–10; Malcolm Heath, *The Poetics of Greek Tragedy* (Stanford, CA: Stanford University Press, 1987), 114–19; Baruch Hochman, *Character in Literature* (Ithaca, NY: Cornell University Press, 1985), 145–46; Christopher Pelling, "Conclusion," in *Characterization and Individuality in Greek Literature* (ed. Christopher Pelling; Oxford: Clarendon Press, 1990), 257–58.

10. Scholes and Kellogg, *The Nature of Narrative*, 161.

11. See, e.g., Jeannine K. Brown, *The Disciples in Narrative Perspective: The Portrayal and Function of the Matthean Disciples* (Leiden: E. J. Brill, 2002), 50–52; Fred. W. Burnett, "Characterization and Reader Construction of Characters in the Gospels," *Semeia* 63 (1993): 6–15; Christopher Gill, "Character-Development in Plutarch and Tacitus," *CQ* 77 (1983): 469–87; Warren Ginsberg, *The Cast of Character: The Representation of Personality in Ancient and Medieval Literature* (Toronto: University of Toronto Press, 1983); David B. Gowler, *Host, Guest, Enemy, and Friend: Portraits of the Pharisees in Luke and Acts* (New York: Peter Lang, 1991), chap. 3; Petri Merenlahti, "Characters in the Making: Individuality and Ideology in the Gospels," in *Characterization in the Gospels: Reconceiving Narrative Criticism* (ed. David Rhoads and Kari Syreeni; JSNTSup 184; Sheffield: Sheffield Academic Press, 1999), 51; Christopher Pelling, ed., *Characterization and Individuality in Greek Literature* (Oxford: Clarendon Press, 1990); Meir Sternberg, *Expositional Modes and Temporal Ordering in Fiction* (Baltimore: Johns Hopkins University Press, 1978), 92; Richard P. Thompson, "Reading beyond the Text, Part II: Literary Creativity and Characterization in Narrative Religious Texts of the Greco-Roman World," *ARC* 29 (2001): 81–122.

12. Pelling, *Characterization and Individuality*, 254.

13. Robert Alter, *The Art of Biblical Narrative* (New York: Basic Books, 1981), 114–15; Erich Auerbach, *Mimesis: The Representation of Reality in Western Literature* (trans. Willard R. Trask; 1953; repr., Princeton, NJ: Princeton University Press, 2003), 20; Shimon Bar-Efrat, *Narrative Art in the Bible* (JSOTSup 70; Sheffield: Almond Press, 1989), 90–92; Adele Berlin, *Poetics and Interpretation of Biblical Narrative* (Sheffield: Almond Press, 1983), 23; Meir Sternberg, *The Poetics of Biblical Narrative: Ideological Literature and the Drama of Reading* (Bloomington, IN: Indiana University Press, 1985), 191, 525 n. 6. Many scholars draw on this understanding in relation to John's characters; e.g., Colleen M. Conway, *Men and Women in the Fourth Gospel: Gender and Johannine Characterization* (SBLDS 167; Atlanta: Society of Biblical Literature, 1999), 61–62; Koester, *Symbolism*, 37–38; Jeffrey L Staley, "Stumbling in the Dark, Reaching for the Light: Reading Character in John 5 and 9," *Semeia* 52 (1991): 55–80.

14. C. K. Barrett, *The Gospel according to St. John* (Philadelphia: Westminster Press, 1978), 169.

15. See also Culpepper, *Anatomy*, 115.

16. Examples of the mimetic view often cited among literary theorists include A. C. Bradley, *Shakespearean Tragedy: Lectures on Hamlet, Othello, King Lear, Macbeth* (1904; repr., London: MacMillan Education, 1986); Maurice Morgann, "Essay on the Dramatic Character of Sir John Falstaff," in *Shakespearian Criticism* (1777; ed. Daniel A. Fineman; Oxford: Clarendon Press, 1972).

17. Chatman, *Story and Discourse*, 116–19; Hochman, *Character in Literature*, 59–61; Shlomith Rimmon-Kenan, *Narrative Fiction: Contemporary Poetics* (2nd ed.; New York: Routledge, 2002), 33–34. The history of interpretation often bears witness to the way in which readers may speculate about the life of a character independent of their role in the text; e.g., see Raimo Hakola, "A Character Resurrected: Lazarus in the Fourth Gospel and Afterwards," in *Characterization in the Gospels: Reconceiving Narrative Criticism* (ed. David Rhoads and Kari Syreeni; JSNTSup 184; Sheffield: Sheffield Academic Press, 1999), 223–63; Jane Schaberg, *The Resurrection of Mary Magdalene: Legends, Apocrypha, and the Christian Testament* (New York: Continuum, 2004), chap. 4.

18. E.g., Jouette M. Bassler, "Mixed Signals: Nicodemus in the Fourth Gospel," *JBL* 108 (1989): 645–46; Culpepper, *Anatomy*, 104.

19. Bassler, "Mixed Signals," 646.

20. Koester, *Symbolism*, 4. See also Raymond F. Collins, "The Representative Figures of the Fourth Gospel—I," *DRev* 94 (1976): 28.

21. Koester, *Symbolism*, 103.

22. In this sense, Koester's understanding of symbolic language corresponds to the "substitution view" of metaphor. For a discussion, see Max Black, "Metaphor," *Proceedings of the Aristotelian Society* 55 (1954–55): 282; Raymond W. Gibbs, *The Poetics of Mind: Figurative Thought, Language, and Understanding* (Cambridge: Cambridge University Press, 1994), 212; George Lakoff and Mark Turner, *More Than Cool Reason: A Field Guide to Poetic Metaphor* (Chicago: University of Chicago Press, 1989), 120.

23. E.g., George Lakoff and Mark Johnson, *Metaphors We Live By* (Chicago: University of Chicago Press, 1980), 5. My view of metaphor comes from conceptual metaphor theorists like Lakoff and Johnson. Other works I have found especially useful include: Black, "Metaphor"; Gibbs, *The Poetics of Mind*; Mark Johnson, *The Body in the Mind: The Bodily Basis of Meaning, Imagination, and Reason* (Chicago: University of Chicago Press, 1987); Lakoff and Turner, *More Than Cool Reason*; Mark Turner, *The Literary Mind* (New York: Oxford University Press, 1996).

24. For further discussion, see Susan Hylen, *Allusion and Meaning in John 6* (Berlin: Walter de Gruyter, 2005), 135–45.

25. See my discussion in chap. 8, below.

26. Cf. D. François Tolmie, "The (Not So) Good Shepherd: The Use of Shepherd Imagery in the Characterisation of Peter in the Fourth Gospel," in *Imagery in the Gospel of John: Terms, Forms, Themes, and Theology of Johannine Figurative*

Language (ed. Jörg Frey, Jan G. van der Watt, and Ruben Zimmerman; WUNT 200; Tübingen: Mohr Siebeck, 2006), 353–67.

27. Elsewhere I address additional aspects of the usefulness of metaphor for reading John. See Hylen, *Allusion*, 59–74, 186–94.

28. Lakoff and Johnson, *Metaphors We Live By*, 158.

29. The emphasis on plot is partly the result of structuralism, which identified a character's role in relation to the plot. Algirdas Julien Greimas, *Sémantique structurale: Recherche de méthode* (Paris: Librairie Larousse, 1966), 172–79; Vladimir Propp, *Morphology of the Folktale* (trans. Laurence Scott; 2nd ed.; Austin: University of Texas Press, 1968), 25–65, 78–83. Although structuralism has fallen out of favor among literary critics, its influence is still seen in the emphasis on plot in understanding character in John. Some interpreters note this influence explicitly; e.g., see Culpepper, *Anatomy*, 102; Meeks, "Man from Heaven," 48–49 n.15.

Yet for some time there has been growing agreement that character is not limited to the function within the plot; e.g., see Chatman, *Story and Discourse*, 111–15; John A. Darr, *On Character Building: The Reader and the Rhetoric of Characterization in Luke-Acts* (Louisville, KY: Westminster/John Knox Press, 1992), 38–39; Frank Kermode, *The Genesis of Secrecy: On the Interpretation of Narrative* (Cambridge: Harvard University Press, 1979), 75–99.

30. Culpepper, *Anatomy*, 88. Bultmann does not discuss Jesus' identity as a matter of plot, but his understanding of Jesus' purpose permeates his commentary. He regularly refers to Jesus as "the Revealer." Rudolf Bultmann, *The Gospel of John* (Philadelphia: Westminster Press, 1971).

31. Rudolf Bultmann, *Theology of the New Testament* (2 vols.; New York: Scribner, 1951–55), 2:66, with original italics.

32. Culpepper, *Anatomy*, 89.

33. E. M. Forster, *Aspects of the Novel* (New York: Harcourt, Brace & World, 1927), chaps. 3–4; W. J. Harvey, *Character and the Novel* (London: Chatto & Windus, 1965), chap. 3.

34. Hochman, *Character in Literature*, 86–140. Hochman uses the term "symbolic" rather than "metaphorical." For the sake of clarity, and for the reasons outlined above with regard to metaphor, I avoid the use of the word "symbolic." This does not affect the usefulness of Hochman's analytic categories.

35. For discussion, see chap. 5, below.

36. See Gowler, *Host, Guest, Enemy, and Friend*, 55–75. Cf. Alter, *The Art of Biblical Narrative*, 116–17; Berlin, *Poetics*, 34–42; Adeline Fehribach, *The Women in the Life of the Bridegroom: A Feminist Historical-Literary Analysis of the Female Characters in the Fourth Gospel* (Collegeville, MN: Liturgical Press, 1998), 16; Elizabeth Struthers Malbon, *In the Company of Jesus: Characters in Mark's Gospel* (Louisville, KY: Westminster John Knox Press, 2000), 9–10; Mark Alan Powell, *What Is Narrative Criticism?* (Minneapolis: Fortress Press, 1990), 52; James L. Resseguie, *The Strange Gospel: Narrative Design and Point of View in*

John (BibInt 56; Leiden: E. J. Brill, 2001), 110; Rimmon-Kenan, *Narrative Fiction*; William H. Shepherd, *The Narrative Function of the Holy Spirit as a Character in Luke-Acts* (Atlanta: Scholars Press, 1994), 88–89; Joel F. Williams, *Other Followers of Jesus: Minor Characters as Major Figures in Mark's Gospel* (JSNTSup 102; Sheffield: JSOT Press, 1994), 61–66.

37. For a discussion of the role of the reader, see John A. Darr, "Narrator as Character: Mapping a Reader-Oriented Approach to Narration in Luke-Acts," *Semeia* 63 (1993): 43–60; Darr, *Character Building*, chap. 1; Francis J. Moloney, *Belief in the Word: Reading the Fourth Gospel: John 1–4* (Minneapolis: Fortress Press, 1993), chap. 1. As Darr notes, critics also build readers, an activity that includes historical inquiry. Darr, "Narrator as Character," 47–48.

38. On criteria for recognizing allusions, see Richard B. Hays, *Echoes of Scripture in the Letters of Paul* (New Haven, CT: Yale University Press, 1989), 29–32; Hylen, *Allusion*, 53–59.

39. Many interpreters make similar arguments regarding John's use of irony, metaphor, and misunderstanding; e.g., see Culpepper, *Anatomy*, 199; Hylen, *Allusion*, 193–94; Gail R. O'Day, *Revelation in the Fourth Gospel: Narrative Mode and Theological Claim* (Philadelphia: Fortress Press, 1986), 29–32.

Chapter 2: Nicodemus

1. With the exception of John Bligh, "Four Studies in St. John, II: Nicodemus," *HeyJ* 8 (1967): 40–51. Gabi Renz points out that a majority of premodern commentators viewed Nicodemus more positively. Gabi Renz, "Nicodemus: An Ambiguous Disciple? A Narrative Sensitive Investigation," in *Challenging Perspectives on the Gospel of John* (ed. John Lierman; WUNT 219; Tübingen: Mohr Siebeck, 2006), 272–73.

2. Craig L. Blomberg, "The Globalization of Biblical Interpretation: A Test Case—John 3–4," *BBR* 5 (1995): 1–15; J. Bryan Born, "Literary Features in the Gospel of John (An Analysis of John 3:1–12)," *Direction* 17, no. 2 (1988): 3–17; J. Duncan M. Derrett, "Correcting Nicodemus (John 3:2, 21)," *ExpTim* 112 (2001): 126; William C. Grese, "'Unless One Is Born Again': The Use of a Heavenly Journey in John 3," *JBL* 107 (1988): 677–93; M. Michel, "Nicodème ou le non-lieu de la vérité," *RSR* 55 (1981): 227–36; Jerome H. Neyrey, "John III—A Debate over Johannine Epistemology and Christology," *NovT* 23 (1981): 115–27; Karl Olav Sandnes, "Whence and Whither: A Narrative Perspective on Birth ἄνωθεν (John 3, 3–8)," *Bib* 86 (2005): 153–73; Kiyoshi Tsuchido, "The Composition of the Nicodemus-Episode, John ii 23–iii 21," *AJBI* 1 (1975): 91–103; Don Williford, "John 3:1–15—*gennēthēnai anōthen*: A Radical Departure, a New Beginning," *RevExp* 96 (1999): 451–61.

3. Jean-Marie Auwers, "La nuit de Nicodème (Jean 3, 2; 19, 39) ou l'ombre du langage," *RB* 97 (1990): 481–503; D. A. Carson, *The Gospel according to John*

(Grand Rapids: Wm. B. Eerdmans Publishing Co., 1991), 629; F. P. Cotterell, "The Nicodemus Conversation: A Fresh Appraisal," *ExpTim* 96 (1984–85): 237–42; Julius Graf, "Nikodemus," *TQ* 132 (1952): 65; Barnabas Lindars, *The Gospel of John* (NCB; London: Oliphants, 1972), 592; Francis J. Moloney, *Belief in the Word: Reading the Fourth Gospel: John 1–4* (Minneapolis: Fortress Press, 1993), 120; idem, *The Gospel of John* (SP 4; Collegeville, MN: Liturgical Press, 1988), 510; Gail R. O'Day, *The Gospel of John* (NIB 9; Nashville: Abingdon Press, 1995), 835; James L. Resseguie, *The Strange Gospel: Narrative Design and Point of View in John* (BibInt 56; Leiden: E. J. Brill, 2001), 120–27; Rudolf Schnackenburg, *The Gospel according to St. John* (3 vols.; New York: Seabury Press, 1982–90), 3:160; Mark F. Whitters, "Discipleship in John: Four Profiles," *WW* 18 (1998): 422–27.

4. Marinus de Jonge, *Jesus: Stranger from Heaven and Son of God: Jesus Christ and the Christians in the Johannine Perspective* (trans. John E. Steely, SBLSBS 11; Missoula, MT: Scholars Press, 1977), 39; Andreas J. Köstenberger, *John* (Grand Rapids: Baker Academic, 2004), 555; David Rensberger, *Johannine Faith and Liberating Community* (Louisville, KY: Westminster John Knox Press, 1996), 40; Dennis D. Sylva, "Nicodemus and His Spices," *NTS* 34 (1988): 148–49.

5. Jouette M. Bassler, "Mixed Signals: Nicodemus in the Fourth Gospel," *JBL* 108 (1989): 635. Other interpreters who read Nicodemus as ambiguous include Craig R. Koester, *Symbolism in the Fourth Gospel: Meaning, Mystery, Community* (2nd ed.; Minneapolis: Fortress Press, 2003), 45–47; Craig R. Koester, "What Does It Mean to Be Human? Imagery and the Human Condition in John's Gospel," in *Imagery in the Gospel of John: Terms, Forms, Themes, and Theology of Johannine Figurative Language* (ed. Jörg Frey, Jan G. van der Watt, and Ruben Zimmerman; WUNT 200; Tübingen: Mohr Siebeck, 2006), 418–19; Margaret Pamment, "Focus in the Fourth Gospel," *ExpTim* 97 (1985): 73.

6. Bassler, "Mixed Signals," 646. Cf. Blomberg, "Globalization," 7; Colleen M. Conway, *Men and Women in the Fourth Gospel: Gender and Johannine Characterization* (SBLDS 167; Atlanta: Society of Biblical Literature, 1999), 86; Edwyn Clement Hoskyns, *The Fourth Gospel* (ed. F. N. Davey; London: Faber & Faber, 1947), 211.

7. Contra Renz, "Nicodemus," 279–80, who argues that the reader must push Nicodemus into either a positive or negative category.

8. E.g., Bassler, "Mixed Signals," 637; Born, "Literary Features," 7; Raymond Brown, *The Gospel according to John* (2 vols., AB 29–29A; New York: Doubleday, 1966–70), 1:129, 135, 137. Bultmann argues that there is a connection between the story of Nicodemus and the preceding verses, but that Nicodemus should not be understood as a believer in signs; Rudolf Bultmann, *The Gospel of John* (Philadelphia: Westminster Press, 1971), 133.

9. D. Moody Smith argues that belief on this basis is at least a beginning. See D. Moody Smith, *John* (ANTC; Nashville: Abingdon Press, 1999), 94. Bassler

points out that Jesus' disciples also seem to have believed on the same basis in 2:11; Bassler, "Mixed Signals," 638.

10. On the relationship between signs and belief, see, e.g., Craig Koester, "Hearing, Seeing, and Believing in the Gospel of John," *Bib* 70 (1989): 327–48.

11. E.g., Auwers, "La nuit de Nicodème," 489–90; C. K. Barrett, *The Gospel according to St. John* (Philadelphia: Westminster Press, 1978), 171; Brown, *John*, 1:137–38.

12. Meeks understands Nicodemus's opening statement as a declaration of faith; see Wayne A. Meeks, "The Man from Heaven in Johannine Sectarianism," *JBL* 91 (1972): 54. Cf. O'Day, *John*, 549; Williford, "John 3:1–15," 453.

13. Cf. "Rabbi," in John 1:49; 4:31; 9:2; 11:8. In comparison with other characters, then, Nicodemus looks much like the disciples.

14. Cf. Barrett, *St. John*, 171; O'Day, *John*, 549.

15. Contra Derrett, who argues that God being "with" Jesus is not an adequate understanding; Derrett, "Correcting Nicodemus," 126.

16. Contra Brown, who writes, "It would be difficult to explain Jesus' unfavorable reaction if Nicodemus' faith were that profound"; Brown, *John*, 1:137.

17. E.g., Bultmann, *John*, 133; Raymond F. Collins, "The Representative Figures of the Fourth Gospel—I," *DRev* 94 (1976): 31, 36; de Jonge, *Jesus*, 30; C. H. Dodd, *The Interpretation of the Fourth Gospel* (Cambridge: Cambridge University Press, 1953), 303.

18. E.g., R. Alan Culpepper, *Anatomy of the Fourth Gospel: A Study in Literary Design* (Philadelphia: Fortress Press, 1983), 135.

19. Brown, *John*, 1:46, 50, 51; cf. 1:45.

20. Bassler, "Mixed Signals," 636–37.

21. E.g., Hoskyns, *Fourth Gospel*, 203; Félix Mosur, "Missverständnis und Ironie in der johanneischen Argumentation und ihr Gebrauch in der heutigen pfarramtlichen Praxis," in *Johannes-Studien: Interdisziplinäre Zugänge zum Johannes-Evangelium* (ed. Martin Rose; Zurich: Theologischer Verlag, 1991), 53; Williford, "John 3:1–15," 454.

22. E.g., Barrett, *St. John*, 171; Moloney, *John*, 92; O'Day, *John*, 549.

23. See, e.g., Exod. 4:22; Deut. 32:6; Hos. 11:1. Cf. *Jub.* 1:22–25. Other texts point to individuals as God's child: i.e., 2 Sam. 7:14; Ps. 89:27; cf. Wis. 5:5. For discussion, see Brown, *John*, 1:139–40; Bultmann, *John*, 137 n. 1.

24. A couple of other interpreters read these words in a more sympathetic manner, as I have here, although their interpretations differ from mine. See Bligh, "Four Studies," 44, 46; Hugo Odeberg, *The Fourth Gospel: Interpreted in Its Relation to Contemporaneous Religious Currents in Palestine and the Hellenistic-Oriental World* (Chicago: Argonaut, 1968), 48–49.

25. If Jesus' words are understood as harsh, this indicates that he has already passed judgment on Nicodemus's level of understanding. E.g., Bassler, "Mixed Signals," 637; Meeks, "Man from Heaven," 68.

26. Hoskyns, *Fourth Gospel*, 203, italics original.

27. Robert Kysar, "The Making of Metaphor: Another Reading of John 3:1–15," in *"What Is John?" Readers and Readings of the Fourth Gospel* (ed. Fernando F. Segovia; Atlanta: Scholars Press, 1996), 25–26; O'Day, *John*, 550.

28. Cf. Isa. 32:15; 44:3; Ezek. 36:25–26; Joel 2:28–29. For further parallels, see Barrett, *St. John*, 169; Brown, *John*, 1:131, 139; Cotterell, "Nicodemus Conversation," 241; Schnackenburg, *St. John*, 1:368–70.

29. Cf. Barrett, *St. John*, 175; Bultmann, *John*, 140–41; Moloney, *John*, 93; Schnackenburg, *St. John*, 1:371.

30. E.g., Moloney, *John*, 93–94; O'Day, *John*, 550.

31. Barrett, *St. John*, 175.

32. For some interpreters, Nicodemus's response here indicates that he is "honest" (Brown) or "objective" (Bultmann), not that he believes. See Brown, *John*, 1:330; Bultmann, *John*, 311; Hoskyns, *Fourth Gospel*, 325; Smith, *John*, 177.

33. E.g., Barrett, *St. John*, 274; Culpepper, *Anatomy*, 136.

34. E.g., Bassler, "Mixed Signals," 640; Brown, *John*, 1:325; Schnackenburg, *St. John*, 1:160.

35. Moloney, *John*, 255; Severino Pancaro, *The Law in the Fourth Gospel: The Torah and the Gospel, Moses and Jesus, Judaism and Christianity according to John* (NovTSup 42; Leiden: E. J. Brill, 1975), 142. Cf. Pancaro's earlier article on the subject: Severino Pancaro, "The Metamorphosis of a Legal Principle in the Fourth Gospel: A Closer Look at Jn 7, 51," *Bib* 53 (1972): 340–61.

36. Cf. Moloney, *John*, 255.

37. For Nicodemus as a representative of secret disciples in John's community, see Culpepper, *Anatomy*, 136; J. Louis Martyn, *History and Theology in the Fourth Gospel* (3rd ed.; Louisville, KY: Westminster John Knox Press, 2003), 88; Rensberger, *Johannine Faith*, 55; Smith, *John*, 94. Brown disagrees: Raymond Brown, *The Community of the Beloved Disciple* (New York: Paulist Press, 1979), 72 n.128.

38. Culpepper, *Anatomy*, 136; cf. Bassler, "Mixed Signals," 641.

39. Auwers, "La nuit de Nicodème," 499, 503.

40. E.g., Meeks, "Man from Heaven," 55; Sylva, "Nicodemus and His Spices," 148–49.

41. Smith, *John*, 101. Other interpreters argue that John must not have the law in view, because if he does so, Nicodemus would understand what he says. See Bultmann, *John*, 137 n. 1; Julius Wellhausen, *Das Evangelium Johannes* (Berlin: Georg Reimer, 1908), 16–17.

42. E.g., Born, "Literary Features," 5, 15; Culpepper, *Anatomy*, 135; Meeks, "Man from Heaven," 53. Renz is correct in pointing out that, whatever conclusion the reader draws about Nicodemus, the same process of shaping the reader takes place; Renz, "Nicodemus: An Ambiguous Disciple?" 280.

Chapter 3: The Samaritan Woman

1. For the first opinion, see Rudolf Bultmann, *The Gospel of John* (Philadelphia: Westminster Press, 1971), 192. For the second, Gail R. O'Day, *The Gospel of John* (NIB 9; Nashville: Abingdon Press, 1995), 570.

2. Clifton C. Black, "Rhetorical Criticism," in *Hearing the New Testament: Strategies for Interpretation* (ed. Joel B. Green; Grand Rapids: Wm. B. Eerdmans Publishing Co., 1995), 265.

3. See David Daube, "Jesus and the Samaritan Woman: The Meaning of συγχράομαι," *JBL* 69 (1950): 137–47.

4. Many interpreters note the implicit contrast between this story and that of Nicodemus. E.g., see Margaret M. Beirne, *Women and Men in the Fourth Gospel: A Genuine Discipleship of Equals* (JSNTSupp 242; Sheffield: Sheffield Academic Press, 2003), 67–104; Winsome Munro, "The Pharisee and the Samaritan in John: Polar or Parallel?" *CBQ* 57 (1995); O'Day, *John*, 546; Mary Margaret Pazdan, "Nicodemus and the Samaritan Woman: Contrasting Models of Discipleship," *BTB* 17 (1987): 145–48; Sandra M. Schneiders, "Feminist Hermeneutics," in *Hearing the New Testament: Strategies for Interpretation* (ed. Joel B. Green; Grand Rapids: Wm. B. Eerdmans Publishing Co., 1995), 357; Mark F. Whitters, "Discipleship in John: Four Profiles," *WW* 18 (1998): 424.

5. Most commentators read the nighttime setting of the Nicodemus story as reflective of his character but do not read the time frame of John 4 as a positive indication of the Samaritan woman's character; e.g., Raymond Brown, *The Gospel according to John* (2 vols., AB 29–29A; New York: Doubleday, 1966–70), 1:130, 169; Edwyn Clement Hoskyns, *The Fourth Gospel* (ed. F. N. Davey; London: Faber & Faber, 1947), 211, 240–41; O'Day, *John*, 548, 565.

6. For a few commentators, the setting at noon is not positive because of its association with light; it is a metaphor for the woman's disrepute. Women did not normally draw water in the heat of the day, so the woman's choice to do so points to her status in the community. If she were not viewed by others as a pariah, she would draw water in the morning with the rest of the women; e.g., see Whitters, "Discipleship," 424. This interpretation only makes sense if the woman is already understood to be a sinner. The timing of the story may be unusual, but drawing water at midday would not automatically have brought associations of sinfulness. For Whitters, both the darkness of Nicodemus's visit and the noon setting of the Samaritan woman's conversation have negative associations.

7. A number of interpreters read the woman's response as a rejection or mocking of Jesus; see Brown, *John*, 1:177. Others read her response simply as conveying surprise; e.g., Bultmann, *John*, 178; Hoskyns, *Fourth Gospel*, 241; O'Day, *John*, 565–66; Rudolf Schnackenburg, *The Gospel according to St. John* (3 vols.; New York: Seabury Press, 1982–90), 1:425.

8. Most interpreters convey some version of this approach; e.g., see George R. Beasley-Murray, *John* (WBC 36; Waco, TX: Word, 1987), 61; Beirne,

Women and Men, 88; Black, "Rhetorical Criticism," 268, 272; Brown, *John*, 1:177; Bultmann, *John*, 181; C. H. Dodd, *The Interpretation of the Fourth Gospel* (Cambridge: Cambridge University Press, 1953), 313; Robert Gordon Maccini, *Her Testimony Is True: Women as Witnesses according to John* (JSNTSupp 125; Sheffield: Sheffield Academic Press, 1996), 128, 131, 142; Stephen D. Moore, "Are There Impurities in the Living Water That the Johannine Jesus Dispenses? Deconstruction, Feminism, and the Samaritan Woman," *BibInt* 1 (1993): 209; Gail R. O'Day, "Narrative Mode and Theological Claim: A Study in the Fourth Gospel," *JBL* 105 (1986): 667; idem, *Revelation in the Fourth Gospel: Narrative Mode and Theological Claim* (Philadelphia: Fortress Press, 1986), 57–66; Steven M. Sheeley, "Lift Up Your Eyes: John 4:4–42," *RevExp* 92 (1995): 83.

9. John MacDonald, *Memar Marqah: The Teaching of Marqah* (BZAW 84; Berlin: A. Töpelmann, 1963), 2:47, 81. The metaphor also continues in Jewish writings: see *Sipre Deut.* 48; *y. Sukkah* 5a; *Gen. Rab.* 64b.

10. Contra Graydon Snyder, who argues that there are "inside" readers who would understand Jesus' words, and "outside" readers who would not. While an "outside" reader is possible in theory, the vast majority of readers, whether Christian or not, understand this water as metaphorical. See Graydon F. Snyder, "The Social Context of the Ironic Dialogues in the Gospel of John," in *Putting Body and Soul Together* (ed. Virginia Wiles, Alexandra Brown, and Graydon F. Snyder; Valley Forge, PA: Trinity Press International, 1997), 3–23.

11. This example comes from George Lakoff and Mark Johnson, *Metaphors We Live By* (Chicago: University of Chicago Press, 1980), 4–6.

12. The literal and figurative readings are not necessarily mutually exclusive. Cf. C. K. Barrett, *The Gospel according to St. John* (Philadelphia: Westminster Press, 1978), 197; Brown, *John*, 1:171; Schnackenburg, *St. John*, 1:420–21.

13. Craig Farmer argues that the Reformation interpreters first emphasized the idea that the woman is sinful; Craig S. Farmer, "Changing Images of the Samaritan Woman in Early Reformed Commentaries on John," *CH* 65 (1996). Many modern interpreters reiterate this approach; e.g., see Jo Ann Davidson, "John 4: Another Look at the Samaritan Woman," *AUSS* 43 (2005): 162; Charles Homer Giblin, "What Was Everything He Told Her She Did? (John 4.17–18, 29, 39)," *NTS* 45 (1999): 151; Hoskyns, *Fourth Gospel*, 237; Peter J. Scaer, "Jesus and the Woman at the Well: Where Mission Meets Worship," *CTQ* 67 (2003): 4, 6.

14. There are different versions of the literal interpretation of her husbands. Some commentators focus on the woman's entire sexual history as sinful: see Beasley-Murray, *John*, 61; Brown, *John*, 1:177; Dodd, *Interpretation*, 313; Giblin, "What Was Everything He Told Her She Did?" 151; William Hendriksen, *Exposition of the Gospel according to John* (vol. 4 of *New Testament Commentary*; Grand Rapids: Baker Book House, 1953), 164–65; Hoskyns, *Fourth Gospel*, 242; Teresa Okure, *The Johannine Approach to Mission: A Contextual Study of John 4:1–42* (WUNT 31; Tübingen: Mohr Siebeck, 1988), 184; Scaer, "Jesus and the Woman at the Well," 4. For others, it is her present state: Davidson, "Another

Look," 15; George Hogarth Carnaby MacGregor, *The Gospel of John* (New York: Harper & Brothers Publishers, 1937), 101; Francis J. Moloney, *The Gospel of John* (SP 4; Collegeville, MN: Liturgical Press, 1988), 127. Craig Farmer points out that this interpretation first gained credence in the Reformation, when Reformers saw the woman as needing to recognize her own sinful nature; Farmer, "Changing Images." Cf. Jean Calvin, *The Gospel according to St. John 1–10* (ed. David W. Torrance and Thomas F. Torrance; Grand Rapids: Wm. B. Eerdmans Publishing Co., 1961), 93–94.

15. See Davidson, "Another Look," 165; Peter F. Lockwood, "The Woman at the Well: Does the Traditional Reading Still Hold Water?" *LTJ* 36 (2002): 15–17; O'Day, *John*, 567.

16. Some rabbinic writings point to the idea that one should marry no more than three times; see Hermann L. Strack and Paul Billerbeck, *Kommentar zum Neuen Testament* (Munich: C. H. Becksche Verlangsbuchhandlung, 1924), 2:437. However, this textual evidence is not sufficient to show that such a view was widespread or that those who did marry more frequently were understood as sinners as a result.

17. Black, "Rhetorical Criticism," 270. Black's elaboration of this allusion is helpful. A number of other scholars have identified the allusion, usually drawing on Robert Alter's understanding of the well betrothal as an OT "type story." Robert Alter, "Biblical Type-Scenes and the Uses of Convention," in *The Art of Biblical Narrative* (New York: Basic Books, 1981), 47–62; cf. e.g., Ellen B. Aitken, "At the Well of Living Water: Jacob Traditions in John 4," in *The Interpretation of Scripture in Early Judaism and Christianity* (ed. Craig A. Evans; JSPSup 33; Sheffield: Sheffield Academic Press, 2000), 342–52; Calum M. Carmichael, "Marriage and the Samaritan Woman," *NTS* 26 (1980), 332–46; Joan E. Cook, "Wells, Women, and Faith," in *Proceedings of the Eastern Great Lakes and Midwest Biblical Societies* (ed. Benjamin Fiore; Buffalo, NY: Eastern Great Lakes and Midwest Biblical Societies, 1997), 11–19; Sandra M. Schneiders, "Inclusive Discipleship (John 4:1–42)," in *Written That You May Believe: Encountering Jesus in the Fourth Gospel* (New York: Herder & Herder, 1999), 135.

18. Cf. Carmichael, "Marriage," 332–46; Dodd, *Interpretation*, 313; Hoskyns, *Fourth Gospel*, 242–43; Craig Koester, "The Savior of the World (John 4:42)," *JBL* 109 (1990): 669; Lockwood, "Woman at the Well," 15–16; Scaer, "Jesus and the Woman at the Well," 7–8; Schneiders, "Feminist Hermeneutics," 360–61; Sandra M. Schneiders, *Written That You May Believe: Encountering Jesus in the Fourth Gospel* (New York: Herder & Herder, 1999), 138.

19. For a discussion of criteria for evaluating allusions, see Richard B. Hays, *Echoes of Scripture in the Letters of Paul* (New Haven, CT: Yale University Press, 1989), 29–32; Susan Hylen, *Allusion and Meaning in John 6* (Berlin: Walter de Gruyter, 2005), 57–59. By the same criteria, the interpretation of the woman's five husbands as symbolic of the five Samaritan cults or five nations that colonized Samaria seems less likely to be recognized by early readers; see Dodd, *Interpretation*,

313; Koester, "Savior," 675. The reading relies on the idea that the number five would immediately call to mind Samaria's colonizers or cults. On the other hand, the topic of "husbands" as an OT metaphor for idolatry seems likely to have been known. If recognized by a reader, the idea of five cults could contribute to the idolatry metaphor. But this is not a necessary step in recognizing the idolatry allusion.

20. See O'Day, *John*, 569; Scaer, "Jesus and the Woman at the Well," 9; Schneiders, "Feminist Hermeneutics," 363; Whitters, "Discipleship," 425. Many take it literally, as a simple detail that John includes: e.g., Beasley-Murray, *John*, 63; Bultmann, *John*; Daube, "συγχράομαι," 138; Schnackenburg, *St. John*, 1:443.

21. O'Day, "Narrative Mode," 667.

22. Jesus' "I am" statement may also be read as a revelation of Jesus as God, because the Greek phrase alludes to the name of God (Exod. 3:14; cf. John 8:24; 18:5, 6, 8). There is no indication that the Samaritan woman understands this at this point.

23. For some interpreters, the woman never does understand Jesus adequately; e.g., see Maccini, *Her Testimony Is True*, 142; O'Day, *Revelation*, 76.

24. The Greek construction of the question can be construed either as expecting a negative answer or as simply tentative. The latter seems more likely in this case, given the context. She is at least holding out the possibility that Jesus is the Messiah, an identification that the Samaritan people later confirm (4:42). For a discussion of the Greek syntax, see Friedrich Blass and Albert Debrunner, *Grammatik des neutestamentlichen Griechisch* (14th ed. Göttingen: Vandenhoeck & Ruprecht, 1975), 356; James Hope Moulton, *A Grammar of New Testament Greek* (Edinburgh: T&T Clark, 1963), 283.

25. E.g., Maccini, *Her Testimony Is True*, 121.

26. See, e.g., David E. Aune, *Prophecy in Early Christianity and the Ancient Mediterranean World* (Grand Rapids: Wm. B. Eerdmans Publishing Co., 1983).

27. A few interpreters read these verses as contrasting the disciples and Jesus; e.g., see Élian Cuvillier, "La figure des disciples en Jean 4," *NTS* 42 (1996): 253; Pazdan, "Nicodemus and the Samaritan Woman," 148; Sheeley, "Lift Up," 85.

28. As elsewhere, John indicates that the eschaton has already begun in the life of Jesus, although a future element is also maintained (i.e., "the hour is coming and is now here," 4:23; cf. 6:40).

29. Frances Taylor Gench, "The Samaritan Woman: John 4:1–42," in *Back to the Well: Women's Encounters with Jesus in the Gospels* (Louisville, KY: Westminster John Knox Press, 2004), 118–19.

Chapter 4: The Disciples

1. On the importance of belief in the disciples' character, see Rudolf Bultmann, *The Gospel of John* (Philadelphia: Westminster Press, 1971), 589; Claude Coulot, "Les figures du maître et de ses disciples dans les premiere communautés chrétiennes," *RevScRel* 59 (1985): 10; R. Alan Culpepper, *Anatomy of the Fourth*

Gospel: A Study in Literary Design (Philadelphia: Fortress Press, 1983), 115; Rudolf Schnackenburg, *The Gospel according to St. John* (3 vols.; New York: Seabury Press, 1982–90), 3:206; Fernando F. Segovia, "'Peace I Leave with You; My Peace I Give to You': Discipleship in the Fourth Gospel," in *Discipleship in the New Testament* (ed. Fernando F. Segovia; Minneapolis: Fortress Press, 1985), 78, 90.

2. In each instance the Greek is in the aorist tense, which suggests that the disciples' belief is a onetime event that has not happened yet. John could also have employed the present tense, which would imply that the disciples already believe and will continue to do so when certain events come to pass. The aorist tense carries a stronger sense that the disciples do not yet believe.

3. Culpepper, *Anatomy*, 115; cf. Schnackenburg, *St. John*, 3:207; Segovia, "Peace I Leave with You," 90–91.

4. Wayne A. Meeks, "The Man from Heaven in Johannine Sectarianism," *JBL* 91 (1972): 68.

5. E.g., ibid., 69.

6. See my discussion of the Samaritan woman in chap. 3, above.

7. Cf. Élian Cuvillier, "La figure des disciples en Jean 4," *NTS* 42 (1996): 245–59.

8. See also C. K. Barrett, *The Gospel according to St. John* (Philadelphia: Westminster Press, 1978), 201; Bultmann, *John*, 195 n. 2; Schnackenburg, *St. John*, 2:446.

9. Cuvillier, "Figure des disciples," 253.

10. Segovia discusses this as "counterbalancing"; see Segovia, "Peace I Leave with You," 76–102.

11. Francis J. Moloney, *The Gospel of John* (SP 4; Collegeville, MN: Liturgical Press, 1988), 140; Gail R. O'Day, *The Gospel of John* (NIB 9; Nashville: Abingdon Press, 1995), 572.

12. See Susan Hylen, *Allusion and Meaning in John 6* (Berlin: Walter de Gruyter, 2005), 131–34; Gail R. O'Day, "John 6:15–21: Jesus Walking on Water as Narrative Embodiment of Johannine Christology," in *Critical Readings of John 6* (ed. R. Alan Culpepper; BibInt 22; Leiden: E. J. Brill, 1997), 149–59.

13. For a discussion of the background of the "I am" sayings in John, see Raymond Brown, *The Gospel according to John* (2 vols., AB 29–29A; New York: Doubleday, 1966–1970), 2:535–38.

14. See Bultmann, *John*, 433–51.

15. E.g., Barrett, *St. John*, 251.

16. Ludger Schenke, "Das johanneische Schisma und die 'Zwölf' (Johannes 6.60–71)," *NTS* 38 (1992): 113.

17. See Schnackenburg, *St. John*, 2:73; cf. Barrett, *St. John*, 251; Moloney, *John*, 228.

18. John rarely uses the designation "the twelve" (cf. 20:24) and more commonly indicates an unspecified group of disciples, including places where the Twelve might be expected, such as the Last Supper (cf. Matt. 26:20).

19. E.g., Brown, *John*, 1:301; Bultmann, *John*, 443; Edwyn Clement Hoskyns, *The Fourth Gospel* (ed. F. N. Davey; London: Faber & Faber, 1947), 302; Andreas J. Köstenberger, *John* (Grand Rapids: Baker Academic, 2004), 218.

20. Cf. Brown, *John*, 1:432; O'Day, *John*, 687.

21. Cf. Barrett, *St. John*, 326–27; Hoskyns, *Fourth Gospel*, 401.

22. Culpepper sees this as a repeated pattern in the Gospel; Moloney argues that their misunderstanding is intensified here. See Culpepper, *Anatomy*, 117–18; Moloney, *John*, 327.

23. Cf. J. A. du Rand, "Narratological Perspectives on John 13:1–38," *HvTSt* 46 (1990): 376–80; Segovia, "Peace I Leave with You," 86. See also Segovia's discussion of 13:31–38; Fernando F. Segovia, "The Structure, *Tendenz*, and *Sitz im Leben* of John 13:31–14:31," *JBL* 104 (1985): 479–81.

24. Cf. Bultmann, *John*, 557.

25. The Greek syntax can also be translated as a sentence, as in the NIV: "You believe at last." However, the question fits the context better. See O'Day, *John*, 783. Either way, Jesus' words about the disciples' scattering contrast with their presumed belief.

26. Cf. Hoskyns, *Fourth Gospel*, 491.

27. Brown, *John*, 1:78.

28. Culpepper, *Anatomy*, 116.

29. O'Day, *John*, 531.

30. The disciples are spoken of in John 7:3 and 8:31, but not in ways that indicate their presence.

31. Segovia, "John 13:31–14:31," 478.

32. Wayne A. Meeks, "The Man from Heaven in Johannine Sectarianism," *JBL* 91 (1972): 69.

33. Both Meeks and Segovia describe the perfection of the disciples in contrast to the character of the Jews; ibid.; Segovia, "Peace I Leave with You," 81, 85, 89. On this subject, see chapter 7.

34. Segovia, "John 13:31–14:31," 475. Cf. Brown, *John*, 2:736; Köstenberger, *John*, 478; Uta Poplutz, "Paroimia und Parabole: Gleichniskonzepte bei Johannes und Markus," in *Imagery in the Gospel of John: Terms, Forms, Themes, and Theology of Johannine Figurative Language* (ed. Jörg Frey, Jan G. van der Watt, and Ruben Zimmerman; WUNT 200; Tübingen: Mohr Siebeck, 2006), 117–20; Marianne Meye Thompson, "The Breath of Life: John 20:22–23 Once More," in *Holy Spirit and Christian Origins: Essays in Honor of James D. G. Dunn* (ed. Graham N. Stanton, Bruce W. Longenecker, and Stephen Barton; Grand Rapids: Wm. B. Eerdmans Publishing Co., 2004), 69–78.

35. Cf. Moloney, *John*, 530, 532–33; O'Day, *John*, 846.

36. Cf. Moloney, *John*, 531; O'Day, *John*, 849–50.

37. Cf., e.g., Bultmann, *John*, 692; Hoskyns, *Fourth Gospel*, 474; Thompson, "Breath of Life," 69–78.

38. Cf. O'Day, *John*, 849.

39. Barrett, *St. John*, 482. Brown argues that this incongruity suggests that the fishing story was originally an independent resurrection story; Brown, *John*, 2:1070.

40. For example, see Bultmann, *John*, 261; Rudolf Bultmann, "Ζάω," in *Theological Dictionary of the New Testament* (ed. Gerhard Kittel; vol. 2; Grand Rapids: Wm. B. Eerdmans Publishing Co., 1964), 870–71. Cf. Brown's discussion of composition and eschatology: Brown, *John*, 1:cxx–cxxi. See also Thompson's critique of this approach: Marianne Meye Thompson, *The God of the Gospel of John* (Grand Rapids: Wm. B. Eerdmans Publishing Co., 2001), 81.

41. Moloney, *John*, 533.

42. Contra Thompson, who argues that John reserves "resurrection" as a future event, while offering "life" to believers in the present; see Thompson, *God*, 86; Marianne Meye Thompson, "When the Ending Is Not the End," in *The Ending of Mark and the Ends of God* (ed. Beverly Roberts Gaventa and Patrick D. Miller; Louisville, KY: Westminster John Knox Press, 2005), 73. See my discussion of John 11 in chap. 5, below.

For a discussion of expectations of the last day such as life, resurrection, and judgment, see C. H. Dodd, *The Interpretation of the Fourth Gospel* (Cambridge: Cambridge University Press, 1953), 144–50; Schnackenburg, *St. John*, 2:428.

43. I am indebted to Ted A. Smith for his understanding of an eschatological perspective on history; see Ted A. Smith, *The New Measures: A Theological History of Democratic Practice* (Cambridge: Cambridge University Press, 2007), 10–13.

44. Culpepper, *Anatomy*, 115.

Chapter 5: Martha and Mary

1. Sandra M. Schneiders, "Death in the Community of Eternal Life: History, Theology, and Spirituality in John 11," *Int* 41 (1987): 52.

2. Francis J. Moloney, "The Faith of Martha and Mary: A Narrative Approach to John 11, 17–40," *Bib* 75 (1994): 493.

3. Francis J. Moloney, "Can Everyone Be Wrong? A Reading of John 11.1–12.8," *NTS* 49 (2003): 514–15.

4. Rudolf Schnackenburg, *The Gospel according to St. John* (3 vols.; New York: Seabury Press, 1982–90), 2:333.

5. E.g., George R. Beasley-Murray, *John* (WBC 36; Waco, TX: Word, 1987), 190; Schnackenburg, *St. John*, 2:329. Calvin comes closest to a negative view of Martha's words, though he writes, "I acknowledge that her words came from faith partly; but I say that disorderly passions were mixed with them and carried her beyond proper bounds." See Jean Calvin, *The Gospel according to St. John 11–21 and the First Epistle of John* (ed. David W. Torrance and Thomas F. Torrance; trans. T. H. L. Parker; Edinburgh: Oliver & Boyd, 1961), 7.

6. E.g., C. K. Barrett, *The Gospel according to St. John* (Philadelphia: Westminster Press, 1978), 328; Rudolf Bultmann, *The Gospel of John* (Philadelphia:

Westminster Press, 1971), 401; Wendy Sproston North, "Jesus' Prayer in John 11," in *The Old Testament in the New Testament: Essays in Honour of J. L. North* (ed. Steve Moyise; JSNTSup 189; Sheffield: Sheffield Academic Press, 2000), 169; Barbara E. Reid, "The Cross and Cycles of Violence," *Int* 58 (2004): 381–82.

7. Francis J. Moloney, *The Gospel of John* (SP 4; Collegeville, MN: Liturgical Press, 1988), 327.

8. Ibid.

9. E.g., Edwyn Clement Hoskyns, *The Fourth Gospel* (ed. F. N. Davey; London: Faber & Faber, 1947), 401–2; Gail R. O'Day, *The Gospel of John* (NIB 9; Nashville: Abingdon Press, 1995), 688; Satako Yamaguchi, "Christianity and Women in Japan," *JJRS* 30 (2003): 331.

10. E.g., Beasley-Murray, *John*, 190; Hoskyns, *Fourth Gospel*, 402; Schnackenburg, *St. John*, 2:330.

11. Contra Thompson, who argues that Jesus' gift of life is present, while resurrection remains in the future; see Marianne Meye Thompson, *The God of the Gospel of John* (Grand Rapids: Wm. B. Eerdmans Publishing Co., 2001), 82–83; idem, "When the Ending Is Not the End," in *The Ending of Mark and the Ends of God* (ed. Beverly Roberts Gaventa and Patrick D. Miller; Louisville, KY: Westminster John Knox Press, 2005), 73.

12. I find this position most clearly articulated by Gail O'Day and C. H. Dodd; see C. H. Dodd, *The Interpretation of the Fourth Gospel* (Cambridge: Cambridge University Press, 1953), 148; O'Day, *John*, 688–89.

13. E.g., Donald L. Bretherton, "Lazarus of Bethany: Resurrection or Resuscitation?" *ExpTim* 104 (1993): 171; Bultmann, *John*, 403–4; James P. Martin, "History and Eschatology in the Lazarus Narrative: John 11.1–44," *SJT* 17 (1964): 338; Thompson, "When the Ending Is Not the End," 73. Similarly, for many interpreters the raising of Lazarus prefigures later Christian resurrection; see Philip F. Esler and Ronald A. Piper, *Lazarus, Mary and Martha: A Social-Scientific and Theological Reading of John* (London: SCM Press, 2006), 125, 153.

14. This definition of "eternal life" is similar to what the Synoptic Gospel writers seem to mean by the term. They speak of eternal life as a future inheritance (e.g., Matt. 19:29; 25:46; Mark 10:30; Luke 18:30).

15. Schneiders, "Death," 53. See also W. H. Cadman, "The Raising of Lazarus (John 10, 40–11, 53)," in *Studia evangelica*, vol. 1 (ed. Kurt Aland et al.; TU 73; Berlin: Akademie-Verlag, 1959), 432–33; Raymond F. Collins, "The Representative Figures of the Fourth Gospel—I," *DRev* 94 (1976): 46; Colleen M. Conway, *Men and Women in the Fourth Gospel: Gender and Johannine Characterization* (SBLDS 167; Atlanta: Society of Biblical Literature, 1999), 142; Miguel Rodríguez-Ruiz, "Significado cristológico y soteriológico de Jn 11, 25–27," *EstBíb* 55 (1997): 199; Turid Karlsen Seim, "Roles of Women in the Gospel of John," in *Aspects on the Johannine Literature* (ed. Lars Hartman and Birger Olsson; ConBNT 18; Uppsala: Almqvist & Wiksell International, 1987), 71.

A number of interpreters applaud Martha's faith because she believes before Jesus' sign. Her faith is not dependent on signs; e.g., Adele Reinhartz, "From Narrative to History: The Resurrection of Mary and Martha," in *Women Like This: New Perspectives on Jewish Women in the Greco-Roman World* (ed. Amy-Jill Levine; Atlanta: Scholars Press, 1991), 178; John Rena, "Women in the Gospel of John," *ÉgT* 17 (1986): 141. This conclusion is weakened by Martha's previous words in 11:21–22, where she has declared her belief in Jesus' ability to heal. Also see my discussion of faith and signs in chapter 2, above.

16. Francis Moloney suggests that the use of the perfect tense in the words "I believe" (πεπίστευκα, *pepisteuka*) in 11:27 shows Martha's prior belief in Jesus, indicating that what she believes is not affected by her current conversation with him. Moloney, "Can Everyone Be Wrong?" 513–14. Many interpreters reject this reading of *pepisteuka*; e.g., see Barrett, *St. John*, 330; Conway, *Men and Women*, 141; O'Day, *John*, 689.

17. Many interpreters argue that Martha's expression of faith is a good one, although she does not fully understand what she says; e.g., see Raymond Brown, *The Gospel according to John* (2 vols., AB 29–29A; New York: Doubleday, 1966–70), 1:434–35. Francis Moloney goes further to argue that Martha's faith is inadequate. Moloney, "Can Everyone Be Wrong?" 509, 511, 514, 520; idem, "The Faith of Martha and Mary," 477.

Interpreters who explain Martha's reaction as human nature or as beyond what is humanly possible include Esler and Piper, *Lazarus, Mary and Martha*, 120; O'Day, *John*, 691; Sandra M. Schneiders, *Written That You May Believe: Encountering Jesus in the Fourth Gospel* (New York: Herder & Herder, 1999), 159–60. Conway concludes that Martha is ambiguous, yet her overall evaluation of her character does not reflect this ambiguity; see Conway, *Men and Women*, 150, 201.

18. The metaphors John uses here speak to one of the deepest mysteries of the life of faith and are difficult to describe in terms other than the metaphors John uses. Descriptions of this "life" as "spiritual life" fall short of capturing the force of John's language here, because the "life" that Lazarus receives is the most visceral, physical sort. See Beasley-Murray, *John*, 191; Brown, *John*, 1:434.

19. E.g., O'Day, *John*, 690.

20. E.g., Moloney, "Can Everyone Be Wrong?" 516.

21. E.g., T. E. Pollard, "The Raising of Lazarus (John xi)," *Studia evangelica*, vol. 6 (ed. Elizabeth A. Livingstone; TU 112; Berlin: Akademie-Verlag, 1973): 440; Rena, "Women in the Gospel of John," 141; Schnackenburg, *St. John*, 2:333; Mark W. G. Stibbe, "A Tomb with a View: John 11:1–44 in Narrative-Critical Perspective," *NTS* 40 (1994): 47.

22. E.g., Barrett, *St. John*, 331; Bultmann, *John*, 405; Reid, "Cross and Cycles of Violence," 382.

23. Some suggest that Martha returns to Mary "privately" (λάθρα, *lathra*, verse 28) "because of the known hostility of the Jews to Jesus." Thus Hoskyns,

Fourth Gospel, 405. However, others argue that the word simply identifies Martha's message as directed to Mary; e.g., see Bultmann, *John*, 405.

24. E.g., O'Day, *John*, 689–90.

25. Cf. Conway, *Men and Women*, 146.

26. Moloney, "Can Everyone Be Wrong?" 518.

27. E.g., Bultmann, *John*, 406; Hoskyns, *Fourth Gospel*, 405. For O'Day, Jesus' anger is directed only toward the Jews: O'Day, *John*, 690.

28. E.g., Barnabas Lindars, "Rebuking the Spirit: A New Analysis of the Lazarus Story of John 11," *NTS* 38 (1992): 89–104.

29. A few interpreters take Jesus' anger to be internally directed: e.g., see Cullen I. K. Story, "The Mental Attitude of Jesus at Bethany: John 11:33, 38," *NTS* 37 (1991): 51–66.

30. Jesus is not usually so agitated by the people's lack of faith or understanding. He elsewhere states his understanding that "no one can come to me unless drawn by the Father" (6:44; cf. 6:45, 65; 10:27–29).

31. Bultmann writes that "for the man who tarries in the earthly life and is a believer, there is no death in an ultimate sense; death for him has become unreal." See Bultmann, *John*, 403. See also the views of Moloney cited above.

32. Lazarus's death is in view here, but Jesus may also have in mind and be deeply disturbed by his own impending "hour." The link between Lazarus's death and Jesus' death has been identified in the prelude to the story (11:8) and becomes clear in the response of the council that follows (11:45–53). The verb "troubled" (ταράσσω, *tarassō*) occurs alongside *embrimaomai* in verse 33. It is also found in 12:27, where Jesus is clearly troubled about his own death. In 13:21, Jesus is also "troubled," either about his death and/or the fact of his betrayal.

33. Matthew and Mark include a similar objection, but only John's Gospel attributes this response to Judas (cf. Matt. 26:8–9; Mark 14:4–5).

34. E.g., Hoskyns, *Fourth Gospel*, 416; Moloney, "Can Everyone Be Wrong?" 525.

35. E.g., Brown, *John*, 1:441, 454; Bultmann, *John*, 416.

36. Dodd, *Interpretation*, 365.

37. O'Day, *John*, 701.

38. A similar argument is made by Yamaguchi, "Christianity and Women in Japan," 332.

39. O'Day, *John*, 703.

Chapter 6: The Beloved Disciple

1. The first quote is from Edwyn Clement Hoskyns, *The Fourth Gospel* (ed. F. N. Davey; London: Faber & Faber, 1947), 530. The second is from John J. Gunther, "The Relation of the Beloved Disciple to the Twelve," *TZ* 37 (1981): 134.

2. David J. Hawkin, "The Function of the Beloved Disciple Motif in the Johannine Redaction," *LTP* 33 (1977): 144.

3. E.g., Richard Bauckham, "The Beloved Disciple as Ideal Author," *JSNT* 49 (1993): 37; James H. Charlesworth, *The Beloved Disciple: Whose Witness Validates the Gospel of John?* (Valley Forge, PA: Trinity Press International, 1995), 326–36.

4. E.g., Paul Sevier Minear, "The Beloved Disciple in the Gospel of John," *NovT* 19 (1977): 117–18; Kevin Quast, *Peter and the Beloved Disciple: Figures for a Community in Crisis* (JSNTSup 32; Sheffield: Sheffield Academic Press, 1989), 71–89; John K. Thornecroft, "The Redactor and the 'Beloved' in John," *ExpTim* 98 (1987): 135–39. As Charlesworth argues, the use of the phrase "the other disciple" in reference to the Beloved in 20:2 does not provide sufficient evidence for this claim; Charlesworth, *Beloved Disciple*, 325–26. Interpreters have a tendency to interpret 18:15–16 on the basis of their understanding of the relationship between the Beloved and Peter elsewhere; the passage itself adds little to our understanding of this disciple. He functions only to facilitate Peter's entry into the courtyard of the high priest; his own actions are not narrated.

5. E.g., Rudolf Bultmann, *The Gospel of John* (Philadelphia: Westminster Press, 1971), 484; Eduard Meyer, "Sinn und Tendenz der Schlusszene am Kreuz im Johannesevangelium," in *Sitzungsberichte der Preussischen Akademie der Wissenschaften* (Berlin: Verlag der Akademie der Wissenschaften, 1924), 157–62.

6. E.g., E. F. Scott, *The Fourth Gospel: Its Purpose and Theology* (2nd ed.; Edinburgh: T&T Clark, 1908), 74–76; R. H. Strachan, *The Fourth Gospel: Its Significance and Environment* (London: SCM Press, 1941), 319.

7. For an example of those who do not support authorship by John, son of Zebedee, see Gail R. O'Day, *The Gospel of John* (NIB 9; Nashville: Abingdon Press, 1995), 498–500. For a modern expression of the traditional view, see Rudolf Schnackenburg, *The Gospel according to St. John* (3 vols.; New York: Seabury Press, 1982–90), 1:75–104.

8. I can do none of these arguments justice in such a small space. Many other possibilities exist. For a discussion, see Charlesworth, *Beloved Disciple*, chap. 3.

For identifications of the Beloved as Lazarus, see, e.g., Hugues Garcia, "Lazare, du mort vivant au disciple bien-aimé: Le cycle et la trajectoire narrative de Lazare dans le quatrième évangile," *RevScRel* 73 (1999): 259–92; Raimo Hakola, "A Character Resurrected: Lazarus in the Fourth Gospel and Afterwards," in *Characterization in the Gospels: Reconceiving Narrative Criticism* (ed. David Rhoads and Kari Syreeni; JSNTSup 184; Sheffield: Sheffield Academic Press, 1999), 223–63.

For identifications of the Beloved as Mary Magdalene, see Esther A. de Boer, "Mary Magdalene and the Disciple Jesus Loved," *Lectio* 1 (2000): 1–17; Sandra M. Schneiders, *Written That You May Believe: Encountering Jesus in the Fourth Gospel* (New York: Herder & Herder, 1999), 211–32.

For identification of the Beloved as Thomas, see Charlesworth, *Beloved Disciple*.

9. Adele Reinhartz offers a variety of functions of anonymity. Adele Reinhartz, *Why Ask My Name? Anonymity and Identity in Biblical Narrative* (New York: Oxford University Press, 1998). In studies of John, some scholars conclude that

anonymity helps render the Beloved an ideal or representative character; e.g., see David R. Beck, *The Discipleship Paradigm: Readers and Anonymous Characters in the Fourth Gospel* (BibInt 27; Leiden: E. J. Brill, 1997); Margaret Pamment, "The Fourth Gospel's Beloved Disciple," *ExpTim* 94 (1983): 363. Others suggest that anonymity helps to distinguish this disciple: Bauckham, "Beloved Disciple as Ideal Author," 43–44.

10. O'Day, *John*, 840. See also Raymond Brown, *The Gospel according to John* (2 vols., AB 29–29A; New York: Doubleday, 1966–70), 2:577.

11. E.g., Gunther, "Relation of the Beloved Disciple to the Twelve," 129–30; Arthur H. Maynard, "The Role of Peter in the Fourth Gospel," *NTS* 30 (1984): 536; Francis J. Moloney, *The Gospel of John* (SP 4; Collegeville, MN: Liturgical Press, 1988), 383; Graydon F. Snyder, "John 13:16 and the Anti-Petrinism of the Johannine Tradition," *BR* 16 (1971): 11–12; Sjef van Tilborg, *Imaginative Love in John* (Leiden: E. J. Brill, 1993), 91.

12. E.g., Richard Bauckham, "The Martyrdom of Peter in Early Christian Literature," in *ANRW* 26.1 (1992): 549–50; O'Day, *John*, 729; Quast, *Peter and the Beloved Disciple*, 69.

13. C. K. Barrett, *The Gospel according to St. John* (Philadelphia: Westminster Press, 1978), 373. A number of interpreters suggest that the Beloved Disciple, and in some cases Peter, should be understood as exceptions to the statement that no one understood; e.g., see Brown, *John*, 2:575; Robert Mahoney, *Two Disciples at the Tomb: The Background and Message of John 20.1–10* (Bern: Herbert Lang, 1974), 92–93.

14. This seems to be the case whether or not one reads the verb "believe" here as an aorist subjunctive or (according to some manuscripts) as a present subjunctive. The disciples do believe in Jesus (2:11), and yet Jesus uses the aorist (without any known variants) in at least one other instance to indicate that they may in the future begin to believe (11:15). The variation may suggest that both are true: they both believe in him and do not (see my discussion of the disciples in chap. 4). While the variant smoothes over the blatant contradiction with 2:11, it does not change the overall sense that the disciples' faith is incomplete.

15. Interpreters differ on how to understand the number of women present. For a discussion, see Brown, *John*, 2:904–6.

16. For the first view, see, e.g., Barrett, *St. John*, 459; Hoskyns, *Fourth Gospel*, 530. For the second, see, e.g., Bultmann, *John*, 521; A. Loisy, *Le quatrième évangile* (Paris: Nourry, 1921), 488. For a discussion of the varieties of viewpoints, including premodern examples, see Brown, *John*, 2:922–27; O'Day, *John*, 832; Max Thurian, *Mary: Mother of All Christians* (New York: Herder & Herder, 1963), 144–49.

17. E.g., F. G. Beetham and P. A. Beetham, "A Note on John 19:29," *JTS* 44 (1993): 162–69; Brown, *John*, 2:909–910, 930; Schnackenburg, *St. John*, 3:284.

18. E.g., Brown, *John*, 2:944–56; C. H. Dodd, *Historical Tradition in the Fourth Gospel* (Cambridge: Cambridge University Press, 1963), 133–36;

A. F. Sava, "The Wound in the Side of Christ," *CBQ* 19 (1957): 343–46; Schnackenburg, *St. John*, 3:289–94.

19. It is hard to determine with any certainty to whom the ἐκεῖνος (*ekeinos*, "that one") of 19:35 refers. What is clear is that the narrator confirms the Beloved's testimony and points to either the Beloved himself or another witness (God, Jesus) as further verification.

20. Dodd, *Tradition*, 127.

21. Sandra M. Schneiders, "The Face Veil: A Johannine Sign (John 20:1–10)," *BTB* 13 (1983): 95, 96. See also Barrett, *St. John*, 466; Bultmann, *John*, 684; Hoskyns, *Fourth Gospel*, 541; Moloney, *John*, 520.

22. R. Alan Culpepper, *Anatomy of the Fourth Gospel: A Study in Literary Design* (Philadelphia: Fortress Press, 1983), 121.

23. E.g., Brendan Byrne, "The Faith of the Beloved Disciple and the Community in John 20," *JSNT* 23 (1985): 83; Hawkin, "Function of the Beloved Disciple," 144.

24. For belief in Mary's report, see, e.g., Paul Sevier Minear, "We Don't Know Where, John 20:2," *Int* 30 (1976): 127. On the belief that Jesus is alive, see, e.g., Craig Koester, "Hearing, Seeing, and Believing in the Gospel of John," *Bib* 70 (1989): 344.

25. Cf. O'Day, *John*, 841.

26. Schneiders, "Face Veil," 96–7.

27. E.g., Bauckham, "Beloved Disciple as Ideal Author," 38; Byrne, "Faith of the Beloved Disciple," 90; Barnabas Lindars, *The Gospel of John* (NCB; London: Oliphants, 1972), 602; Quast, *Peter and the Beloved Disciple*, 158.

A few interpreters take these words to reflect the Beloved Disciple's belief independent of (or prior to) his understanding of Scripture. See Gunther, "Relation of the Beloved Disciple to the Twelve," 132; Lindars, *The Gospel of John*, 602.

28. Cf. Ismo Dunderberg, "The Beloved Disciple in John: Ideal Figure in an Early Christian Controversy," in *Fair Play* (ed. Heikki Räisänen et al.; Leiden: E. J. Brill, 2002), 255; Koester, "Hearing," 344; O'Day, *John*, 841.

29. E.g., Gunther, "Relation of the Beloved Disciple to the Twelve," 132; Maynard, "Role of Peter," 540.

30. See Colleen M. Conway, *Men and Women in the Fourth Gospel: Gender and Johannine Characterization* (SBLDS 167; Atlanta: Society of Biblical Literature, 1999), 199.

31. Sandra M. Schneiders, "John 21:1–14," *Int* 43 (1989): 73.

32. Some interpreters find additional evidence in the fishing episode. Because Peter initiates the fishing expedition (21:3), and then brings the net to shore (2:11), some understand him as pastoral leader of the group, mirroring the role to which Jesus calls him in 21:15–19; e.g., see ibid., 72–73. For a discussion of Peter's "rehabilitation" to a pastoral role, see Majella Franzmann and Michael Klinger, "The Call Stories of John 1 and John 21," *SVTQ* 36 (1992): 7–15;

Moloney, *John*, 555. However, the net of fish would never make it to shore without the efforts of the other disciples, since Peter has abandoned ship.

33. E.g., M.-J. Lagrange, *Évangile selon St. Jean* (ed. J. Gabalda; 5th ed., Ébib; Paris: Libraire Lecoffre, 1936), 532. For a detailed discussion of the traditions of Peter's martyrdom, see Bauckham, "Martyrdom," 539–95.

34. Raymond E. Brown, "The Resurrection in John 21: Missionary and Pastoral Directives for the Church," *Worship* 64 (1990): 441. Cf. Max Thurian, "The Ministry of Unity of the Bishop of Rome to the Whole Church," 29 (1986): 12.

35. E.g., Barrett, *St. John*, 488; Hoskyns, *Fourth Gospel*, 558.

36. Translations of the Greek word μένω (*menō*) differ; e.g., the NRSV translates 8:31 as "continue" rather than "abide."

37. Hoskyns, *Fourth Gospel*, 559.

38. E.g., Culpepper, *Anatomy*, 122; Frans Neirynck, "John 21," *NTS* 36 (1990): 321–36.

39. E.g., Maynard, "Role of Peter," 454; Quast, *Peter and the Beloved Disciple*, 166. The designation "apostolic Christians" is strange since it suggests that the Beloved Disciple is not considered an apostle, or that Johannine Christianity lies outside a discernible "mainstream" of ancient Christianity. Likewise, Hawkin argues that the Gospel makes a claim for "orthodoxy" through the character of the Beloved; see Hawkin, "Function of the Beloved Disciple," 150.

40. Bauckham, "Beloved Disciple as Ideal Author," 35–36. Cf. Schneiders, "John 21:1–14," 73.

41. Pamment, "Beloved Disciple," 366.

42. Cf. Ulrich Busse, "The Beloved Disciple," *SK* 15, no. 2 (1994): 219–27; Kelli S. O'Brien, "Written That You May Believe: John 20 and Narrative Rhetoric," *CBQ* 67 (2005): 298, 301.

43. In addition to the first-person plural voice, the following verse includes a single first-person singular voice of the narrator, "I suppose the world itself could not contain . . ." (21:25).

44. E.g., Barrett, *St. John*, 100–101; Brown, *John*, 1:xcix; Bultmann, *John*, 717. Alan Culpepper offers another possibility. He suggests that the "we" voice is that of the narrator, distinct from the author, while the Beloved Disciple is the implied author. To speak of the "implied author" reminds the reader that the text does not give us unmediated access to the historical author; instead, the author creates an image of the author in the act of writing that the reader perceives as the implied author. For a discussion, see Wayne C. Booth, *The Rhetoric of Fiction* (Chicago: University of Chicago Press, 1961), 70–76; Culpepper, *Anatomy*, 15–16.

45. For examples of this view, see Dunderberg, "Beloved Disciple," 246; Moloney, *John*, 7–8; O'Day, *John*, 500. In a slightly different interpretation, Alan Culpepper argues that the "we" of 21:24 identifies the first-person voice as the narrator while the Beloved Disciple is the implied author; see Culpepper, *Anatomy*, 46–48. Some maintain that the Beloved Disciple is the author of the Gospel; e.g., see Donald François Tolmie, "John 21:24–25," *SK* 17 (1996): 422; Kevin

J. Vanhoozer, "The Hermeneutics of I-Witness Testimony: John 21:20–24 and the 'Death' of the 'Author,'" in *Understanding Poets and Prophets* (ed. George W. Anderson and A. Graeme Auld; Sheffield: JSOT Press, 1993), 366–87.

46. E.g., Bauckham, "Beloved Disciple as Ideal Author," 33–36; Dunderberg, "Beloved Disciple," 245; Hawkin, "Function of the Beloved Disciple," 136; Vanhoozer, "Hermeneutics," 366.

Chapter 7: The Jews

1. Rudolf Bultmann, *The Gospel of John* (Philadelphia: Westminster Press, 1971), 86; cf. Rudolf Bultmann, *Theology of the New Testament* (2 vols.; New York: Scribner, 1951–55), 2:5. Bultmann's interpretation has been widely influential. See the notes below for others who interpret the Jews negatively.

2. Many interpreters have portrayed Pilate as a sympathetic character, who wishes to release Jesus. This leaves the blame for Jesus' death on the shoulders of the Jews. See, e.g., C. K. Barrett, *The Gospel according to St. John* (Philadelphia: Westminster Press, 1978), 442–45; C. H. Dodd, *Historical Tradition in the Fourth Gospel* (Cambridge: Cambridge University Press, 1963), 104–7. Although I do not treat Pilate as a character in this book, see the excellent interpretation of David Rensberger, "The Politics of John: The Trial of Jesus in the Fourth Gospel," *JBL* 103 (1984): 401–6.

3. John Ashton, "The Identity and Function of the ΙΟΥΔΑΙΟΙ in the Fourth Gospel," *NovT* 27 (1985): 40. Cf. Reimund Bieringer, Didier Pollefeyt, and Frederique Vandecasteele-Vanneuville, "Wrestling with Johannine Anti-Judaism: A Hermeneutical Framework for the Analysis of the Current Debate," in *Anti-Judaism and the Fourth Gospel* (ed. Reimund Bieringer, Didier Pollefeyt, and Frederique Vandecasteele-Vanneuville; Louisville, KY: Westminster John Knox Press, 2001), 4.

4. Most scholars argue that the term "the Jews" should be read only with reference to the Jewish authorities. See Gregory Baum, *The Jews and the Gospel: A Re-examination of the New Testament* (Westminster, MD: Newman Press, 1961); Raymond Brown, *The Gospel according to John* (2 vols., AB 29–29A; New York: Doubleday, 1966–70), 1:lxx–lxxiii; G. J. Cuming, "The Jews in the Fourth Gospel," *ExpTim* 60 (1948–49): 290–92; Martinus C. de Boer, "The Depiction of the Jews in John's Gospel: Matters of Behavior and Identity," in *Anti-Judaism and the Fourth Gospel* (ed. Reimund Bieringer, Didier Pollefeyt, and Frederique Vandecasteele-Vanneuville; Louisville, KY: Westminster John Knox Press, 2001), 148; Reinhold Leistner, *Antijudaismus im Johannesevangelium? Darstellung des Problems in der neueren Auslegungsgeschichte und Untersuchung der Leidensgeschichte* (Bern: Herbert Lang, 1974); Gail R. O'Day, *The Gospel of John* (NIB 9; Nashville: Abingdon Press, 1995), 506–7; D. Moody Smith, *John* (ANTC; Nashville: Abingdon Press, 1999), 34–39; Urban C. von Wahlde, "The Johannine 'Jews': A Critical Survey," *NTS* 28 (1982): 33–60; Martin Christopher White, *The Identity*

and Function of the Jews and Related Terms in the Fourth Gospel (Ann Arbor, MI: University Microfilms, 1972).

The main alternative view is that the term should be limited to "the Judeans" (i.e., Jews from Judea as opposed to the diaspora or the Galilee); see e.g., James H. Charlesworth, "The Gospel of John: Exclusivism Caused by a Social Setting Different from That of Jesus," in *Anti-Judaism and the Fourth Gospel* (ed. Reimund Bieringer, Didier Pollefeyt, and Frederique Vandecasteele-Vanneuville; Louisville, KY: Westminster John Knox Press, 2001), 247–59; W. Bauer et al., "'Ιουδαῖος," in BDAG, 478–79; Malcolm Lowe, "Who Were the 'ΙΟΥΔΑΙΟΙ?" *NovT* 18 (1976), 101–30; J. Hugh Michael, "The Jews in the Fourth Gospel," *ExpTim* 60 (1948–49), 290–92.

For a good discussion of the range of viewpoints, see Lars Kierspel, *The Jews and the World in the Fourth Gospel* (Tübingen: Mohr Siebeck, 2006), 13–36.

5. Brown, *John*, 1:lxx. The majority of scholars attribute John's negative depiction of the Jews to the location of the Johannine community following a hostile separation from Judaism. The seminal essays are those of Brown and Martyn: Raymond Brown, *The Community of the Beloved Disciple* (New York: Paulist Press, 1979); J. Louis Martyn, *History and Theology in the Fourth Gospel* (3rd ed.; Louisville, KY: Westminster John Knox Press, 2003). See also Charles Kingsley Barrett, *The Gospel of John and Judaism* (London: SPCK, 1975), 70–71; James H. Charlesworth, "The Gospel of John: Exclusivism Caused by a Social Setting Different from That of Jesus (John 11:54 and 14:6)," in *Anti-Judaism and the Fourth Gospel* (ed. Reimund Bieringer, Didier Pollefeyt, and Frederique Vandecasteele-Vanneuville; Louisville, KY: Westminster John Knox Press, 2001), 254–56; R. Alan Culpepper, "Anti-Judaism in the Fourth Gospel as a Theological Problem for Christian Interpreters," in *Anti-Judaism and the Fourth Gospel* (ed. Reimund Bieringer, Didier Pollefeyt, and Frederique Vandecasteele-Vanneuville; Louisville, KY: Westminster John Knox Press, 2001), 61; R. Alan Culpepper, "The Gospel of John and the Jews," *RevExp* 84 (1987): 280–81; W. D. Davies, "Reflections on Aspects of the Jewish Background of the Gospel of John," in *Exploring the Gospel of John: In Honor of D. Moody Smith* (ed. R. Alan Culpepper and C. Clifton Black; Louisville, KY: Westminster John Knox Press, 1996), 43–64; Paul D. Duke, *Irony in the Fourth Gospel* (Atlanta: John Knox Press, 1985), 150; James D. G. Dunn, "The Embarrassment of History: Reflections on the Problem of 'Anti-Judaism' in the Fourth Gospel," in *Anti-Judaism and the Fourth Gospel* (ed. Reimund Bieringer, Didier Pollefeyt, and Frederique Vandecasteele-Vanneuville; Louisville, KY: Westminster John Knox Press, 2001), 41–60; J. Louis Martyn, "A Gentile Mission That Replaced an Earlier Jewish Mission?" in *Exploring the Gospel of John: In Honor of D. Moody Smith* (ed. R. Alan Culpepper and C. Clifton Black; Louisville, KY: Westminster John Knox Press, 1996), 124–44; Wayne A. Meeks, "'Am I a Jew?' Johannine Christianity and Judaism," in *Christianity, Judaism and Other Greco-Roman Cults: Studies for Morton Smith at Sixty* (ed. Jacob Neusner; SJLA 12; Leiden: E. J. Brill, 1975),

180–83; O'Day, *John*, 506–7; Miroslaw Stanislaw Wróbel, *Who Are the Father and His Children in Jn 8:44? A Literary, Historical and Theological Analysis of Jn 8:44 and Its Context* (Paris: J. Gabalda et Cie Éditeurs, 2005).

A number of scholars have criticized the proposals of Brown and Martyn. See especially Steven T. Katz, "Issues in the Separation of Judaism and Christianity after 70 C.E.: A Reconsideration," *JBL* 103 (1984): 43–76; Reuven Kimelman, "Birkat Ha-Minim and the Lack of Evidence for an Anti-Christian Jewish Prayer in Late Antiquity," in *Jewish and Christian Self-Definition* (ed. E. P. Sanders; vol. 2; Philadelphia: Fortress Press, 1981), 226–44; Adele Reinhartz, *Befriending the Beloved Disciple: A Jewish Reading of the Gospel of John* (New York: Continuum, 2001), 37–53; idem, "The Johannine Community and Its Jewish Neighbors: A Reappraisal," in *What Is John? II, Literary and Social Readings of the Fourth Gospel* (ed. Fernando F. Segovia; Atlanta: Scholars Press, 1998), 111–38.

In addition, Lars Kierspel accepts the hostile portrayal of the Jews but suggests a different social setting; see Kierspel, *Jews and the World*.

6. See also the switch from the Jews to the "authorities" (7:1, 25–26).

7. Von Wahlde, "The Johannine 'Jews,'" 46.

8. See also the discussion by R. Alan Culpepper, *Anatomy of the Fourth Gospel: A Study in Literary Design* (Philadelphia: Fortress Press, 1983), 126.

9. See, e.g., von Wahlde, "The Johannine 'Jews,'" 33, 35.

10. E.g., Barrett, *St. John*, 285; Richard Egenter, "Joh. 8, 31 f. im christlichen Lebensbewusstein," in *Wahrheit und Verkündigung* (ed. Leo Scheffczyk, Werner Dettloff, and Richard Heinzmann; Munich: Verlag Ferdinand Schöningh, 1967), 1589; Edwyn Clement Hoskyns, *The Fourth Gospel* (ed. F. N. Davey; London: Faber & Faber, 1947), 337. Von Wahlde identifies John 11:45 and 12:11 as "neutral" uses and thereby excludes them from the discussion: von Wahlde, "The Johannine 'Jews,'" 46.

11. E.g., Culpepper, "John and the Jews," 280.

12. For examples of this concern, see the essays in Reimund Bieringer, Didier Pollefeyt, and Frederique Vandecasteele-Vanneuville, eds., *Anti-Judaism and the Fourth Gospel* (Louisville, KY: Westminster John Knox Press, 2001).

13. Colleen Conway, "The Production of the Johannine Community: A New Historicist Perspective," *JBL* 121 (2002): 487.

14. See Conway's excellent discussion: ibid., 485–89.

15. Cf. John Darr's discussion of the Pharisees in Luke: John A. Darr, *On Character Building: The Reader and the Rhetoric of Characterization in Luke-Acts* (Louisville, KY: Westminster/John Knox Press, 1992), 94.

16. Borgen observes that the paraphrase of the initial Scripture is a common rabbinic practice; see Peder Borgen, *Bread from Heaven: An Exegetical Study of the Concept of Manna in the Gospel of John and the Writings of Philo* (NovTSup 10; Leiden: E. J. Brill, 1965), 82–90.

17. Susan Hylen, *Allusion and Meaning in John 6* (Berlin: Walter de Gruyter, 2005), 135–45.

18. The most common way of handling the contradiction is to define this faith as false belief or belief that is quickly abandoned; e.g., see Barrett, *St. John*, 344; Brown, *The Community of the Beloved Disciple*, 77; Charles Harold Dodd, "Behind a Johannine Dialogue," in *More New Testament Studies* (Grand Rapids: Wm. B. Eerdmans Publishing Co., 1968), 46; Ernst Haenchen, *John* (2 vols.; Philadelphia: Fortress Press, 1984), 2:28; Martyn, *History and Theology*, 160–62; Leon Morris, *The Gospel according to John* (Grand Rapids: Wm. B. Eerdmans Publishing Co., 1971), 403; James Swetnam, "The Meaning of πεπιστευκότας in John 8, 31," *Bib* 61 (1980): 108.

Others argue that different groups are represented in the text: e.g., see Debbie Hunn, "Who Are 'They' in John 8:33?" *CBQ* 66 (2004): 397; Rudolf Schnackenburg, *The Gospel according to St. John* (3 vols.; New York: Seabury Press, 1982–90), 2:204–5. Still others, that verses were added by a redactor or are a gloss: e.g., see Brown, *John*, 1:351, 354; Barnabas Lindars, *The Gospel of John* (NCB; London: Oliphants, 1972), 323; Morris, *John*, 404.

19. Brown, *John*, 1:347; Urban C. von Wahlde, "Literary Structure and Theological Argument in Three Discourses with the Jews in the Fourth Gospel," *JBL* 103 (1984): 579–80.

20. In 11:31 the verb "believe" occurs in the perfect tense (πρὸς τοὺς πεπιστευκότας, *pros tous pepisteukotas*). Some scholars argue that the change from the aorist tense in verse 30 to the perfect tense in verse 31 is significant. However, the argument stems more from what they understand to be the anachronistic behavior of this group of Jews, who soon afterward are said to seek to kill Jesus; e.g., see Barrett, *St. John*, 285. The perfect tense should not be understood to convey a past belief that is no longer in effect. The same tense is also used to speak of the disciples' belief in 16:27 (πεπιστεύκατε, *pepisteukate*).

21. For additional discussion, see Jörg Augenstein, "'Euer Gesetz'—Ein Pronomen und die johanneische Haltung zum Gesetz," *ZNW* 88 (1997): 311–13.

22. Some interpreters read 8:39 as a contrary expression that Abraham is not the Jews' ancestor; see Adele Reinhartz, "John 8:31–59 from a Jewish Perspective," in *Remembering for the Future: The Holocaust in an Age of Genocide* (3 vols.; ed. John K. Roth and Elisabeth Maxwell; New York: Palgrave, 2001), 2:790. However, as Brown discusses the matter, the manuscript evidence supports a mixed conditional statement rather than a contrary-to-fact condition: "The idea is that the Jews are really Abraham's children, but are denying it by their actions." See Brown, *John*, 1:356–57.

23. Interpreters tend to literalize the language of parentage in the Gospel of John, in part because of a tendency to read "Father" as a synonym for God rather than as an important metaphor that the Gospel employs to express Jesus' (and God's) identity. For a discussion of the tendency, see Gail R. O'Day, "'Show Us the Father and We Will Be Satisfied' (John 14:8)," *Semeia* 85 (1999): 11–17; Adele Reinhartz, "Introduction: 'Father' as Metaphor in the Fourth Gospel," 85 (1999): 1–10. Thompson's approach is metaphorical: Marianne Meye Thomp-

son, *The God of the Gospel of John* (Grand Rapids: Wm. B. Eerdmans Publishing Co., 2001), chap. 2.

24. Luke Timothy Johnson, "The New Testament's Anti-Jewish Slander and the Conventions of Ancient Polemic," *JBL* 108 (1989): 419–41.

25. For a standard definition, see Douglas Colin Muecke, *The Compass of Irony* (London: Methuen & Co., 1969), 19–20. More recent discussions that I found helpful include Katharina Barbe, *Irony in Context* (Amsterdam: John Benjamins Publishing Co., 1995); Claire Colebrook, *Irony* (New York: Routledge, 2004).

26. Allan Rodway, "Terms for Comedy," *RMS* 6 (1962): 113. See also the discussion by Barbe of ironic statements where the ironic meaning is not in opposition to the sentence meaning; e.g., Barbe, *Irony in Context*, 17, 38–39.

27. Reinhartz, "John 8:31–59," 792.

28. For a discussion of "situational irony," see Duke, *Irony in the Fourth Gospel*, 27–29; Muecke, *The Compass of Irony*, chap. 5.

29. The story of the woman caught in adultery, 7:53–8:11, is an interruption that is not found in the earliest manuscripts of the Gospel. Recent translations place the passage in brackets to note that it is an addition to the text of the Gospel. This passage suggests a change in the setting of the rest of John 8, but when the chapters are read without this addition, Jesus' teaching beginning in 8:12 also occurs during the festival. Jesus' discussion with the Jews who believe in him should be read in this context.

30. O'Day, *John*, 823; Rensberger, "Politics of John," 406–7.

31. Wayne A. Meeks, *The Prophet-King* (NovTSup 14; Leiden: E. J. Brill, 1967), 72.

32. On the subject of allusion by narrative paraphrase, see Hylen, *Allusion*, 53–59; Carmela Perri, "On Alluding," *Poetics* 7 (1978): 304.

33. E.g., Colebrook, *Irony*, 12; Gail R. O'Day, *Revelation in the Fourth Gospel* (Philadelphia: Fortress Press, 1986), 29–32.

34. E.g., Culpepper, *Anatomy*, 169, 179; Duke, *Irony in the Fourth Gospel*, 93.

35. For a brief discussion of the topic, see Mary C. Callaway, "A Hammer That Breaks Rock in Pieces: Prophetic Critique in the Hebrew Bible," in *Anti-Semitism and Early Christianity* (ed. Craig A. Evans and Donald Alfred Hagner; Minneapolis: Fortress Press, 1993), 21–38.

36. For examples of the phenomenon, see: Amy-Jill Levine, "The Disease of Postcolonial New Testament Studies and the Hermeneutics of Healing," *JFSR* 20 (2004): 91–99; idem, *The Misunderstood Jew: The Church and the Scandal of the Jewish Jesus* (San Francisco: Harper, 2006), esp. 124–25; E. P. Sanders, "Jesus, Ancient Judaism, and Modern Christianity: The Quest Continues," in *Jesus, Judaism, and Christian Anti-Judaism* (ed. Paula Fredriksen and Adele Reinhartz; Louisville, KY: Westminster John Knox Press, 2002), 31–55; Joseph B. Tyson, "Anti-Judaism in the Critical Study of the Gospels," in *Anti-Judaism and the Gospels* (ed. William R. Farmer; Harrisburg, PA: Trinity Press International, 1999), 216–51.

37. For an ancient example, see Origen, *Comm. Jo.* 20.103. Of John's description of the Jews as "of your father the devil," Origen writes, "In so far as we commit sins, we have not as yet put off the generation of the devil, even if we are thought to believe in Jesus." The Jews are held up in parallel to the Christian community.

Chapter 8: Jesus

1. George Lakoff and Mark Johnson, *Metaphors We Live By* (Chicago: University of Chicago Press, 1980), 5.

2. The work of conceptual metaphor theorists informs my understanding of metaphor in John. See Gilles Fauconnier and Mark Turner, *The Way We Think: Conceptual Blending and the Mind's Hidden Complexities* (New York: Basic Books, 2002); Raymond W. Gibbs, *The Poetics of Mind: Figurative Thought, Language, and Understanding* (Cambridge: Cambridge University Press, 1994); Mark Johnson, *The Meaning of the Body: Aesthetics of Human Understanding* (Chicago: University of Chicago Press, 2007); Lakoff and Johnson, *Metaphors*; George Lakoff and Mark Turner, *More Than Cool Reason: A Field Guide to Poetic Metaphor* (Chicago: University of Chicago Press, 1989); Mark Turner, *The Artful Mind: Cognitive Science and the Riddle of Human Creativity* (Oxford: Oxford University Press, 2006); idem, *The Literary Mind* (New York: Oxford University Press, 1996).

3. The Greek syntax in 6:33 reflects this dual reference. The masculine *ho katabainōn* (ὁ καταβαίνων, "that which/the one who comes down") can refer to the masculine noun bread *ho artos* (ὁ ἄρτος) or to a male person, i.e., Jesus.

4. See my discussion elsewhere: Susan Hylen, *Allusion and Meaning in John 6* (Berlin: Walter de Gruyter, 2005), chap. 4.

5. Craig R. Koester, *Symbolism in the Fourth Gospel: Meaning, Mystery, Community* (2nd ed.; Minneapolis: Fortress Press, 2003), 4. Cf. R. Alan Culpepper, *Anatomy of the Fourth Gospel: A Study in Literary Design* (Philadelphia: Fortress Press, 1983), 80–90; Dorothy A. Lee, *Flesh and Glory: Symbolism, Gender, and Theology in the Gospel of John* (New York: Crossroad, 2002), chap. 1; Sandra M. Schneiders, *Written That You May Believe: Encountering Jesus in the Fourth Gospel* (New York: Herder & Herder, 1999), chap. 5.

6. Rudolf Bultmann, *The Gospel of John* (Philadelphia: Westminster Press, 1971), 364. Bultmann does not describe his view as symbolic, but his description fits the symbolic view as others describe it.

7. Lee, *Flesh and Glory*, 26.

8. Schneiders, *Written That You May Believe*, 68.

9. See Bultmann, *John*, 376, 227.

10. Mark Johnson, *The Body in the Mind: The Bodily Basis of Meaning, Imagination, and Reason* (Chicago: University of Chicago Press, 1987), xxii. Cf. Lakoff and Johnson, *Metaphors*, chaps. 24–27.

11. Many of the theorists I draw on here also argue that many of the expressions we take to be literal are really metaphorical. For a discussion, see, e.g., Johnson, *The Body in the Mind*, chaps. 2–4; Lakoff and Johnson, *Metaphors*, chap. 4.

12. Lee, *Flesh and Glory*, 92; cf. 92–99.

13. John Painter, "Johannine Symbols: A Case Study in Epistemology," *JTSA* 27 (1979): 37.

14. See Gibbs, *The Poetics of Mind*, 217–18.

15. Johnson, *Meaning of the Body*, 190, italics original. For an additional discussion of the way that an objectivist view of language denies metaphor having any cognitive function, see Johnson, *The Body in the Mind*, 66–67.

16. E.g., Craig Koester writes that "to partake of Jesus as the bread of life is to believe that the crucified Messiah is the source of eternal life with God." See Koester, *Symbolism*, 103. Cf. Peder Borgen, *Bread from Heaven: An Exegetical Study of the Concept of Manna in the Gospel of John and the Writings of Philo* (NovTSup 10; Leiden: E. J. Brill, 1965), 186.

17. The cited Scripture in 6:31 is most likely Exod. 16:4, although it is similar in some ways to Exod. 16:15; Neh. 9:15; and Ps. 78:24. In all of these sources, "bread" is a reference to manna.

18. Cf. Philo, *Mut.* 253–263, *Leg.* 3.163–168, 169–173.

19. Painter, "Johannine Symbols," 39. Even symbolic readings that utilize contextual background may assume that the context is not a necessary part of the meaning of the imagery: "John draws much of the pungency of the imagery not just from the symbolism but also from the narrative of failure and rejection with which both images are associated in the Old Testament." See Lee, *Flesh and Glory*, 93. Lee's words suggest that the "symbolism" of the vine is somehow distinct from its OT context at the same time that she draws on the context to understand the symbolism.

20. Johnson, *Meaning of the Body*, 270.

21. E.g., Paul N. Anderson, *The Christology of the Fourth Gospel: Its Unity and Disunity in the Light of John 6* (Tübingen: J. C. B. Mohr, 1996), 203–7; Borgen, *Bread from Heaven*, 172; Ernst Haenchen, *John* (2 vols.; Philadelphia: Fortress Press, 1984), 300.

22. Painter, "Johannine Symbols," 38.

23. For a related discussion, see Marianne Meye Thompson, "'Every Picture Tells a Story': Imagery for God in the Gospel of John," in *Imagery in the Gospel of John: Terms, Forms, Themes, and Theology of Johannine Figurative Language* (ed. Jörg Frey, Jan G. van der Watt, and Ruben Zimmerman; WUNT 200; Tübingen: Mohr Siebeck, 2006), 259–77.

24. J. Louis Martyn, *History and Theology in the Fourth Gospel* (3rd ed.; Louisville, KY: Westminster John Knox Press, 2003), 124–30, 156–57.

25. E.g., Marie-Émile Boismard, *Moses or Jesus: An Essay in Johannine Christology* (trans. B. T. Viviano; Minneapolis: Fortress Press, 1993); Raymond Brown, *The Community of the Beloved Disciple* (New York: Paulist Press, 1979);

Oscar Cullmann, *The Johannine Circle* (trans. J. Bowden; London: SCM Press, 1976).

26. Koester speaks of "core" and "supporting" symbols; see Koester, *Symbolism*, 5.

27. For a summary, see Jan G. van der Watt, *Family of the King: Dynamics of Metaphor in the Gospel according to John* (BibInt 47; Leiden: E. J. Brill, 2000), 406–9. In the end, however, van der Watt is not content with a single image, but creates a hybrid: the "Family of the King." While family and king metaphors are frequent in the Gospel, the blended image of a royal family is not explicitly found within the Gospel.

28. Ibid., 223.

29. Ibid., 228.

30. Mary L. Coloe, *Dwelling in the Household of God: Johannine Ecclesiology and Spirituality* (Collegeville, MN: Liturgical Press, 2007), chap. 4. See also Coloe's earlier work: Mary L. Coloe, *God Dwells With Us: Temple Symbolism in the Fourth Gospel* (Collegeville. MN: Liturgical Press, 2001).

31. In addition to Coloe and van der Watt, see, e.g., Boismard, *Moses or Jesus: An Essay in Johannine Christology*; Coloe, *God Dwells with Us*; Stan Harstine, *Moses as a Character in the Fourth Gospel: A Study of Ancient Reading Techniques* (JSNTSup 229; Sheffield: Sheffield Academic Press, 2002); Larry Paul Jones, *The Symbol of Water in the Gospel of John* (JSNTSup 145; Sheffield: Sheffield Academic Press, 1997).

32. Cited in Semir Zeki, "The Neurology of Ambiguity," in Turner, *The Artful Mind*, 243. Cf. "Ambiguity," *Oxford English Dictionary Online* (cited April 25, 2008). http://dictionary.oed.com/cgi/entry/50006931?single=1&query_type =word&queryword=ambiguity&first=1&max_to_show=10.

33. Zeki, "Neurology of Ambiguity," 245. Zeki writes of multiple interpretations of visual art, yet I found his comments thought-provoking with regard to literary works as well. For further discussions of ambiguity in art and a helpful example, see Mark De May, "Mastering Ambiguity," in Turner, *The Artful Mind*, 271–304.

34. For discussions of these metaphors, see Lakoff and Johnson, *Metaphors*, 7–9, 39, 139–44; Lakoff and Turner, *More Than Cool Reason*, 1–49.

35. Lakoff and Johnson, *Metaphors*, 13, italics original.

36. Lakoff and Turner, *More Than Cool Reason*, 52; cf. Lakoff and Johnson, *Metaphors*, 95.

37. My position is closest to that of Ruben Zimmerman in his *Christologie der Bilder im Johannesevangelium: Die Christopoetik des vierten Evangeliums unter besonderer Berücksichtigung von Joh 10* (ed. Jörg Frey, WUNT 171; Tübingen: Mohr Siebeck, 2004), 421–22; idem, "Imagery in John: Opening Up Paths into the Tangled Thicket of John's Figurative World," in Frey, van der Watt, and Zimmerman, *Imagery in the Gospel of John*, 1–43. Attridge argues for a more unified presentation of Jesus overall than I do: Harold W. Attridge, "The Cubist

Principle in Johannine Imagery: John and the Reading of Images in Contemporary Platonism," in Frey, van der Watt, and Zimmerman, *Imagery in the Gospel of John*, 47–60.

38. For more elaboration, see Hylen, *Allusion*, 120–34.

39. Zimmerman, "Imagery," 38.

40. Lakoff and Johnson, *Metaphors*, 173–74.

41. Ibid., 175.

Chapter 9: Conclusion

1. Rudolf Bultmann, *Theology of the New Testament* (trans. K. Grobel; New York: Charles Scribner's Sons, 1951–55), 2:66.

2. For the formulation of these questions see, e.g., Frank J. Matera, *New Testament Ethics: The Legacies of Jesus and Paul* (Louisville, KY: Westminster John Knox Press, 1996), 92; Wayne A. Meeks, "The Ethics of the Fourth Evangelist," in *Exploring the Gospel of John: In Honor of D. Moody Smith* (ed. R. Alan Culpepper and C. Clifton Black; Louisville, KY: Westminster John Knox Press, 1996), 317–20.

3. Richard B. Hays, *The Moral Vision of the New Testament: A Contemporary Introduction to New Testament Ethics* (San Francisco: Harper Collins, 1996), 4.

4. E.g., ibid., 4, 140; Meeks, "Ethics of the Fourth Evangelist," 317; Johannes Nissen, "Community and Ethics in the Gospel of John," in *New Readings in John: Literary and Theological Perspectives* (ed. Johannes Nissen and Sigfred Pedersen; JSNTSup 182; Sheffield: Sheffield Academic Press, 1999), 199–200; Jan G. van der Watt, "Ethics and Ethos in the Gospel according to John," *ZNW* 97 (2006): 150–52.

5. Meeks, "Ethics of the Fourth Evangelist," 324.

6. Fernando F. Segovia, "The Gospel of John," in *A Postcolonial Commentary on the New Testament Writings* (ed. Fernando F. Segovia and R. S. Sugirtharajah); New York: T&T Clark, 2007), 171. See also Nissen, "Community and Ethics in the Gospel of John," 208.

7. Jey J. Kanagaraj, "The Implied Ethics of the Fourth Gospel: A Reinterpretation of the Decalogue," *TynBul* 52 (2001): 33–60; van der Watt, "Ethics and Ethos," 147–76.

8. Gail R. O'Day, "Jesus as Friend in the Gospel of John," *Int* 58 (2004): 144–57.

9. Meeks, "Ethics of the Fourth Evangelist," 320.

10. Gail R. O'Day, *The Gospel of John* (NIB 9; Nashville: Abingdon Press, 1995), 734.

11. Ibid., 726–28.

Index of Ancient Sources

195

Index of Subjects